"Wooden Man"?

MASCULINITY STUDIES

Literary and Cultural Representations

Josep M. Armengol
General Editor

Vol. 7

This book is a volume in a Peter Lang monograph series.
Every volume is peer reviewed and meets
the highest quality standards for content and production.

PETER LANG
New York • Bern • Frankfurt • Berlin
Brussels • Vienna • Oxford • Warsaw

Daniel Matias

"Wooden Man"?

Masculinities in the Work of J.M. Coetzee (*Boyhood*, *Youth* and *Summertime*)

PETER LANG
New York • Bern • Frankfurt • Berlin
Brussels • Vienna • Oxford • Warsaw

Library of Congress Cataloging-in-Publication Data

Names: Matias, Daniel, author.
Title: "Wooden man"?: masculinities in the work of J.M. Coetzee:
Boyhood, Youth and *Summertime* / Daniel Filipe Mendes Matias.
Description: New York: Peter Lang, 2017.
Series: Masculinity studies: literary and cultural representations; vol. 7 | ISSN 2161-2692
Includes bibliographical references and index.
Identifiers: LCCN 2016043873 | ISBN 978-1-4331-3806-5 (hardcover: alk. paper)
ISBN 978-1-4331-3807-2 (ebook pdf) | ISBN 978-1-4331-3808-9 (epub)
ISBN 978-1-4331-3809-6 (mobi)
Subjects: LCSH: Coetzee, J. M., 1940– —Criticism and interpretation.
Masculinity in literature. | Men in literature.
Classification: LCC PR9369.3.C58 Z84 2017 | DDC 823/.914—dc23
LC record available at https://lccn.loc.gov/2016043873
DOI 10.3726/978-1-4331-3807-2

Bibliographic information published by **Die Deutsche Nationalbibliothek.**
Die Deutsche Nationalbibliothek lists this publication in the "Deutsche
Nationalbibliografie"; detailed bibliographic data are available
on the Internet at http://dnb.d-nb.de/.

The paper in this book meets the guidelines for permanence and durability
of the Committee on Production Guidelines for Book Longevity
of the Council of Library Resources.

© 2017 Peter Lang Publishing, Inc., New York
29 Broadway, 18th floor, New York, NY 10006
www.peterlang.com

Printed in Germany

To Maria Mendes,
(Grand)Mother, Teacher, Friend

It will not do, for instance, to assert in general terms, that the experience of mankind has pronounced in favour of the existing system. Experience cannot possibly have decided between two courses, so long as there has only been experience of one. If it be said that the doctrine of the equality of the sexes rests only on theory, it must be remembered that the contrary doctrine also has only theory to rest upon. All that is proved in its favour by direct experience, is that mankind have been able to exist under it, and to attain the degree of improvement and prosperity which we now see; but whether that prosperity has been attained sooner, or is now greater, than it would have been under the other system, experience does not say.

John Stuart Mill, *The Subjection of Women*

CONTENTS

ACKNOWLEDGEMENTS

The present book being an edited form of my Ph.D. thesis, I should, first of all, like to thank Professor Teresa Pinto Coelho, my main supervisor, whose intellectual rigour allowed me to consider academic inquiry in a different light, particularly on the myriad of possibilities of reading, of doing research, of understanding. Such gusto would, in large part, animate the present work, supporting me through the trials and tribulations that necessarily accompanied it, and for that I am immensely grateful.

I would also like to thank Professor Pedro Aires de Oliveira, co-supervisor, whose helpful guidance proved safe harbour amidst stormy seas. I have learned, with the care and the detail of the historian, to pay attention not only to the past but, perhaps mostly, to the future.

I would like to thank Amal Treacher Kabesh (University of Nottingham) for her insightful comments on an earlier version of this work. I should like to thank Lynne Segal and Stephen Frosh for their insightful comments, and many motivating discussions, in the time that I spent at the Psychosocial Studies Department at Birkbeck College, University of London. I should also like to thank Lisa Baraitser and Derek Hook for their ideas and opinions.

I should like to acknowledge the IHC—Instituto de História Contemporânea (Institute of Contemporary History) of the Faculty of Social Sciences and Humanities of the New University of Lisbon, for harbouring my research and providing me with an exciting, intellectually stimulating community.

I would like to thank José Armengol for involving me in the *Masculinity Series* at Peter Lang.

I should also like to thank the Portuguese funding institution FCT—Fundação para a Ciência e a Tecnologia—for supporting the present work through a PhD scholarship (SFRH/BD/77855/2011).

I would like to thank Editorial Fundamentos for permission to reprint material from "Wooden Man?" Masculinities in the Work of J. M. Coetzee (Boyhood, Youth, and Summertime), first printed in I. D. Gimenez-Rico et al. (Eds.), *Gender Studies: Transatlantic Visions* (pp. 239–252). Madrid: Editorial Fundamentos, 2016.

Finally, I would like to thank my family. Without their continued support, none of this would be possible.

FOREWORD

"I am curious to see what the other women in this man's life have told you...
whether they too found this lover of theirs to be made of wood. Because, you
know, that is what I think you should call your book: *The Wooden Man*."

Although the (unreliable) biographer does not follow Adriana Nascimento's
advice in *Summertime*, Daniel Matias does. But he goes further. In his *Wooden
Man? Masculinities in the Work of J. M. Coetzee*, he extends Coetzee's (the
character) Brazilian lover's concept "wooden" to *Boyhood* and *Youth* showing
how the three texts subvert hegemonic masculinity.

Coined by the Australian sociologist R. W. Connell (Daniel Matias'
theoretical point of departure supported by extensive bibliography on the
subject) who acknowledges the existence of multiple masculinities that vary
across time, culture, region and the individual, the concept has been applied
to several fields of study such as education, health, the military, sports, but
more seldom to literature and, rarely, to Coetzee's *oeuvre*. This is one of Matias' breakthroughs.

Moreover, his book is at the crossroads between gender and postcolonial
studies, a methodology which is most appropriate to approach Coetzee's complex texts and which enables him to write chapters on gender and nationalism, or on imperial codes of masculinity, my favourite ones. For instance, he

cleverly shows how, in the first chapter of *Boyhood*, a house-family-nation symbolic relationship can be drawn, arguing that neither the mother nor the boy (the latter more ambiguously) conform to the norms of Afrikaner nationalism and analysing to what extent the father is the representative of the Afrikaner ideal of masculinity, although he is not the breadwinner and is unfavourably portrayed by his son. He also examines in what way the narrative resists a certain pattern of Afrikaner historiography, the boy not worshipping the national heroes of the Afrikaner canon.

Showing that the three texts reflect on and disrupt dominant, institutionalised formulations of masculinity, Daniel Matias then insightfully advocates that they open spaces for different/Other discourses (in the same way Coetzee—the author—inserts multiple, sometimes, conflicting narrative voices in his fiction), thus dismissing the hegemonic masculine perspective as unique. Various Others become thus heard: the anti-nationalist, the anti-imperial, the black man, women, the poet, the soft man, as well as the "queer" here also interpreted as political activity.

Skilfully resisting genre labeling and elusive of interpretation (like his other works), Coetzee's *Boyhood*, *Youth* and *Summertime* have been discussed as memoirs, or fictionalised memoirs, auto/*autre*biography, confession. Other studies have focused on the role played by women and, in the case of *Summertime*, female narrators.

Daniel Matias' innovative well-researched study follows a different path. He not only reflects on masculinity, but also readdresses the much and ever recurring debated connection between Coetzee's *oeuvre* and South African politics. An unmanly man, as Adriana portrays him ("there is not a quality he did have that a woman looks for in a man, a quality of strength, of manliness"), a lousy lover, according to the women in his life, a bad hunter and inept cricket and rugby player (in *Boyhood*), a son who does not love his father, so Margot says (although the undated fragments of his Notebooks tell otherwise), John defies male dominant authority, as well as colonialist and Afrikaner discourse.

This is, in Matias' opinion, what opens up the possibility of ethical thinking and an ethical account of masculinity, although he acknowledges Coetzee's (provocative) unwillingness to provide the reader with unique definitive answers.

Boyhood, *Youth* and *Summertime* are, in fact, three provocative texts (I resist the term "trilogy," as I keep thinking that Coetzee is also subverting the meaning of it largely through the change in narrative strategy in *Summertime*) about family, the artist's creative process, a more humane, more all inclusive, less judgmental world, the "rainbow nation."

Daniel Matias' rereading of them is also daring and thought provoking, thus opening up new/Other avenues of research not only on masculinities and postcolonial literature, but also and foremost on J. M. Coetzee's work and, as he concludingly proposes, on Coetzee's legacy to the new generation of South African writers.

Teresa Pinto Coelho
Full Professor and Chair
Universidade Nova de Lisboa

INTRODUCTION

Coetzee, Gender and Ethics

But he fears there will be no meeting, not in this life. If he must settle on a likeness for the pair of them, his man and he, he would write that they are like two ships sailing in contrary directions, one west, and the other east. Or better, that they are deckhands toiling in the rigging, the one on a ship sailing west, the other on a ship sailing east. Their ships pass close, close enough to hail. But the seas are rough, the weather is stormy: their eyes lashed by the spray, their hands burned by the cordage, they pass each other by, too busy even to wave.

J. M. Coetzee, *The Nobel Lecture in Literature*

In his Nobel Prize Lecture,[1] the 2003 Laureate in Literature John Maxwell Coetzee, drawing on Daniel Defoe's *Robinson Crusoe*, questioned the possibility of human community and the ethics of Otherness, a theme central to both gender and postcolonial studies.[2]

While criticising the forms of power that constitute the "experiences of cultural exclusion and division under empire," postcolonial writing[3] has sought to harness the capacity to read and resist against frameworks that promote the inequities of colonialism.[4] In such endeavours, it has been left to both gender and postcolonial studies to inquire, in often syncretic ways, on the gendered possibilities of living in a world touched and shaped by such inequities[5]: how one becomes or is a man or a woman, and the multiple meanings and societal norms attached to these terms in a postcolonial world, have been the animating questions of such joint intellectual ventures. The relations between both fields have, however, been fraught in the understanding of such connections. As Elleke Boehmer argues, "the occlusion of the constitutive role of gender … has centrally shaped and informed mainstream postcolonial studies."[6] The field of inquiry, in its mainstream, "constitutes a predominantly 'male province' to which this day relatively few (mostly privileged) women's voices are granted admission."[7]

Promoted by the feminist movement, the analysis and critique of the privileged positioning of masculinist bias within most societies gave rise, in the 1980s, to the creation of the interdisciplinary field of research on masculinities, with Australian sociologist Raewyn Connell's work figuring as an integral part of its theoretical framework.[8] Connell's attention to the intricacies of power present among men would give rise to a series of studies that would evince the multiplicity of arrangements in terms of masculine formations, with the field gaining increased notoriety and with applications in a range of different academic disciplines.

The now global movement of studies on masculinities, increasingly attentive to the tension of the global and the local, has provided valuable vocabulary, constructed in its connections to the feminist movement, which is now being employed to address the construction of masculinities in the postcolonial world.

Within the burgeoning field of studies on postcolonial masculinities, research on South African masculinities in particular, illustrates, for the most part, the necessary interconnections of gender with other social practices, such as race and sexuality. Claiming that the 1994 democratic transition would equally result in "masculinities in transition,"[9] studies have portrayed how South African masculinities are currently constructed in a societal space harbouring promises for change, as well as the continued enactment of oppressive violence towards women and Others, in particular in relation to issues regarding race and dissident sexualities.[10] Thus, the South African context, much like elsewhere in the postcolonial world, is one where the study of men and masculinities figures in an increasingly prominent way, illustrating how the possibilities of change towards more democratic notions, in terms of gender relations, has been one of the principal considerations of the field,[11] coupled still with the need to cope with resistance to such change.[12]

Informed by such a theoretical background, the present work, located in the intersection of gender and postcolonial studies, seeks to interrogate

J. M. Coetzee's trilogy,[13] *Boyhood*, *Youth* and *Summertime*,[14] in its elaboration of masculinities. We seek to understand whether such representations allow for a re-imagining of places where the Self and the Other can meet and, albeit encumbered by cultural and societal norms that tell otherwise, recognise the Other's humanity.[15] The main argument of the present work is that Coetzee's trilogy subverts the main tenets of masculinity as formulated under the guiding premise of masterful dominance over Others, instead opening relational spaces that indicate the promise of masculinities whose formulation is antithetical to cultural traditions whose historical relevance pertains to colonialism.[16]

(1)

In order to properly address such an argument, in this Introduction, we shall first contextualise Coetzee's *oeuvre*, with particular attention towards the trilogy, so as to demonstrate how such work necessarily responds to certain moments in South African history, and how it relates to cultural, literary and social politics. We then seek to understand how Coetzee's specific position within South African culture and towards authority promoted his creation of an ethical framework that necessarily informs much of the available criticism on his work. Such criticism, while preoccupied with a variety of issues has, however, largely eluded the connections between Coetzee's work and masculinities. As such, it should be noted how the present work is one of the few available existing works dealing specifically with such relation, in what is clearly still a burgeoning field. Additionally, and to our knowledge, the present work is the first to explore the connection between the Coetzeean trilogy and the representation of masculinities.

So as to effectively conduct such an exploration, this work is necessarily interdisciplinary in nature, due not only to the innate multiplicity of questions and vectors present when addressing studies on masculinities, but also to the need to contextualise cultural aspects that are at the core of Coetzee's writing. As shall be presented, the mysteries surrounding Coetzee and his work do not necessarily dismiss cultural factors. On the contrary, and as will be argued, such work is necessarily informed by cultural practices, be they literary, historical, political, or otherwise, much as they are addressed in variegated ways, presenting an understanding of writing and its functions that has produced many different responses, never, however, ceasing to surprise and lead to reflection.

The Man and His Mysteries:
Coetzee, Writing, and the Trilogy

Lauded as one of the foremost writers in contemporaneity, the 2003 Nobel Prize and twice Booker Prize winner[17] would exercise the minds and pens of literary and cultural critics around the world over the sparseness of details concerning his biography.[18] Notwithstanding some of his biographical data being available to the wider public, sufficient to draw a summary of his life as an academic, to the frustration of the literary and cultural establishment Coetzee's involvement with intellectual matters would prove to come hand in hand with a recognised tendency for reclusiveness,[19] thus foregoing more explicit understandings of his thoughts on such matters. As such, questions of identity arise as central in dealing with Coetzee's work: who is the man behind the initials,[20] the man whose books "are at the same time both highly abstract—artificial, allegorical, self-conscious—and shockingly actual"?[21]

Not only would questions of identity inform criticism on Coetzee's work, but also those regarding the political validity of his writing. His literary debut, with the publication of *Dusklands* in 1974, would see Coetzee as responsible for introducing Postmodernism in South Africa,[22] an adventurous task in a literary and cultural context where the emphasis was on Realism. The purported capacity for representation of life, the very possibility of verisimilitude: these were characteristics attractive to writers who sought to engage in responsible ways in a context of deep social injustice and violence. Through the espousal of ideas fermenting in a *littérature engagée*,[23] writers had much to say regarding the politics of *apartheid*. In this sense, the state of *apartheid* implied a call to arms in literary terms, in order to fight social repression. "The literary rendering of life under *apartheid*," suggests Louise Bethlehem, "was held to constitute a call to conscience."[24]

One of the major proponents of the realist strand, Nadine Gordimer, herself a Nobel Laureate, would clash with Coetzee's apparently disaffected, apolitical literary work. In a famous reading of Coetzee's 1983 novel *Life and Times of Michael K*, Gordimer suggests that Coetzee's characters are strained from entering the resolutions of the politics that shape them: "No one in this novel has any sense of taking part in determining that course; no one is shown to believe he knows what that course should be. The sense is of the ultimate malaise: of destruction. Not even the oppressor really believes in what he is doing, anymore, let alone the revolutionary."[25]

In a literary field dominated by the notion of "positionality," understood by critic David Attwell as the constant questioning of one's involvement in the wider societal politics,[26] Coetzee would come to inhabit the tense and strange position of the foreigner, the one who considered that the Self who writes is already enmeshed in this political discourse and is thus unable to recreate a clear, pristine view of it. In a particularly poignant reading by Attwell, Coetzee may be said to be looking not at the true nature of the writer, but rather on "what forms of self-definition are *available* within the culture—available, that is, to the *writer*, whose relationship to society rests on the way in which he, or she transmits the discourses of fiction."[27] Coetzee would eventually address some of these issues in his famous Jerusalem Prize speech:

> South African literature is a literature in bondage.... It is a less than fully human literature, unnaturally preoccupied with power and the torsions of power, unable to move from elementary relations of contestation, domination, and subjugation to the vast and complex world that lies beyond them.... In South Africa, there is now too much truth for art to hold, truth by the bucketful, truth that overwhelms and swamps every act of the imagination.[28]

Thus, the meaning of belonging, either to the Afrikaner *volk*,[29] or indeed to South Africa itself, is to Coetzee, as a white man and an intellectual, a politically and affectively charged question.

Those interested in Coetzee's life, or his politics have often resorted to his novelistic work, signaled as the more promising chance of deriving some sort of understanding regarding such nebulous layouts. Such an endeavour, necessarily fraught with perils,[30] has been premised on the notion that some of Coetzee's characters function as the writer's alter egos.[31]

Critics and readers alike would not be prepared for the publication of *Boyhood: Scenes from Provincial Life* in 1997, which came as something of a surprise and shock to the literary system.[32] Although *Boyhood* focuses on the account of a white boy living in *apartheid* South Africa from the age of ten to thirteen, the reader is not given a birthdate, nor a more immediate form of narrative that resembles an autobiography. Instead, the reader is provided with a series of hints, such as the name of the boy being John and belonging to the Coetzee family, from which it becomes increasingly possible to understand it as possessing an autobiographical bent.[33] It would, indeed, be marketed as a memoir, though this genre would seem unfitting, since it is written in the third person and in the present tense.

Youth, published in 2002, and *Summertime: Scenes from Provincial Life*, published in 2009, would add to the increasing controversy on the purported relation to its author's life, dismantling any hope of a coherent reading of the trilogy as strict autobiography. As Hermione Lee suggests, alluding to *Youth*: "It's an autobiography written 'under false pretences': it is never going to tell us how much is 'the truth' about the self, because it doesn't know what that is."[34]

These fictionalised memoirs, as critics have come to regard them,[35] are as such a point of added frustration to scholars and critics alike. As Charles van Onselen remarks in his review of *Boyhood* for the *London Review of Books*: "Anyone trying to discover something as simple as what the M in J. M. Coetzee stands for is not going to find it here.... One longs for detail—he has no date of birth, for instance—but one is always kept at arm's length."[36] Years later, Frank Kermode, while reviewing *Summertime*, would enunciate more clearly the genre-bending aspect of the trilogy: "These books are instalments of a sort of autobiography.... The author's purposes always call for liberty at the frontier between life and the freedoms of fiction."[37] The sentiment is echoed in Tim Parks's review: "*Summertime*'s shifty position between biography and fiction becomes a powerful analogy for Coetzee's difficulties positioning himself in the world; it is as we struggle to get to grips with its mixture of disclosure and secretiveness that we come closest to him."[38] We may then conclude that Coetzee belongs to a group of writers who are experimenting with autobiography, necessarily subverting it.[39]

To the purported inescapable truth that autobiography as genre stands for,[40] made available by what Judith Butler terms "a coherent autobiographer,"[41] Coetzee posits instead an understanding of human subjectivity in which the Self is necessarily split. In this mode, autobiography then becomes an act of narrating the Self as Other, what Coetzee terms "*autre*biography,"[42] an elaboration quickly followed upon by critics.[43]

Contrary, thus, to Jean-Jacques Rousseau's claim to speak true of one's nature,[44] Coetzee's exploration of the autobiographical edifice would indicate how this postcolonial writer recognises, much like Lejeune, and yet with different implications, the nature of autobiography as akin to a pact, negotiated as it is according to specific contexts.[45] For Coetzee, autobiographical truth is always constrained,[46] due to the interplay of psychic resistance and linguistic automatism, and its cultural propension to universalistic truth.[47]

[pig quote]

Coetzee's Ethical Framework

Universal truth would prove to be the hallmark of masculinity, as espoused by Western culture. Reason and mastery over nature through a mathematical understanding of the world (*mathesis*) are central to the formulation of the Cartesian *cogito*, the affirmation of the all-knowing subject of consciousness.[48] Kant, in his 1784 essay *Was ist Aufklärung?* [*What is the Enlightenment?*], advances the notion that the Enlightenment "is man's emergence from his self-incurred immaturity,"[49] with the rational and self-sufficient, masculine "I" as one of its main tenets, and the universal site for knowledge and power.[50]

Masculinity, defined within this strict framework, as the site of violence and domination, "presupposes a belief in individual difference and personal agency. In that sense it is built on the conception of individuality that developed in early-modern Europe with the growth of colonial empires and capitalist economic relations."[51] A prime example of such a mode of masculinity would be Daniel Defoe's Robinson, the solitary man enacting the man of Reason: "So I went to work; and here I must needs observe, that as Reason is the Substance and Original of the Mathematicks, so by stating and squaring every thing by Reason, and by making the most rational Judgment of things, every Man may be in time Master of every mechanick Art."[52]

In Coetzee's Nobel Lecture, suitably titled "He and His Man," the South African author engages with Defoe's ventriloquist ways, underlining both the inspiration he drew from the writer, but also the necessary political distance in terms of considering the Other's place in one's sense of being in the world. On his reading of *Robinson Crusoe*, Coetzee recognises its anthropocentricism, enacted through the paternalistic relation to Friday and the native people. These are the doings of a framework where "all secondary characters in Defoe's I-centred fictions tend to be ciphers."[53]

The paternalistic attitude is an hallmark of the treatment of colonial masculinities, whereby the colonised is attributed a feminine position, contrary to the masculine position of the coloniser. The rational mind, considered as masculine, creates a notion of the world as disenchanted, strained from a relationship to the Other outside an utilitarian scope, and thus enacted through "feelings of omnipotence."[54] The always tense concepts of "masculine" and "feminine" are, therefore, at the core of the imperial experience, whether in its militaristic enactments, or in its wider cultural proposals of symbolic and group adhesion.

In advocating writing Self as Other, Coetzee's work espouses an anti-Cartesian ethics, whereby the Self holds multiplicity,[55] and the Other is not reduced to the Self, such relation being presented as more complex and not exempt of contradictions.[56] As philosopher Jonathan Lear argues, it is in the creation of multiple voices and differing opinions that Coetzee's ethical thinking is foregrounded, so as to better allow for an elaborate reflexive practice on the part of the reader over aspects of power and related issues pertaining to ethical thinking.[57]

Through such strategies, Lear suggests that Coetzee is able to "address different parts of our soul at more or less the same time,"[58] recognising in this the uneasy relation of the individual to power. The anxious placement of Coetzee as heir to the Afrikaner community has sparked in the writer a cautious awareness of his tense positioning regarding the particularly charged topic of the representation of the Other in textual form. Ultimately, both Attridge and Lear agree that Coetzee seeks to deny a single authority in terms of interpretative validity.[59]

Some critics, such as Gayatri Spivak, have understood Coetzee's reluctance in engaging with otherwise more direct representations as a sign of responsibility.[60] More recently, and arguing much in the vein of Attridge and Lear's understanding of Coetzee's ethical framework, Spivak posits how Coetzee's work underlines the difficulty of the continuous, perseverant nature of ethics, which cannot otherwise be defined in a single instant.[61]

Benita Parry, however, criticises Coetzee's lack of overall more direct representations. While acknowledging Coetzee's interrogation of colonial power, Parry suggests that "the consequence of writing the silence attributed to the subjugated as a liberation from the constraints of subjectivity … can be read as re-enacting the received disposal of narrative authority."[62] Replying to this critique, Chris Prentice posits that Coetzee's narrativistic strategy is anchored in the production of unreliableness that "is a gesture against the arrogation of authority to the dominant self as a means either to silence or to represent the other."[63] Equally, it derides other figures of authority, such as the presence of the Author as master signifier of interpretative function.[64] In this, the trilogy also questions the place of Reason,[65] furthermore being intertextually linked to works that question authority and authorship.

The organisation of the trilogy is influenced by Leo Tolstoy's *Childhood, Boyhood, Youth* (published in 1852, 1854, 1857 respectively)[66] and Joseph Conrad's *Youth: A Narrative* (1898).[67] Both Tolstoy and Conrad provide accounts of the exuberance of youth, and the interplay of fantasies and reality, with such adventures resulting in a sense of dismay and melancholy.

As Dominic Head remarks, "Tolstoy, like Coetzee, presents his earlier self in an unfavourable light,"[68] further considering Coetzee's *Youth* to be a post-colonial reworking of Conrad's short story, with the element of transcendence located in colonial youth to be missing from Coetzee's portrayal. Differing experiences of the colonialist project would, then, account for different ways of portraying such experience, with the possibility of arguing that the trilogy is also aligned with other works by Conrad, particularly *Heart of Darkness*,[69] *The Shadow-Line*,[70] and *Lord Jim*,[71] that underscore both the allure and, especially in the case of the latter, the futility of dominant modes of masculinity.

Contrary to the surprise enacted in the literary scene, the vantage point of history enables us to better understand how the cultural context of South Africa's democratic transitioning would be a key force in the making of the trilogy. As André Brink notes, the cultural pull in the young democratic South Africa would be of "a move inward, away from politics as drama and spectacle and social phenomenon towards internalization and interiority."[72] The wider societal turn towards the autobiographical genre would, in the case of white writers, be employed as means to deride, or expiate the until then presiding Afrikaner identity, through pointing out its gaps and ultimate failures, such manoeuvres being highly inadmissible in the tightly controlled and censured *(ok)* environment of *apartheid*. RELAXATION OF CENSORSHIP

It is in recognising such cultural and historical coordinates that one may argue that Coetzee's denial in terms of his clear participation in the moment of public expiation over South Africa's past sins through the autobiographical genre, may be read through a gender and postcolonial lens. This is particularly important for the present work, for Coetzee's doubts on the merits of such an optimistic social discourse,[73] while provocatively delineated and made more available in his novel *Disgrace*, are also reflected in the memoirs.

Contrary, therefore, to societal expectations, the Self that is rendered throughout the trilogy is characterised in deeply unpleasant terms, ultimately being described as "wooden," thus eclipsing the expected narrative of a privileged, important man seeking redemption from the sins of the past attached to his cultural group. Such strategy functions in a number of ways, not only in further deriding the hopes of biographical scrutiny by those interested in Coetzee, but also providing the possibility of not enslaving other voices so as to perform a more narcissistic enacting of the Self.[74] *(?)*

I don't think 'Boyhood' came out as particularly uncritical of Afrikaner ~~...~~

In this movement, and by portraying a deeply flawed individual, Coetzee indicates how expiatory practice cannot be attained by autobiography. Instead, and as persuasively argued by Rita Barnard, Coetzee's acknowledgement of creative work as the composite site of both unwanted and desired aspects of oneself,[75] indicates how redemption, if achievable at all, necessarily holds a relational quality. His subversion of autobiography, thus, carries not only a questioning of the writer's position within the new South Africa. It equally suggests a message in terms of gender politics, often disregarded by the available scholarly criticism to date, namely in terms of masculinities.

The Possibilities of Imagining Otherwise

The aforementioned tense politics of representation necessarily reflect the differing views of critics on Coetzee's representation of gendered life. As we have seen, Coetzee oftentimes adopts the imaginative portrayal of women to introduce himself in the public eye, performing a sort of "textual transvestism," in Lucy Graham's felicitous expression.[76] Coetzee's genealogy of female narrators, as much as it constitutes an entry into the politics of the disenfranchised, also underlines a mode of identification wherein Coetzee recognises his own ambiguous position in South Africa, as underlined by Laura Wright.[77] And yet, Elleke Boehmer, commenting on *Disgrace*, suggests frustration over the always tactful way of Coetzee's engagement with representation, in that Lucy Lurie, the white woman, remains the *locus* of sacrifice even in the renewed political landscape of democratic South Africa.[78]

An added question may be, however, and as Rosemarie Buikema suggests, whether such frustration may not be understood as the main function of art, resulting in a necessary engagement towards the recognition of the still prevalent predicament of women and other groups even within the new democratic nation.[79] While cognisant of the validity of the appeal for fiction to transcend its context of origin, one could note how such a request would also play its part in the continued silencing of the interplay between the formation of masculinities in South Africa and the still perilous situation of the disenfranchised.

The claims of such an argument rest in Rosemary Jolly's assertion that the common denominator of masculinity in South Africa remains its link with violence.[80] In *Disgrace*, David Lurie embodies the discomforting tensions of post-*apartheid* for the white privileged man, now evicted from political power,

yet whose patriarchal lineage, as exhibited in Coetzee's work, is one that exhibits hyper-masculinity as integral to the formation of the coloniser. Much
like the burgeoning field of South African studies on masculinities deals with
the tensions revolving around change, in the field of post-*apartheid* literary
fiction one can witness a somewhat reluctant view in terms of the possibilities
of reshaping masculinity. Issues of control remain at the foreground, revealing
the troubling—yet expected—notion that formations of masculinity in the
democratic polity still engage with the traditions of its past, re-enacting, or
possibly deriding them, in often confusing and, in many ventures, conservative ways.

Much of the available published criticism on the relation between Coetzee and masculinities is, then, on the topic of crisis, namely on how the privileged white male acts in a different political context in which his political and
cultural power is now largely diminished. Elahe Yekani argues that Coetzee's
work may be understood in the context of the renegotiation of hegemonic
masculinity presenting a critique of the white masculine dominant Self as a
"failing Self."[81] Emily Davis, reading *Waiting for the Barbarians*, considers how
the dominant tenets of imperial masculinity are revisited in the encounter
with the racialised Other's suffering. It is in bearing witness to the Other's
pain that masculinity redraws its coordinates, questioning its foundations.
And yet, according to Davis, imperial masculinity is never entirely imagined
otherwise, the lack of alternatives becoming clear.[82]

Brenna Munro provides a more persuasive reading of masculinity in crisis
as portrayed by Coetzee. The democratic transition saw Gordimer and Coetzee introduce gay characters, in part a response to the hopeful times, in part
the recognition of the gay person as a welcomed sign of novelty espoused by
the new nation. While Munro agrees with the relatively stunted characterisation of these queer characters, her understanding of South African politics
allows her to consider how *Disgrace* argues that the utopian dreams core to
democratic South Africa may never be realised in the midst of the reconciliatory pull if justice over land and property is not given its due political
attention. To this end, the queer children of South Africa inherit a past of
violence that is still being played out, though in differing ways. The narrative
then is twofold: theirs is the future, though inquisitive doubt remains over the
possibility of creating newness.[83]

Such future, as should by now be clear, is in large part dependent on how
scholarship engages with issues pertaining to masculinities and the possibilities of cultural (re)formulation according to tenets other than the traditional

not real yet

ones, infused as they are with violence and destruction. As a site of recon-figuration of the tensions related to inhabiting the place of the white South African, Pieter Vermeulen argues that Coetzee understands the imperative of the continuing struggles of the South African polity, and the need to carry its aspirations in writing, purporting literature to be a space of renewed search for the ethical in terms of the disenfranchised.[84] To this, Sam Cardoen's intima-tion that the trilogy, in particular *Summertime*, employs gossip as community-making is telling, for it is a discourse enacted after the event of John's death, the textual marker of the wounded aspirations of the white dominant man in South Africa. Cardoen argues that the trilogy's depiction of John as a failed man may be read as an overly "satirical response to [Coetzee's] sense of shame or paranoia,"[85] thus alluding to Coetzee's own sense of shame and guilt over his position as a man of a privileged background, and its confusing ramifica-tions.[86]

As Eckard Smuts suggests, Coetzee introduces accountability through the espousal of doubt, delineating how political predicaments necessarily organise one's selfhood, while at the same time nodding towards the need of not sub-merging oneself in such a discourse, so as to retain a modicum of criticism.[87]

Outline

Aware of the complex cultural, historical and political landscape portrayed in the trilogy, the present work, through its engagement with the largely silenced theme of masculinities in Coetzee's *oeuvre*, seeks also to account for the neces-sity of such scholarly inquiry.

In the first part, "Masculinities," we begin by tracing the significance of masculinity in the core work of postcolonial studies. The double effect of masculinity is noticed, for while it informs the central characteristics of such work, its influence is largely absent from direct critique. We thus argue that it is in the syncretic meeting of postcolonial and gender studies that the pos-sibility of such critique arises. Reaching such a point, we move to a possible historical delineation of the rise of studies on masculinities, its problematics as well as its theoretical tools.

The second part, "Making Men: Places of Masculinities," focuses on the institutionalised sites that provide the social templates for approved codes of masculinity. The chapter "Fathers of the Nation," will draw on existing dis-cussions of gender and nationalism in order to question the trilogy's relation to these, much as it also provides a questioning look on the difficulties that the new South Africa provides in its democratic promises to the formation of new gendered identities.

"Family Outcast" interrogates the relation of the trilogy to the enactment of masculinity through sports. In this, British Empire's gendered codes and aspirations are questioned in their articulation with the trilogy. The aesthetics of heroism, drawn from imperialist-induced readings of history and morality, play an alluring role particularly in the boy's formative years. The remote control of patriarchy is, however, understood in its forced administrative dynamic of the rule-bound game. The main argument provided is that heroism as a mandate of imperial masculinity is recognised in its alluring seduction, but ultimately shown to be a societal construction that denies creativity and freer expression of oneself.

Having suggested that Coetzee's trilogy may be read as harbouring seeds of dissidence regarding established myths of nationalistic becoming, and thus fracturing imperialistic notions of rule over Others, in "Art of One," the focus will be on the sphere of cultural kinship. Writing, for Coetzee, functions as an homosocial event, through the exploration of the intellectual debt to one's literary fathers. This, however, is accompanied with the understanding that canonical disposition, as a result of ingrained societal powers, disavows more liberatory views of the Other. Attending to the gendered realities of the Sixties, the decade of untold promises and commited political activism, and the tensions found in the play between provincial life and life in the metropole,[88] we seek to demonstrate how literary influence may still prove to be the saving gusto for political insertion.

In the third part, "Making the Other: Alternatives to Hegemony," we reflect on how the difficult, paradoxical nature of the moment of recognition between Self and Other is one of the animating themes of the trilogy. Here the focus will be on the spaces that the trilogy provides the often non-privileged Others in the hierarchical notions of a gender system. We seek to demonstrate how the shame and guilt of the protagonist over his privileged position enact already a Other-led ethics that questions the politics that affords the white, male and heterosexual population its status as the dominant group.

In "Race and Masculinities" we interrogate how black men are portrayed in the trilogy. To this end, we delineate the continuous portrayal, per European tenets, of the racialised Other as monstrous, a being filled with the projected excess of European desires and frustrations. Contrary to such fantastical enactments, we argue that the trilogy seeks to redraw some sense of justice, by positing the racialised Other as the true inheritor to the land, in the process considering the European progeny as traitors to such a land.

In "Shades and Shadows of Life: Women in Dark Times," we argue that women are, in the context of Coetzee's work, the privileged point of entry into more obvious enactment of politics. Drawing from the contextualised tensions of South African women's movement towards recognition, we discuss that it is through the voicing of women, even if always from the imaginative point of a man, that Coetzee draws the terms of recognition further into the negotiation between mastery and intersubjectivity.

In "Queer Other," the national metaphor of South Africa as coming out of the closet of its dark times, into the happier days of multiculturalism and diversity, is questioned in its possibility. Depicting the troubling relations between colonialism and homosexuality, we argue that the trilogy disrupts a discourse of the latter as stranger to the African polity, instead arguing for the collaborative potential in accepting the queer Other as source of creativity, compassion and friendship. Such politics of friendship necessarily disrupt the dominant notion of masculinity, as they create the necessary mental and physical space for communion with the stranger. We further argue that the trilogy plays with intimations of queering John, that is, of placing him as the site of difference according to societal norms. In playfully portraying the heir to white dominant masculinity as himself a possible queer Other, we surmise that Coetzee is necessarily advancing anticolonial thinking, deriding imperialism in favor of human connection.

We conclude that Coetzee creates a narrative that resists the normative pull of traditional masculinity, by allowing for an understanding of the ambivalence that one faces when presented with the ideal that is hegemonic masculinity. Coetzee does not present, however, a simplistic account, as he is masterful at showcasing the allure of the normative pulls towards homogeneity (disguised as greatness) that constitutes the place of hegemony in gendered terms. One can argue, though, that by showcasing such ambivalence, the contradictions that preside to gender formations, Coetzee provides an ethical account of masculinity, thus creating certain spaces for further imaginative play of the consequences that such spaces can have and how they may be achieved in an outside world that is itself deeply charged with its own set of fantasies.

Notes

1. J. M. Coetzee, *The Nobel Lecture in Literature* (New York: Penguin, 2004).
2. See Robert Young, *Postcolonialism: A Very Short Introduction* (Oxford: Oxford University Press, 2003); Manuela Ribeiro Sanches, "Afinidades Selectivas. Edward W. Said e a Perspectiva Pós-Colonial," in *Pensamento Crítico Contemporâneo*, ed. UNIPOP (Lisboa: Edições 70, 2014), 344–62.
3. Whereas the hyphenated term "post-colonial" is oftentimes employed in a strict chronological sense, usually referring to the projects of decolonisation that occurred in the twentieth century, the non-hyphenated term "postcolonial" seeks to draw attention to the possibilities of reading and interpreting texts which preceded such movements of decolonisation through a framework of adherence, or resistance to imperialist and colonialist norms. In this sense, postcolonial literature is that which allows to read otherwise regarding the colonial outlook, "to resist colonialist perspectives" and to seek resistance to them. See Elleke Boehmer, *Colonial and Postcolonial Literature: Migrant Metaphors*, 2nd ed. (Oxford: Oxford University Press, 2005 [1995]), 3.
4. We understand colonialism as "the practice of planting and securing colonies' and imperialism as a set of 'attitudes, structures, philosophies or processes that facilitate the practice of colonialism." See Julie Mullaney, *Postcolonial Literatures in Context* (London: Continuum, 2010), 3.
5. As Robert Young argues, "postcolonial critique focuses on forces of oppression and coercive domination that operate in the contemporary world: the politics of anti-colonialism and neocolonialism, race, gender, nationalisms, class and ethnicities define its terrain." *Postcolonialism: An Historical Introduction* (Oxford: Blackwell, 2001), 11.
6. See Elleke Boehmer, "Edward Said and (the Postcolonial Occlusion of) Gender," in *Edward Said and the Literary, Social, and Political World*, ed. Ranjan Ghosh (New York: Routledge, 2009), 126.
7. Boehmer, "Postcolonial Occlusion," 134.
8. R. W. Connell, *Masculinities*, 2nd ed. (Cambridge: Polity Press, 2005 [1995]).
9. Robert Morrell, "The Times of Change: Men and Masculinity in South Africa," in *Changing Men in Southern Africa*, ed. Robert Morrell (London: Zed Books, 2001), 3–37.
10. Robert Morrell, "Men, Movements, and Gender Transformation in South Africa," in *African Masculinities: Men in Africa from the Late Nineteenth Century to the Present*, ed. Ouzgane Lahoucine and Robert Morrell (New York: Palgrave Macmillan, 2005), 271–88.
11. Robert Morrell and others, "Hegemonic Masculinity: Reviewing the Gendered Analysis of Men's Power in South Africa," *South African Review of Sociology* 44, no. 1 (2013): 3–21.
12. Kopano Ratele, "Currents against Gender Transformation of South African Men: Relocating Marginality to the Centre of Research and Theory of Masculinities," *NORMA: International Journal for Masculinity Studies* 9, no. 1 (2014): 30–44.
13. Following available criticism on the three works, we consider them as a trilogy. See, for instance, Paulina Grzeda, "The Ethico-Politics of Autobiographical Writings: J. M. Coetzee's *Boyhood*, *Youth* and *Summertime*," *Werkwinkel* 7, no. 2 (2012): 77–101. The latest anthology of essays on Coetzee's *oeuvre* also considers the three works as forming a trilogy.

See Sue Kossew, "Scenes from Provincial Life (1997–2009)," in *A Companion to the Works of J. M. Coetzee*, ed. Tim Mehigan (Rochester, New York: Camden House, 2011), 9–22.

14. *Boyhood: Scenes from Provincial Life* (London: Vintage, 1998 [1997]); *Youth* (London: Vintage, 2003 [2002]); *Summertime: Scenes from Provincial Life* (London: Vintage, 2010 [2009]). Henceforth references to these texts in the present work will appear only with the respective initial and, where applicable, the page(s) of the passage(s) that are being referred to.

15. As Ania Loomba argues, the dialectic between Self and Other has, in the scope of colonial discourse, necessarily been understood as a manichean allegory of a "us *versus* them" mentality, whereby the Self of the coloniser seeks to obliviate the colonised, represented as the Other. *Colonialism/Postcolonialism*, 2nd ed. (New York: Routledge, 2005 [1998]). We understand the Self to be a historical being, a singularity that is irremediably in relation to an alterity, the Other. See Jessica Benjamin, *Like Subjects, Love Objects: Essays on Recognition and Sexual Difference* (New Haven and London: Yale University Press, 1995), in particular 35–39.

16. For methodological purposes, it should be noted that, in order to augment our understanding of the trilogy's representation of masculinities, we shall be addressing various other works by Coetzee, interrelated as they are in the presentation of themes that are central to our arguments.

17. Coetzee was the first novelist to win the Booker Prize twice: in 1983 for *Life and Times of Michael K*, and in 1999 for *Disgrace*. See J. M. Coetzee, *Life & Times of Michael K* (London: Vintage, 2004 [1983]); *Disgrace* (London: Vintage, 2000 [1999]). It should also be noted how Coetzee would reach international success after the publication of his third novel, *Waiting for the Barbarians* (London: Vintage, 2004 [1980]).

18. The first biography on Coetzee is by renowned biographer J. C. Kannemeyer. See J. M. *Coetzee: A Life in Writing*, trans. Michiel Heyns (Johannesburg and Cape Town: Jonathan Ball Publishers, 2012).

19. A topic Coetzee himself would address in *Doubling the Point*, a collection of essays and interviews with David Attwell. For more on this matter, see *Doubling the Point*, ed. David Attwell (Cambridge, MA: Harvard University Press, 1992 [1986]), especially 65.

20. A question posed more intently in Imraan Coovadia, "Coetzee In and Out of Cape Town," *Kritika Kultura* 18 (2012): 103–15.

21. Hedley Twidle, "Getting Past Coetzee," *Financial Times*, December 28, 2012, http://www.ft.com/cms/s/2/d2a3d68a-4923-11e2-9225-00144feab49a.html#axzz2Gk4csP8i [accessed 28 September 2013] (para 19 of 29).

22. As Dominic Head further comments, Coetzee "is the first South African writer to produce overtly self-conscious fictions drawing explicitly on international postmodernism." See J. M. *Coetzee* (Cambridge: Cambridge University Press, 1997), 1.

23. As André Brink suggests, while *apartheid*'s attack on imagination would prove successful to some degree, it would meet with a degree of resistance, namely on the part of writers, as "it imposed certain priorities on a writer's choice of themes," notwithstanding the various ways in which such would happen, be it in a more overt or nuanced way. "Stories of History: Reimagining the Past in Post-Apartheid Narrative," in *Negotiating the Past: The Making*

of Memory in South Africa, ed. Sarah Nuttall and Carli Coetzee (Cape Town: Oxford University Press, 1998), 29.

24. Louise Bethlehem, "The Pleasures of the Political: *Apartheid* and *Postapartheid* South African Fiction," in *Teaching the African Novel*, ed. Gaurav Desai (New York: The Modern Language Association of America, 2009), 226.

25. Nadine Gordimer, "The Idea of Gardening," *New York Review of Books*, February 2, 1984, http://www.nybooks.com/articles/archives/1984/feb/02/the-idea-of-gardening/ [accessed 3 April 2012] (para 15 of 22).

26. David Attwell argues that "in South Africa a writer's worldliness expresses itself within a fragmented national context in which *positionality* is always at issue; thus, certain questions continually resurface: Who is the self-of-writing? What is his or her power, representativeness, legitimacy, and authority?" *J. M. Coetzee: South Africa and the Politics of Writing* (Berkeley: University of California Press, 1993), 3.

27. Attwell, *South Africa and the Politics of Writing*, 13.

28. J. M. Coetzee, "Jerusalem Prize Acceptance Speech," in *Doubling the Point*, 98–99.

29. The term "Afrikaner" (the Afrikaans word for African) will be employed in its more widespread usage, that of designing white-Afrikaans speakers in South Africa, especially after 1875 and during the mid-twentieth century. It should be noted, though, that the term is rife with different usages, being first employed in 1707 and eventually coming to designate Europeans who spoke Dutch or Afrikaans. "Afrikaans" is a creolised version of Dutch. See Herman Giliomee, *The Afrikaners: Biography of a People* (London: C. Hurst & Co, 2011). One of its first uses was by Estienne Barbier, a political insubordinate towards the Dutch East India Company (VOC, *Vereenigde Oost-Indisch Compagnie*), displeased by the contracts between the company and the Khoikhoi. See Nigel Penn, "Estienne Barbier: An Eighteenth-Century Cape Social Bandit," in *Rogues, Rebels and Runaways: Eighteenth-Century Cape Characters*, ed. Nigel Penn (Cape Town: David Philip Publishers, 1999), 101. Barbier's life would also be fictionalised by the hands of André Brink in *On the Contrary: Being the Life of a Famous Rebel, Soldier, Traveller, Explorer, Reader, Builder, Scribe, Latinist, Lover and Liar* (London: Martin Secker & Warburg Limited, 1993).

30. Here it is worth mentioning David Attwell's latest work on Coetzee, based on his study of the archive of Coetzee's manuscripts made recently available to the public at the Harry Ransom Center, located at the University of Texas at Austin. See David Attwell, *J. M. Coetzee and the Life of Writing* (New York: Viking, 2015). Characteristically, Attwell's main argument is that Coetzee's entire *oeuvre* is autobiographical in nature, though necessarily reworked, reframed, retouched with various layers of fiction. Attwell aptly summarises his argument in the following way: "The ant boring its way through rock is a good metaphor for all of Coetzee's writing" (2).

31. The most obvious case would be that of Elizabeth Costello, a character depicted as an aging Australian academic and public speaker, who would act as a stand-in for her author in various of his public appearances. Her "debut" would be in the 1996 Ben Belitt Lecture at Bennington College, wherein Coetzee gave the lecture addressing the audience as Costello. Costello's most famous "appearance" would be in the Tanner Lectures on Human Values at Princeton University, to which Coetzee was invited in 1997. The two lectures, presented in *The Lives of Animals* (Princeton: Princeton University Press, 1999),

would be recollected in the novel *Elizabeth Costello: Eight Lessons* (London: Secker & Warburg, 2003). Costello would also figure in the novel *Slow Man* (London: Vintage, 2006 [2005]). According to critics, Coetzeean alter egos seem to be more prominent in the author's latter half of his career, namely in the post-*apartheid* era. See Dominic Head, *Cambridge Introduction to J. M. Coetzee* (Cambridge: Cambridge University Press, 2009) for this possible division of Coetzee's works.

32. As suggested by Derek Attridge, *J. M. Coetzee and the Ethics of Reading* (Chicago and London: University of Chicago Press, 2004), particularly 138–61.

33. A preliminary exploration of elements that would form the recognisable basis for Coetzee's quasi-autobiographical trilogy first appeared, most explicitly, in Coetzee and David Attwell's last interview in *Doubling the Point*. In this revealing event, Coetzee provides the outline of the story of a white South African man living in the latter half of the twentieth century who leaves his country while pursuing a career in the field of mathematics, until eventually favouring an academic life, a decision that seems partly to reflect his having been seduced by Samuel Beckett's literary style. Coetzee, *Doubling the Point*, 393.

34. Hermione Lee, "Heart of Stone: J. M. Coetzee," in *Body Parts: Essays on Life-Writing* (London: Pimlico, 2008), 168.

35. See Kossew, "Scenes from Provincial Life (1997–2009)," 9. The recent publication of the collected edition of the three books is also marketed as such. J. M. Coetzee, *Scenes from Provincial Life* (London: Harvill Secker, 2011).

36. Charles van Onselen, "A Childhood on the Edge of History," *London Review of Books*, February 5, 1998, http://www.lrb.co.uk/v20/n03/charles-van-onselen/a-childhood-on-the-edge-of-history [accessed 17 July 2012] (para 10 of 17).

37. Frank Kermode, "Fictioneering," *London Review of Books*, October 9, 2009, http://www.lrb.co.uk/v31/n19/frank-kermode/fictioneering [accessed 23 July 2012] (para 1 of 18).

38. Tim Parks, "The Education of 'John Coetzee'", *New York Review of Books*, February 11, 2010, http://www.nybooks.com/articles/archives/2010/feb/11/the-education-of-john-coetzee/ [accessed 11 July 2012] (para 32 of 32).

39. Patrick Madden argues to this effect. See "The 'New Memoir'", in *The Cambridge Companion to Autobiography*, ed. Maria DiBattista and Emily Wittman (Cambridge: Cambridge University Press, 2014), 234.

40. According to Linda Anderson, it is a notion of "intentionality" that informs the edifice of autobiography, an understanding that "the author is behind the text, controlling its meaning; the author becomes the guarantor of the 'intentional' meaning or truth of the text, and reading a text therefore leads back to the author as origin." *Autobiography*, 2nd ed. (New York: Routledge, 2011 [2001]), 2. French theorist Philippe Lejeune, based on a post-1770 European body of work, provides the working definition of "autobiography" as "a retrospective prose narrative produced by a real person concerning his own existence, focusing on his individual life, in particular on the development of his personality." "The Autobiographical Contract," in *French Literary Theory Today*, ed. Tzvetan Todorov (Cambridge: Cambridge University Press, 1982), 193. Eventually, Paul de Man would polemicise the central argument of autobiography as being created from the unitary subject, instead suggesting that the author of an autobiography is enacting a series of defacements

that demonstrate the impossibility of a strictly true, unchallengeable account of oneself. See "Autobiography as De-Facement," *MLN* 94, no. 5 (1979): 919–30.

41. Judith Butler, *Giving an Account of Oneself* (New York: Fordham University Press, 2005), 64. It should be noted how Butler is highly critical of the possibility of autobiography as coherent narrative, sharing alongside Coetzee a deep suspicion of the genre's claim to truth.

42. Coetzee, *Doubling the Point*, 394.

43. On this point, see: Kossew, "Scenes from Provincial Life (1997–2009)," 21; Margaret Lenta, "*Autre*biography: J. M. Coetzee's *Boyhood* and *Youth*," *English in Africa* 30, no. 1 (2003): 157–69 and Sheila Collingwood-Whittick, "Autobiography as *Autre*biography: The Fictionalisation of the Self in JM Coetzee's *Boyhood: Scenes from Provincial Life*," *Commonwealth* 24, no. 1 (2001): 13–23.

44. "Je forme une entreprise qui n'eut jamais d'exemple et dont l'exécution n'aura point d'imitateur. Je veux montrer à mes semblables un homme dans toute la vérité de la nature; et cet homme ce sera moi." Jean-Jacques Rousseau, *Les Confessions* (Paris: Gallimard, 2009 [1782–1789]), 33.

45. "An autobiographer is not only a man who once upon a time lived a life in which he loved, fought, suffered, strove, was misunderstood, and of which he now tells the story; he is also a man engaged in writing a story. That story is written within the limits of a pact, the pact of autobiography, one of the many pacts negotiated over the years between writers and readers (and always open to renegotiation) for each of the genres and sub-genres, pacts which cover, among other things, what demands may be made of each genre and what may not, what questions may be asked and what may not, what one may see and what one must be blind to. (Another of the clauses is that one shall be blind to the existence of the pact.)" J. M. Coetzee, "Truth in Autobiography" (unpublished inaugural lecture, University of Cape Town, 1984), 5. See also J. M. Coetzee, "A Fiction of the Truth," *Sydney Morning Herald*, November 27, 1999.

46. See J. M. Coetzee, "Confession and Double Thoughts: Tolstoy, Rousseau, Dostoevsky," in *Doubling the Point*, 251–93.

47. Such elements are discussed in the recently published series of exchanges between Coetzee and psychotherapist Arabella Kurtz. Coetzee's argument should by now be familiar; yet the following passage is still worth quoting so as to ascertain the permanence of such matters in his current work: "The claim is that in making up our autobiography we exercise the same freedom that we have in dreams, where we impose a narrative form that is our own, even if influenced by forces that are obscure to us, on elements of a remembered reality." See J. M. Coetzee and Arabella Kurtz, *The Good Story: Exchanges on Truth, Fiction and Psychotherapy* (London: Harvill Secker, 2015), 3.

48. René Descartes, *A Discourse on the Method*, trans. Ian Maclean (Oxford: Oxford University Press, 2008).

49. Immanuel Kant, *An Answer to the Question: "What is Enlightenment?"*, trans. H. B. Nisbet (London: Penguin, 1991 [1784]), 1.

50. As Leela Gandhi argues: "Cartesian philosophy of identity is premised upon an ethically unsustainable omission of the Other." *Postcolonial Theory: A Critical Introduction* (Crows Nest: Allen & Unwin, 1998), 39.

51. R. W. Connell, "The Social Organization of Masculinity," in *The Masculinities Reader*, ed. Stephen M. Whitehead and Frank J. Barrett (Cambridge: Polity Press, 2001), 31.

52. Daniel Defoe, *Robinson Crusoe* (Oxford: Oxford University Press, 2007 [1719]), 59.

53. J. M. Coetzee, "Daniel Defoe, *Robinson Crusoe*," in *Stranger Shores: Essays 1986–1999*, ed. J. M. Coetzee (London: Vintage, 2001), 20–26.

54. Laurenz Volkmann, "Fortified Masculinity: Daniel Defoe's *Robinson Crusoe* as a Literary Emblem of Western Male Identity," in *Constructions of Masculinity in British Literature from the Middle Ages to the Present*, ed. Stefan Horlacher (New York: Palgrave Macmillan, 2011), 137.

55. This reading is in accord with an earlier essay by Coetzee, where the writer talks of his understanding of the human Self as akin to a zoo: "The self, as we understand the self today, is not the unity it was assumed to be by classical rationalism. On the contrary, it is multiple and multiply divided against itself. It is, to speak in figures, a zoo in which a multitude of beasts have residence, over which the anxious, overworked zookeeper of rationality exercises a rather limited control. At night the zookeeper sleeps and the beasts roam about, doing their dream-work." J. M. Coetzee, *Giving Offense: Essays on Censorship* (Chicago: Chicago University Press, 1996), 37. It should be noted that Coetzee provides an inclusion of the unconscious as contrary to rationality's hyper-vigil. For another, earlier, understanding of the Self by Coetzee, see the essay "Achterberg's 'Ballade van de gasfitter'", in *Doubling the Point*, where Coetzee considers how "all versions of the *I* are fictions of the *I*. The primal *I* is not recoverable" (75).

56. As indicated by Martin Woessner, "Coetzee's Critique of Reason," in *J. M. Coetzee and Ethics*, ed. Anton Leist and Peter Singer (New York: Columbia University Press, 2010), 223–47.

57. Jonathan Lear, "The Ethical Thought of J. M. Coetzee," *Raritan* 28, no. 1 (2008): 72.

58. Lear, "The Ethical Thought of J. M. Coetzee," 74.

59. See Attridge, *J. M. Coetzee and the Ethics of Reading*, 7; Lear, "The Ethical Thought of J. M. Coetzee," 71.

60. Gayatri Chakravorty Spivak, "Theory in the Margin: Coetzee's *Foe* Reading Defoe's *Crusoe/Roxana*," *English in Africa* 17, no. 2 (1990): 1–23.

61. Gayatri Chakravorty Spivak, "Ethics and Politics in Tagore, Coetzee, and Certain Scenes of Teaching," in *An Aesthetic Education in the Era of Globalization*, ed. Gayatri Chakravorty Spivak (Cambridge, MA: Harvard University Press, 2012), 316–34.

62. Benita Parry, "Speech and Silence in The Fictions of J. M. Coetzee," in *Writing South Africa: Literature, Apartheid, and Democracy, 1970–1995*, ed. Derek Attridge and Rosemary Jolly (Cambridge: Cambridge University Press, 1998), 150.

63. Chris Prentice, "Foe," in *A Companion to the Works of J. M. Coetzee*, ed. Tim Mehigan (Rochester, New York: Camden House, 2011), 100–101.

64. The "author-function," as observed by Michel Foucault, constitutes a principle of unity in writing, supposed to quell the inconsistencies of the text, a staple of authority to whom the reader accedes in seeking to understand the ultimate meaning of the text. See "What is an Author?", in *Language, Counter-Memory, Practice: Selected Essays and Interviews*, ed. Donald F. Bouchard (New York: Cornell University Press, 1977 [1969]), 128. As Roland Barthes would suggest: "To give the text an Author is to impose a limit on that text, to

furnish it with a final signified, to close the writing. Such a conception suits criticism very well, the latter then allotting itself the important task of discovering the Author." See "The Death of the Author," in *Image-Music-Text*, trans. Stephen Heath (London: Fontana, 1977 [1968]), 147.

65. Dirk Klopper argues that both *Boyhood* and *Youth* "point in the direction of a kind of thinking that is both inclusive and singular, that pays attention to context and to detail, that invokes the generality of reason and the particularity of feeling." "Critical Fictions in JM Coetzee's *Boyhood* and *Youth*," *Scrutiny2: Issues in English Studies in Southern Africa* 11, no. 1 (2006): 30.

66. Leo Tolstoy, *Childhood, Boyhood, Youth*, trans. Rosemary Edmonds (London: Penguin Books, 1964 [1852, 1854, 1857]).

67. Joseph Conrad, "Youth: A Narrative," in *Heart of Darkness and Other Tales*, ed. Cedric Watts, rev. ed. (New York: Oxford University Press, 2002 [1902]), 69–99.

68. Head, *Cambridge Introduction to J. M. Coetzee*, 10.

69. Joseph Conrad, "Heart of Darkness," in *Heart of Darkness and Other Tales*, ed. Cedric Watts, rev. ed. (New York: Oxford University Press, 2002 [1899]), 101–87.

70. Joseph Conrad, *The Shadow-Line* (Oxford: Oxford University Press, 2009 [1917]).

71. Joseph Conrad, *Lord Jim* (Oxford: Oxford University Press, 2008 [1900]).

72. André Brink, "Post-Apartheid Literature: A Personal View," in *J. M. Coetzee in Context and Theory*, ed. Elleke Boehmer, Katy Iddiols and Robert Eaglestone (London: Continuum, 2009), 11.

73. As Rita Barnard notes, "optimistic terms like the 'rainbow nation' or 'the new South Africa' pervaded political discourse during the 1990s"; yet there is now a clear acknowledgement of the shortcomings of its policies in terms of changing the country's inequalities. See "Rewriting the Nation," in *The Cambridge History of South African Literature*, ed. David Attwell and Derek Attridge (Cambridge: Cambridge University Press, 2012), 652.

74. Robert Kusek, "Writing Oneself, Writing the Other: J. M. Coetzee's Fictional Autobiography in *Boyhood, Youth* and *Summertime*," *Werkwinkel* 7, no. 1 (2012): 97–116.

75. Rita Barnard, "Coetzee in/and Afrikaans," *Journal of Literary Studies* 25, no. 4 (2009): 84–105. See, especially, 103.

76. Lucy Graham, "Textual Transvestism: The Female Voices of J. M. Coetzee," in *J. M. Coetzee and the Idea of the Public Intellectual*, ed. Jane Poyner (Ohio: Ohio University Press, 2006), 217–35.

77. As Laura Wright argues: "That Coetzee chooses to address such issues from the perspective of white female narrators is illustrative of his own tendency to identify with the position of white women as both complicit with, and victimised by, patriarchal and colonial institutions like those of *apartheid* and literary production." "Displacing the Voice: South African Feminism and JM Coetzee's Female Narrators," *African Studies* 67, no. 1 (2008): 11–31.

78. Elleke Boehmer, "Not Saying Sorry, Not Speaking Pain: Gender Implications in Disgrace," *Interventions: International Journal of Postcolonial Studies* 4, no. 3 (2002): 342–51. In a later essay, Boehmer would further comment on how Lucy's predicament underlines her still precarious notion of agency in the novel: "Lucy has abnegation forced on her and has herself committed no wrong ... Lurie in this sense remains a subject, even if a self-subsituting one; Lucy's self-substitution involves becoming reconciled to the position

of conventional object." "Sorry, Sorrier, Sorriest. The Gendering of Contrition in J. M. Coetzee's *Disgrace*", in J. M. *Coetzee and the Idea of the Public Intellectual*, ed. Jane Poyner (Athens: Ohio University Press, 2006), 145.

79. Rosemarie Buikema, "O Conteúdo da Forma e Outras Políticas Textuais. Configurações de Nação e Cidadania em *Disgrace* e *Agaat*," *Revista Crítica de Ciências Sociais*, 89, trans. Isabel Pedro dos Santos (2010): 55–69.

80. Rosemary Jolly, *Cultured Violence: Narrative, Social Suffering, and Engendering Human Rights in Contemporary South Africa* (Liverpool: Liverpool University Press, 2013), 47.

81. Elahe Haschemi Yekani, *The Privilege of Crisis: Narratives of Masculinities in Colonial and Postcolonial Literature, Photography and Film* (Frankfurt: Campus Verlag, 2011), 262.

82. Emily S. Davis, "1980s South African Fiction and the Romance of Resistance," in *Rethinking the Romance Genre: Global Intimacies in Contemporary Literary and Visual Culture*, ed. Emily S. Davis (New York: Palgrave Macmillan, 2013), 27–62.

83. Brenna M. Munro, *South Africa and the Dream of Love to Come: Queer Sexuality and the Struggle for Freedom* (Minneapolis: Minneapolis University Press, 2012). See, specifically, 173–97.

84. Pieter Vermeulen, "Wordsworth's Disgrace: The Insistence of South Africa in J. M. Coetzee's *Boyhood* and *Youth*," *Journal of Literary Studies* 23, no. 3 (2007): 179–99.

85. Sam Cardoen, "The Grounds of Cynical Self-Doubt: J.M. Coetzee's *Boyhood*, *Youth* and *Summertime*," *Journal of Literary Studies* 30, no. 1 (2014): 111.

86. As evidenced by J. U. Jacobs, "(N)either Afrikaner (n)or English: Cultural Cross-over in J. M. Coetzee's *Summertime*," *English Academy Review: Southern African Journal of English Studies* 28, no. 1 (2011): 39–52.

87. Eckard Smuts, "J. M. Coetzee and the Politics of Selfhood," *English in Africa* 39, no. 1 (2012): 21–36.

88. The continuous, intimate connection between Coetzee and South Africa is evidenced in *Youth*, as argued by Lars Engle, "Being Literary in the Wrong Way, Time, and Place: J. M. Coetzee's *Youth*," *English Studies in Africa* 49, no. 2 (2006): 29–49; and Paul Sheehan, "The Disasters of Youth: Coetzee and Geomodernism," *Twentieth-Century Literature* 57, no. 1 (2011): 20–33.

PART I

MASCULINITIES

· 1 ·

BECOMING A MAN

Je voulais tout simplement être un homme parmi d'autres hommes. J'aurais voulu arriver lisse et jeune dans un monde nôtre et ensemble édifier.

Frantz Fanon, *Peau Noire, Masques Blancs*

Masculinity is riddled with attendant expectations. If one were to perform and attain a series of goals, one would become a man, though not without first going through a series of conditions, Rudyard Kipling assures us in his poem *If*, published in 1910. Inspired by the actions of Leander Starr Jameson, the protagonist of the Jameson Raid (1895–1896), an attempted coup against the South African Republic instigated by Cecil John Rhodes that would eventually fail in toppling Paul Kruger's government, the poem is a purported transgenerational masculine transmission of advice on how to successfully walk the path towards manhood: "If you can fill the unforgiving minute/With sixty seconds' worth of distance run,/Yours is the Earth and everything that's in it,/ And-which is more-you'll be a Man, my son!."[1]

To become a man is then to overcome a series of trials, to never forget one's goals and yet, at the same time, to be able to tailor oneself according to different situations. This is not an easy, linear path. In the assessment of one scholar of imperial masculinity, "the test of manhood is the ability to transcend and survive the horror of life as a pit of unending trial and torment, deceit and loss."[2] No wonder then that the reward for such hard work is the world itself, though it pales in comparison to the real reward: masculinity is the real treasure of the overcoming of obstacles and the fine manicure of the tailoring of the Self, much as the poem underlines its many anxieties and frustrations.

This fatherly transmission of advice on how to achieve masculinity may be read in the more traditional understanding of masculinity as something—we are never given an exact, precise depiction of what this "something" is—that is propagated from fathers to sons. This heritage is one of the themes of Coetzee's most recent novel *The Childhood of Jesus*, wherein the main couple of protagonists, a man (Simón) and a boy (David), whose past is eclipsed when arriving at a new land, experience the difficulties of naming their relationship.[3] From the outstart, Simón is adamant in dismissing any filiation to David: "Not my grandson, not my son. We are not related,"[4] he curtly states to the immigration officer, focused as he is on an apparent understanding of fatherhood as lacking when compared to motherhood. The following summary is indicative of such an understanding:

> Because, you know, fathers aren't very important, compared to mothers. A mother brings you out of her body into the world. She gives you milk, as I mentioned. She holds you in her arms and protects you. Whereas a father can sometimes be a bit of a wanderer, like Don Quixote, not always there when you need him. He helps to make you, right at the beginning, but then he moves on. By the time you come into the world he may have vanished over the horizon in search of new adventures.[5]

Mothers are important as nurturers, to raise the children, whereas men are conveyed as strictly attached to the biological making, soon pursuing the need for adventure. Wanderers men may be, in search of renewed chances of proving themselves, but it quickly becomes apparent that a different possibility of reading and being is made available, though this new mode may be shier and more cautious than the previous. As a definition of parenthood is given as resting strictly in a reproductive sphere—"Being a father isn't a career, Simón," he is told by one of his female liaisons, "you don't have to like the woman, she doesn't have to like you. You have intercourse with her, and lo and behold, nine months later you are a father. It's simple enough. Any man can do it."—Simón is somewhat reluctant to accept this matter of fact reasoning: "Not so. Fatherhood is not only a matter of having intercourse with a woman, just as motherhood is not only a matter of providing a vessel for male seed,"[6] and he eventually comes to a place of understanding of his importance in David's life by affirming his affective bond towards the boy: "I was the one who brought him here ... I am his guardian. I am in all respects that matter his father."[7]

It becomes then patent that the attaining of masculinity is never an entirely simple aspect of life. Kipling's famous boy, *Kim*, wanderer of Indian roofs and terraces, is split between two cultures, both demanding to make a man out of the boy: "We'll make a man of you at Sanawar—even at the price o' making you a Protestant,"[8] goads Father Victor, the injunction of becoming a man tellingly surmised in Mahbub Ali's summary: "Colonel Sahib, only once in a thousand years is a horse born so well fitted for the game as this our colt. And we need men."[9]

As Edward Said comments on *Kim*, it "is an overwhelmingly male novel," with men being the subjects of attention and women poorly characterised: "The women in the novel are remarkably few by comparison, and all of them are somehow debased or unsuitable for male attention—prostitutes, elderly widows, or importunate and lusty women."[10] These "importunate women" are one of the challenges, as Said notes, that Kim finds in his path to masculinity, such a challenge being transparent in the novel: "'How can a man follow the Way or the Great Game when he is eternally pestered by women? ... Now I am a man, and they will not regard me as a man. Walnuts indeed!'",[11] wonders the irritated boy. Women are thus the obstacle to one's attaining of masculinity, those who cast restlessness and suspicion over a masculine identity—one of the main tenets of adventure fiction.[12]

But if Said is quick to understand some of the gendered aspects of Kipling's novel, his arguments are also dismissive of its wider politics. His analysis and reading of *Kim* for its 1987 Penguin edition would prove to be an ambitious literary event. Harish Trivedi comments that "it was as if they had sponsored and won exclusive broadcasting rights to a world heavyweight boxing championship match between the arch-colonial of all times and the arch-postcolonial of our times," the encounter being understood as an homosocial one,[13] "when two strong men stand face to face."[14]

In this literary standoff, itself drawn in masculinist terms,[15] Said assures the reader that *Kim* should not be understood as political tract, rather as an aesthetic way of looking at India.[16] Trivedi considers this to be a reading that is dismissive of the politics espoused in the novel, with Said providing "an apolitical and artistic shield for the most famously imperialist of all British novelists."[17] The reason may be one of an affective nature. As Said's memoir illustrates, English literature would prove crucial in providing the material for the rituals of his childhood[18]; yet, mischaracterising gendered aspects as apolitical implies a canonical reading, Robyn Wiegman tells us:

> Before feminism's constitution of men and masculinity as discrete objects of study, these identities became known as the effect of the way knowledge was produced. The English literary canon, traditional history: these arenas taught us a great deal about the relation of men to masculinity, but only as evidence of the male body's abstraction into the normative domain of the universal where, shielded by humanism, both specificity and diversity were lost in the generic function of "man".[19]

And yet, going against canonical understanding was the hallmark of Said's career, though, as we have seen, with its limitations. Paradoxically, we can see in *Orientalism* the hints of how gender was an important factor in the creation of empires and the wider understanding of the "Orient".[20] Namely, in his treatment of Napoleon, Said writes about how the emperor-to-be "had been attracted to the Orient since his adolescence," as can be seen in his writing as a youth. This was a received understanding of what the Orient was, a fascination with its Otherness that enticed Napoleon to the degree of wanting to master it: "Thus the idea of reconquering Egypt as a new Alexander proposed itself to him," an idea that was attractive due to the fantastical notion of what the "Orient" was, which is why: "For Napoleon Egypt was a project that acquired reality in his mind, and later in his preparations for conquest, through experiences that belong to the realm of ideas and myths culled from texts, not empirical reality."[21]

Myths and ideas over Egypt would make real for Napoleon how the enterprise of conquering it would place him in the company of great men, such as Alexander. Thus, the enterprise of colonialism could be determined as founded in fantasies of masculine power and Self-realisation. The capacity to read gendered realities with a critical eye, namely in terms of gender relations, would eventually only be possible through the application of concepts and frameworks whose delineation was formed within the scope of the second women's movement, emerging in the late 1960s.[22]

Feminism and Gender

The so-called second wave of the women's movement[23] sought to distinguish itself from other contemporary lines of thought by exposing the intrinsic misogyny and masculine centrality that permeated much of contemporary thought. Feminist theory, here conceptualised as multiple in its theoretical and practical approaches, takes its commonality in the understanding of the power-laden relations between women and men, and the ensuing possibilities for change stemming from such an analysis, through attempts at redefining such relations.[24] Efforts of change-making have been met with their own degrees of resistance, by recurrent attempts at denigrating the feminist movement.[25] Thus the public face of feminism, Lynne Segal argues, must engage with all the criticisms, discussion and partnerships that are elaborated in feminist thinking and action,[26] a self-critique that feminist scholar bell hooks understands as being the main point of feminism as a social movement: "There has been no other movement for social justice in our society that has been as self-critical as the feminist movement."[27]

Always a politically and affectively charged term, bell hooks attempts to define feminism as "a movement to end sexism, sexist exploitation, and oppression."[28] As a social movement, feminism targets the systemic oppression of women, reproduced and maintained through an array of norms, customs and symbols that are present in everyday life. The term "oppression", philosopher Iris Marion Young argued, is central to the political discourse advanced by social movements, as it provides the necessary *locus* of shared social experience.[29] The use of the concept, according to Young, rests on its propagation by the new social movements of the 1960s and 70s, which shifted the meaning of oppression from one designating the tyrannical ways of the dominant group to one that emphasises its multifaceted, structural aspect:

> Its causes are embedded in unquestioned norms, habits, and symbols, in the assumptions underlying institutional rules and the collective consequences of following those rules.... In this extended structural sense oppression refers to the vast and deep injustices some groups suffer as a consequence of often unconscious assumptions and reactions of well-meaning people in ordinary interactions, media and cultural stereotypes, and structural features of bureaucratic hierarchies and market mechanisms—in short, the normal processes of everyday life.[30]

Such constraints are visible in the access to material resources, being "systematically reproduced in major economic, political, and cultural institutions."[31] Oppression is also located at a psychological level, in the self-deprecating thoughts and reduced expectations that members of subordinated groups portray.[32]

The feminist project of reconceptualising relations between women and men met routine resistance and obstacles from men who, as a group, are privileged. "Privilege", Peggy McIntosh suggests, is generally understood as a favoured state, with positive attributes and implications. However, in its more critical meaning, privilege is a term that "confers *dominance*, gives permission to control, because of one's race or sex."[33] Such privilege is, according to McIntosh, a knapsack of invisibility, a set of conditions that must be reflected upon, lest it remain "an elusive and fugitive subject."[34] As Michael Kimmel and Abby Ferber argue, "to be white, or straight, or male, or middle class is to be simultaneously ubiquitous and invisible."[35] This invisibility is of a political nature, as it has largely been left to those who have felt the effect—in this case the negative effect of privilege—to deploy the theoretical and practical tools to make some sense of it:

> It is the "victims," the "others," who have begun to make these issues visible to contemporary scholars and lay people alike. This is, of course, political, as it should be: The marginalized always understand first the mechanisms of their marginalization; it remains for them to convince the center that the processes of marginalization are in fact both real and remediable.[36]

As a group, men are privileged over women, due to what R. W. Connell calls the "male dividend", a term reflecting the institutionalised gender inequalities in various sectors, from economic to technological sites, an arrangement from which men derive a surplus of resources, not available to women:

> I call this surplus the *patriarchal dividend*: the advantage to men as a group from maintaining an unequal gender order. The patriarchal dividend is reduced as overall gender equality grows. Monetary benefits are not the only kind of benefit. Others are authority, respect, service, safety, housing, access to institutional power, and control over one's own life. It is important to note that the patriarchal dividend is the benefit to men *as a group*. Individual men may get more of it than others, or less, or none, depending on their location in the social order.[37]

As we have observed, the existing tensions between gender and postcolonial studies indicate, among other aspects, a variety of power relations between women themselves. In this vein, bell hooks considers that "racism abounds in the writings of white feminists, reinforcing white supremacy and negating the possibility that women will bond politically across ethnic and racial boundaries."[38]

Attempts at hierarchising different sites of power have garnered various critiques from differently located feminists. Thus, various scholars have argued that a "feminism without borders" would vie for attention over how knowledge is produced and often universalised, while being equally aware of the ways in which the category of gender is always produced in relation to other social categories. As we shall see, and as most feminist theorists would later address, such demands would largely rest on issues of race, ethnicity, class, geographical location, sexuality, religion, disability, etc., all relevant in the mainstream production of knowledge.[39]

This implies that power, the "enduring capacity or disposition to do something, regardless of whether this capacity is actually being exercised,"[40] is as such not monolithic, as it exists in different temporalities and contexts.[41]

Such remarks allow us then to ponder over the possible definition of "gender". Etymologically, the term means "to produce". In its origin a grammatical term, it originally referred to distinctions of anatomical sex.[42] As Lynne Segal argues, the expansion of the concept is closely linked to the second wave of feminism, developing from a grammatical to an analytical tool.[43] Gender would come to designate "the cultural or social construction of sex,"[44] in an attempt to displace the prescriptive role of biology in determining the meanings of "masculinity" and "femininity".

The distinction between "sex" and "gender" would first be introduced by American psychologist and sexologist John Money in 1955,[45] a distinction that was further elaborated in the social sciences and the humanities by psychoanalyst Robert Stoller in 1968, with his book *Sex and Gender: On the Development of Masculinity and Femininity*.[46]

These advances would, whether in the more descriptive field of feminism or in the more prescriptive field of medicine, engage as well with Freudian theories of sexuality. For example, in a later footnote to his famous text of 1905, *Three Essays on Sexual Theory*, Freud would question the meanings of the terms "masculine" and "feminine", "whose content seems so unambiguous to ordinary opinion," yet which he "considered to be among the most confused in science."[47] Freud's own work would engage in paradoxical ways with such complexities. In his lecture on femininity, Freud admitted his own shortcomings: "That is all I have to say to you about femaleness. It is most certainly incomplete and fragmentary; it may also sound unfriendly at times."[48]

Freud would, for the most part, be an ambivalent figure in relation to these questions of sexual difference: a pioneer in promoting an understanding of the complexities of the mind, he would also prove largely unable to follow up on some of the richer contradictions he uncovered, namely on womanhood. His legacy was to prove very contentious within the feminist movement, resulting in what Lynne Segal calls a "century of contradiction".[49] As New York psychoanalyst Ken Corbett asserts, "while it could be said that much has been written about men and masculinity throughout the history of psychoanalysis,

it would be more correct to say that much has been *presumed* about masculinity through the repetition of Sigmund Freud's normative Oedipal model."[50]
To this, Corbett concludes that "masculinity is just as likely to be transferred
from mother to son as it is from father to son. Femininity is just as likely to be
transferred from father to son as it is from mother to son."[51]

What is also being addressed here is the issue between gender as essence,
the notion that certain characteristics are intrinsic to men or to women in an
exclusive manner; or gender as relational, the notion that gender is a social
structure that is itself in relation to other structures.

For Simone de Beauvoir, "on ne naît pas femme; on le devient ... c'est
l'ensemble de la civilisation qui élabore ce produit intermédiaire entre le mâle
et le castrat qu'on qualifie de féminin."[52] Gender in this perspective is not
something one *has*, but rather something one *becomes*. As Judith Butler famously argues in *Gender Trouble*, published in 1990, gender is a performance,
a series of acts produced through and maintained in "political and cultural in-
tersections" that are always negotiated in spheres of recognition and validity.[53]

In this vein, Ken Corbett considers how gender is not something static,
but can rather be conceptualized as a "field", "with a dense median, and an
assiduously controlled mythos, but a field nevertheless that demonstrates how
multiple acts of gendered address, affect, and embodiment are equally robust
and intelligible, however majoritized or minoritized they may be."[54] In recognising how gender is organised according to societal norms, Corbett also
provides an understanding of the need to dissent from such norms, to establish
an idiosyncratic perspective on the need to defer and the need to rebel,[55] due
to the inherent complexities and mutabilities of the field:

> Gender is built through the complex accrual of an infinite array of parent-child ex-
> changes, social-child exchanges, symbolic-child exchanges, and body-child exchang-
> es, including the child's experience of his or her body and genitals, the observation of
> morphological sexual differences, as well as the physiological components of sexual
> development. This complex matrix (open as it is to enigmatic transfer layered on
> enigmatic transfer) starts to operate at birth (or even before birth, now that a child's
> sex is often known to a parent prior to birth) and is crisscrossed by an infinite array of
> conscious and unconscious meanings for both parent and child.[56]

From the moment of birth, the child is confronted with a world that is complex, where meaning proliferates at accelerated speed and is always multifari-
ous, and to a certain extent incomprehensible. For the French psychoanalyst
Jean Laplanche, this encounter between child and world is provided through

a series of enigmatic messages, enigmatic not only to the child who does not possess a cognitive system capable of interpreting them, or other methods to understand such messages, but enigmatic also to the adults imparting them, who certainly provide conscious messages, but also unconscious ones as well.[57] The unconscious aspects of the adult become inscribed in the child, and thus an internal foreign object is created; this is, according to Ilka Quindeau, a notion of human development where the Other is an inviolable part of it,[58] "is *causal in the constitution of subjectivity*, profoundly passionate yet utterly mysterious, and right there at the centre of psychic life."[59]

Gender is thus *done* in connection with others, a social structure (re)produced at an individual level (and here one must account for the possibility of creativity and subversion, the myriad of ph/fantasies that inhabit such connections), cultural and institutional level (institutions such as the family, school, the boy scouts, amongst others). As psychologist Lígia Amâncio argues, demands for a "true womanhood", a "true manhood", "the traditional family", are largely a skewed view of gender relations as formed by historical contingencies, ultimately resulting in the continued reproduction of social inequalities.[60]

Gender as relation implies that it is in the intersection between various factors that gender is formed; to this end, the term "intersectionality" would be employed by Kimberlé Crenshaw, in 1989, and by many others since then.[61] As Leslie McCall reflects, the term appears as the necessary answer to the awareness of "the limitations of gender as a single analytic category,"[62] with Kathy Davis defining it as referring to "the interaction between gender, race, and other categories of difference in individual lives, social practices, institutional arrangements, and cultural ideologies and the outcomes of these interactions in terms of power."[63] Taking into account these diverse elaborations of sexual difference and gender theory, gender theorists, such as Connell, came to define gender as "the structure of social relations that centres on the reproductive arena, and the set of practices that bring reproductive distinctions between bodies into social processes."[64]

Masculinities and Empire

The aspects of privilege that we have signaled earlier explain why the investigation of men as gendered beings is a relatively new event. Emerging out of second-wave feminism, the bulk of research on men and masculinity appears only at the close of the 1980s.[65] From this time, ethnographic and historical studies have demonstrated the existence not only of one, but multiple masculinities, exhibiting differences across cultures,[66] and within any one culture itself.[67]

The essentialist understanding of masculinity was heavily challenged by several social movements, in particular the feminist, gay and anti-racist movements.[68] Divergent masculinities are thus the result of various factors, among others, historical, cultural and even geographical aspects.[69] Following such an understanding, according to Segal, masculinity may be defined as follows:

> Masculinity ... is best understood as transcending the personal, as a heterogeneous set of ideas, constructed around assumptions of social *power*, which are lived out and reinforced, or perhaps denied and challenged, in multiple and diverse ways within a whole social system in which relations of authority, work, and domestic life are organised, in the main, along hierarchical gender lines.[70]

Now in its middle-age, the field has been fruitful in its scale of research,[71] especially after its own Kuhnian paradigm shift in 1995, with the publishing of Connell's *Masculinities*. Connell presented new concepts that highlighted the internal fractures one can witness amongst men, according to differing positions of power in society, basing her work, in particular, on the writings of Antonio Gramsci. For Gramsci, hegemony is exercised by the dominant group throughout society.[72] As Toby Miller considers, hegemony may be understood as "a contest of meanings in which a ruling class gains consent to the social order by making its power appear normal and natural."[73] As Connell argues, relations between men are constructed through experiences of hegemony, subordination, complicity and marginalisation.

Different masculinities are interrelated in a complex game of hierarchy and hegemony. The dominant form of masculinity is coined by Connell as hegemonic masculinity, and defined as "the configuration of gender practice which embodies the currently accepted answer to the legitimacy of patriarchy, which guarantees (or is taken to guarantee) the dominant position of men and the subordination of women."[74] Hegemonic masculinity serves largely as an ideal "type" of masculinity, though as with any other ideal, it is highly contestable and largely unachievable for the majority of men, while also being subject to historical change.

Though largely unachievable, men inevitably absorb and mostly remain complicit with these norms, as they gain at various levels from the patriarchal dividend that stems from upholding them. On the other hand, men who disrupt these norms are symbolically excluded from hegemonic/ideal notions of masculinity, being largely placed at a subordinate level, as in the case of gay men, or heterosexual men who defy the gender order.[75]

The interplay of gender with other structures, such as class and race, creates further tensions between men, exacerbating the marginalisation of some. This is particularly true of colonial and, to a certain extent, of postcolonial masculinities.

Current academic concern over phenomena such as globalisation and mass migration[76] has engendered a further paradigmatic change in the field of study on masculinities. In a globalised, increasingly inter-connected and inter-dependent world, there is a need to understand the ways in which local and global masculinities are mutually constituted.[77] Coupled with shifts in global politics and criticism regarding the ways knowledge is produced and validated in Western societies,[78] the field has demonstrated an increased interest on research on non-Western societies.[79]

In his essay on masculinity, *Are you a Man or a Mouse?*, Homi K. Bhabha addresses the question, and its added provocation, as meriting only a call for withdrawal. It allows for no possible answer, lest it launches the subject into its "prosthetic reality", the appeal to universalism and rationality.[80] What Bhabha seeks to erase then, is a discourse that is self-generative, "reproduced over the generations in patrilineal perpetuity, that masculinity seeks to make a name for itself."[81]

This masculine presence is, in a postcolonial framework, an indication of continuing imperial struggles. It occurs in the shadow of Western powers, whose universalistic conceptions of the term reflect a disavowal of localised practices of gender.[82]

Scholarship on gender in Africa would follow the international trend of multidisciplinary interrogation: in recent years, scholarship on gender in Africa has become ever more multi-disciplinary, encompassing an ever wider terrain. In this, two concurrent motions may be noted. For one, the advances of twentieth-century Western feminism have met with a generalised distrust by African scholarship and practice in these areas, the rationale being that such narratives, though necessarily local in their fomulation, in claiming to provide solution to most, if not all, situations of oppression, forego the specificities of certain contexts.[83] Equally, and as noted by political anthropologist Andrea Cornwall, closer attention has been given to "the imbrication of gender identities with other dimensions of difference, and to men's, as well as women's, gendered experiences."[84]

Andrea Cornwall further suggests that "early writing on gender in Africa was largely about women and by women,"[85] with primary interests in economic issues and the position of women in society. Furthermore, Nancy Rose Hunt posits a chronological framework whereby this first phase, located primarily in the early 1970s, would be superseded by a second one, originating in the late 1980s, that focused on customary law, motherhood, sexuality and the body.[86] As "women's studies came to embrace the study of the construction of gender relations, attention turned to processes and structures through which women's and men's identities and relationships were mediated,"[87] whereby a third phase would arise in Hunt's chronology, the field evolving from a centrality in women's experiences and identities, to a more encompassing notion of social justice,[88] one that would allocate increasingly more space for additional intellectual and practical pursuits:

> Recent work situates "gender" on a broader canvas of translocal and transnational cultural currents…and goes beyond a focus on "women". A series of exciting edited collections trace the contours of the new landscape of gender studies in Africa, from the history and ethnography of masculinities, to gendered colonialisms and the reconfiguration of gender in Africa.[89]

The turn from a focus on "women" to a focus on "gender", while fraught with expected and understandable dissension and questioning on the worthiness of such a shift, would provide increasing opportunities for addressing the diverse positions of men in relations of power, thus proving its relevance. Concurrent with the increasingly global interest on masculinities, this paradigmatic turn would acknowledge men as gendered beings, even as it tried to introduce some different aspects to Western scholarship on the matter, namely the adamant recognition of how gender must be analysed alongside the effects of colonialism, specifically the questions surrounding racial identities.[90] This motion is remindful of how colonial masculinities were constituted in such relations of power:

> The masculinised ethos of aggressive-but-gentlemanly competition among the British was accepted by much of the nineteenth-century Indian male elite … who took the existence of British domination as proof of a masculine superiority that they should emulate…. Gandhi's profound challenge to British colonialism [lies] precisely in his refusal to accept the inherent superiority of a "masculinity" that was increasingly equated with rationality, materialism, and physical strength.[91]

As we have seen, empires needed men. The British Empire was a man's world, encapsulated within the fantasies of Self-improvement and social ascendancy. As Phillipa Levine argues, speaking of the British case, empire can be conflated with a man's world, not only because of the sheer number of men involved, but also necessarily because of the values embedded in such an enterprise, with maleness being equated with authority and power and thus befitting masculinity as an essential aspect of colonisation.[92]

What Karen Lawrence understands as the "heterosexual paradigm of adventure"[93] sustains the trope of the quest as privileged site for Self-affirmation. This, however, was possible only through a dichotomous system of gendered attribution, whereby the coloniser was the "masculine" and the colonised the "feminine".[94] British masculinity was focused on tailoring militaristic qualities,[95] with landscapes being imprinted as metaphors of the female object, the correlation of validating excursions and quests into such a land within the scope of heterosexual and homosocial environment. As Graham Dawson suggests:

> The soldier heroes composed in adventure narratives, being ideally powerful and free from contradictions, function psychically and socially as positive imagos to set against the fragmenting and undermining effects of anxiety. They offer the psychic reassurance of triumph over the sources of threat, promising the defeat of enemies and the recovery of that which is valued and feared lost. Having accomplished their quest, they win recognition and bask in the affirmation of their public, for whom they become idealized vessels preserving all that is valued and worthwhile. Identification with these heroes meets the wish to fix one's own place within the social world, to feel oneself to be coherent and powerful rather than fragmented and contradictory. It offers the assurance of a clearly recognizable gender identity and, through this, the security of belonging to a gendered national collectivity that imagines itself to be superior in strength and virtue to others.[96]

Through the *locus* of adventure, masculine identity would find its validating codes. These would largely be constructed in action-oriented terms, with the goal of achieving virtues such as "courage, fortitude, cunning, strength, leadership, and persistence."[97] Thus activities such as hunting, excursions, or the gathering over scientific activities constituted the main sites of constructing a masculinity that was bent on proving its superiority to "feminine" others.

These "feminine" others, namely the colonised male subjects, "frequently witnessed their fathers and grandfathers struggling for authority, power and status."[98] To such men, humiliation and the impossibility to reciprocate would prove to be the hallmarks of colonialism, leading to the creation of subjugated masculinities, and thus denying the colonised the acquisition of power or control over their own lives.[99]

Acknowledging such figurations of power, certain scholarly work would come to challenge the often dichotomous and polarising representations of black women and men. African women's traditional representations would be under the auspices of a polarising binary of submissive, voiceless victims, or one where they would be portrayed as feminist heroes, "African women as feisty, assertive, self-reliant heroines."[100] African men would also be equally polarised in their representations: "They appear either as powerful, dominant figures, colluding with colonial and post-colonial institutions to deepen women's subordinations; fleetingly as the objects of women's successful resistance; or as rather useless characters that women can do without."[101]

The specificities of gender formations in South Africa, both in the *apartheid* and post-*apartheid* periods, would hold a powerful, and in many ways, constant relation to colonialism's ideological exportations. In this vein, masculinities in South Africa would be articulated between local and imported social codes of gender. As Nigel Worden argues, eighteenth-century Cape Town exhibited traces of social organisation in what pertains to gender structuring reminiscent of Holland in the same period. The Dutch considered their colonies not only as economic sources, but also as sites of national pride.[102] With the goal of maintaining a certain cohesion in terms of identity, certain strategies would be employed, such as establishing a brewing production that would not only benefit the local economies, but also the colony's sense of community: "Good Dutch beer would help to make the colony properly Dutch."[103]

That is to say, Cape Town in its gender makeup was enacted through the social codes ruling masculinity in European contexts, particularly in Holland,[104] with Nigel Worden arguing for a parallel between the ritualised masculine violence of eighteenth-century Netherlands and the Cape Colony in the same period. Whereas in the seventeenth and early eighteenth centuries violence was largely an affair between "relative strangers" and of an "impulsive" nature, from "the mid- to late eighteenth-century planned and premeditated assaults on those known to the perpetrators came to predominate."[105] This signals a passage from public violence to domestic assaults. If Carl Sagan chooses to consider seventeenth-century Dutch society a clear follower of European Enlightenment's codes, a society whose creativity rested on its rationality and orderliness,[106] it is important also to stress its violence, largely caused by the actions of young men, for whom "committing violence often symbolized masculine character traits such as courage and the ability to take risks," such as excessive drinking.[107]

The very political articulation of the nation implies the recognition of borders, of constitutive mapping that seeks to separate and organise the "we" from "them", by enmeshing the "we" in a narrative of origins that denies historical accuracy. Maps exert their political expression and influence, constituting a narrative that may be presented as the necessary reality upon which the nation is based. As scholars uncover the imaginary underpinnings of such maps, however, one is persuaded that maps often lie, both in their assumption to tell the truth and the ability to convince us of its authority to do so.[108]

An attempt at redrawing such maps, the movement of decolonisation that arose from the political demands of the post-1945 European world would be met, overall, with salutation from colonised people, who would themselves be already engaged in what Chatterjee understands to be an "anticolonial nationalism,"[109] derived from a place of difference regarding European nationalisms. That is, nationalisms in the postcolonial world occur through a series of resistances that are extensions of those enacted against the colonial enterprise, namely against the framework of modernity that is considered as the largest European import. This is achieved, according to Chatterjee, by understanding the division occurring in colonised societies between the domain of the material, the turf of modernity by excellence, and westernised in its conceptions, and the domain of the spiritual, whereby the colonial system is barred from entrance. Anticolonial nationalism then creates its own sovereignty by upholding the spiritual dimension as its recognised property and symbol of its cultural identity, the national community thus being imagined as national culture before its struggle for political power. The upkeep of culture and the dealings with the necessary constraints of the nation-state's development is, in part, the job of writers. As Neil Lazarus points out:

> Through their contestatory troping, counteridentification, valorization and revalorization of community, environment, and social order, writers in the historical context of decolonisation bring the "worlds" of the "new" nations to conceptuality and cognition. They "world" these nations, so to speak, defining them through grammars, lexicons, registers, habitus that have had to be fought for and fought over, seized from the grasp of colonial definition, colonial understanding, colonial discursivity, and conceptuality.[110]

If the imagining of communities that turn into nations in the postcolonial world is different from the imagination of the European nations, postcolonial scholarship seems at fault for failing to recognise these different imaginative ventures, "that some of the most adamantine and far reaching resistance to the violence and repressiveness of the postcolonial state has been undertaken precisely in the name of alternative nationalisms, of different national imaginings."[111]

The nation as *locus* of contested fantasies would be one of the main tenets argued by Frantz Fanon. It is in returning to Fanon's writings on the mechanisms of liberation from colonial systems that one can perceive the possible difference of anticolonial nationalism. For Fanon, in *Les Damnés de la Terre*, national sovereignty that seeks to constitute the coming postcolonial nation arises from the spontaneity of people, whereby politics is confounded with militarism: "Chaque colonisé en armes est un morceau de la nation désormais vivante.... Dans les vallées et dans les forêts, dans la jungle et dans les villages, partout, on rencontre une autorité nationale."[112] However, Fanon understands that the immediacy of such acts of nation-building, embedded in what seems like inevitable violence and its ecstatic moments, constitute a reproduction of the manichean mode of thinking and social organisation that is, in Fanonian analysis, the very basis of colonial exploitation:

> Le peuple, qui au début de la lutte avait adopté le manichéisme primitif du colon: les Blancs et les Noirs, les Arabes et les Roumis, s'aperçoit en cours de route qu'il arrive à des Noirs d'être plus blancs que les Blancs et que l'éventualité d'un drapeau national, la possibilité d'une nation indépendante n'entrâinent pas automatiquement certaines couches de la population à renoncer à leurs privilèges ou à leurs intérêts.... Le militant qui fait face, avec des moyens rudimentaires, à la machine de guerre colonialiste se rend compte que dans le même temps où il démolit l'oppression coloniale il contribue par la bande à construire un autre appareil d'exploitation. Cette découverte est désagréable, pénible et revoltante. Tout était simple pourtant, d'un côté les mauvais, de l'autre les bons.[113]

Fanon decries the European model as a succession of failures in creating humane ways of living, thus advancing the general need to do otherwise when it comes to community building. Challenging European narcissism, other ways of creating subjectivity must be promoted: "Il faut faire peau neuve, développer une pensée neuve, tenter de mettre sur pied un homme neuf."[114]

The masculine noun is not coincidental. In terms of imagining the nation, women are largely excluded from such a function, considered unimportant in the scheme of nation-building. Lois West considers this invisibility the effect of a masculinist bias, persisting "at all levels, from the family to the nation."[115] This becomes clear in the trilogy, as Coetzee's protagonist's complex interaction with those who are socially marginalised, mired in tensions derived from privilege, is an enactment of the anxieties that would later come to be perceived as the basis for the need by Afrikaner men to "rethink and reinvent a male identity that is not intimately connected to power and domination" in post-*apartheid* South Africa.[116]

The transition from the *apartheid* regime to democracy indicated not only a reshaping of the country's attitudes towards race, but also a seeking of new ways of dealing with the gendered aspects of life itself. Such a project would imply, for political validity of the new democratic way of living, a re-assessment of the very history of the nation, indeed, of the path built by its many fathers, and whether the sons would be creative in designing new routes towards justice.

Notes

1. Rudyard Kipling, "If," in *Selected Poems* (London: Penguin, 1993 [1910]), 134.
2. Zohreh T. Sullivan, *Narratives of Empire: The Fictions of Rudyard Kipling* (Cambridge: Cambridge University Press, 1993), 33.
3. J. M. Coetzee, *The Childhood of Jesus* (London: Harvill Secker, 2013).
4. Coetzee, *Childhood of Jesus*, 2.
5. Coetzee, *Childhood of Jesus*, 221.
6. Coetzee, *Childhood of Jesus*, 189.
7. Coetzee, *Childhood of Jesus*, 252.
8. Rudyard Kipling, *Kim* (Oxford: Oxford University Press, 2008 [1901]), 95.
9. Kipling, *Kim*, 167.
10. Edward Said, *Culture and Imperialism* (London: Vintage, 1994 [1993]), 165. Said's analysis of Kipling's novel first appeared as an introduction to the Penguin edition; it would later emerge, in rewritten form, in *Culture and Imperialism*.
11. Kipling, *Kim*, 257.
12. Maria Teresa Pinto Coelho, *Ilhas, Batalhas e Aventura: Imagens de África no Romance de Império Britânico do Último Quartel do Século XIX e Início do Século XX* (Lisboa: Edições Colibri, 2004), namely 61–88.
13. The concept of "homosociality" is found in Eve Kosofsky Sedgwick's study where it is understood, in its more general sense, as describing "social bonds between persons of the same sex" (1). See *Between Men: English Literature and Male Homosocial Desire* (New York: Columbia University Press, 1985). Sedgwick further problematises the concept through the refusal to ascertain its limits in a more identificatory basis; on the contrary, the critic ascertains the social use of the concept, by demonstrating that it is the site of a plethora of desires and identifications that are never entirely resolubable, "the potential unbrokenness of a continuum between homosocial and homosexual—a continuum whose visibility, for men, in our society, is radically disrupted" (1–2).

14. See Harish Trivedi, "'Arguing with the Himalayas'? Edward Said on Rudyard Kipling," in *Kipling and Beyond: Patriotism, Globalisation and Postcolonialism*, ed. Caroline Rooney and Kaori Nagai (New York: Palgrave Macmillan, 2010), 120.
15. By "masculinism" we understand "the ideology that justifies and naturalizes male domination." See Arthur Brittan, "Masculinities and Masculinism," in *The Masculinities Reader*, ed. Stephen M. Whitehead and Frank J. Barrett (Cambridge: Polity Press, 2001), 53. In Brittan's understanding of the term, masculinism does not consider that the relationships between men and women are themselves a product and site of politics; rather, these are understood as being natural: "Masculinism takes it for granted that there is a fundamental difference between men and women, it assumes that heterosexuality is normal, it accepts without question the sexual division of labour, and it sanctions the political and dominant role of men in the public and private spheres" (53).
16. Said, *Culture and Imperialism*, 196.
17. Trivedi, *Kipling and Beyond*, 141.
18. Edward Said, *Out of Place: A Memoir* (New York: Alfred A. Knopf, 1999), 48.
19. Robyn Wiegman, "Unmaking: Men and Masculinity in Feminist Theory," in *Masculinity Studies & Feminist Theory: New Directions*, ed. Judith Kegan Gardiner (New York: Columbia University Press, 2002), 33.
20. Edward Said, *Orientalism* (London: Penguin, 2003 [1978]). On the question of gender and sexuality, and regarding his seminal work, Said would be criticised for subsuming such areas as simply a sub-domain of Orientalism. See Meyda Yegenoglu, *Colonial Fantasies* (Cambridge: Cambridge University Press, 1998), namely 14–38.
21. Said, *Orientalism*, 80.
22. Deepika Bahri, "Feminism in/and Postcolonialism," in *The Cambridge Companion to Postcolonial Literary Studies*, ed. Neil Lazarus (Cambridge: Cambridge University Press, 2004), 199–220.
23. The second wave refers to the late 1960s until the mid-1970s period of the women's movement. See Lynne Segal, *Why Feminism?: Gender, Psychology, Politics* (New York: Columbia University Press, 1999). This cultural moment as lived experience is discussed in greater detail in Lynne Segal, *Making Trouble: Life and Politics* (London: Serpent's Tail, 2007). For a wider understanding of the women's movement, in its different phases, see Rosemarie Putnam Tong, *Feminist Thought*, 3rd ed. (Boulder, CO: Westview Press, 2008 [1998]).
24. See Madalena Barbosa, *Que Força é Essa* (Lisboa: Sextante Editora, 2008) and Lynne Segal, *Is the Future Female?: Troubled Thoughts on Contemporary Feminism* (New York: Peter Bedrick Books, 1988).
25. As an example, in the Portuguese case one can see how feminism has largely been understood as a "movement led by radical women in their struggle against men" (103, our translation). See Manuela Tavares, *Movimentos de Mulheres em Portugal—Décadas de 70 e 80* (Lisboa: Livros Horizonte, 2000).
26. Segal, *Is the Future Female*, namely ix–xvi.
27. bell hooks, *Feminist Theory: From Margin to Center*, 2nd ed. (London: Pluto Press, 2000 [1984]), xiii.
28. bell hooks, *Feminism is for Everybody: Passionate Politics* (London: Pluto Press, 2000), 1.

29. Iris Marion Young, *Justice and the Politics of Difference* (Princeton: Princeton University Press, 1990).
30. Iris Marion Young, *Justice and the Politics of Difference*, 41.
31. Iris Marion Young, *Justice and the Politics of Difference*, 41.
32. See Isaac Prilleltensky and Geoffrey Nelson, *Doing Psychology Critically: Making a Difference in Diverse Settings* (New York: Palgrave Macmillan, 2002). For the authors' discussion of oppression and cognate terms, see especially Chapter I (1–20).
33. Peggy McIntosh, "White Privilege and Male Privilege: A Personal Account of Coming to see Correspondences Through Work in Women's Studies," in *Privilege: A Reader*, ed. Michael S. Kimmel and Abby L. Ferber (Cambridge: Westview Press, 2003), 155.
34. McIntosh, *Privilege: A Reader*, 153.
35. Michael S. Kimmel and Abby L. Ferber, "Toward a Pedagogy of the Oppressor," in *Privilege: A Reader*, ed. Michael S. Kimmel and Abby L. Ferber (Cambridge: Westview Press, 2003), 3.
36. See Kimmel and Ferber, *Privilege: A Reader*, 2.
37. See R. W. Connell, *Gender* (Cambridge: Polity Press, 2002), 142.
38. See hooks, *Feminist Theory*, 3.
39. On the trials of the feminist movement over such issues, see bell hooks, *Ain't I a Woman: Black Women and Feminism* (Cambridge: South End Press, 1981), Chandra Talpade Mohanty, *Feminism Without Borders: Decolonizing Theory, Practicing Solidarity* (Durham and London: Duke University Press, 2003) and Susana López Penedo, *El Laberinto Queer* (Barcelona: EGALES, 2008).
40. John Scott, *Power* (Cambridge: Polity Press, 2001), 5.
41. Isaac Prilleltensky, "The Role of Power in Wellness, Oppression, and Liberation: The Promise of Psychopolitical Validity," *Journal of Community Psychology* 36, no. 2 (2008): 116–36.
42. Raewyn Connell, *Gender: In World Perspective*, 2nd ed. (Cambridge: Polity Press, 2009). See especially 9–11.
43. "Gender and second-wave feminism were born together, at the close of the 1960s." Segal, *Why Feminism*, 38.
44. Judith Butler, "Gender," in *Feminism and Psychoanalysis: A Critical Dictionary*, ed. Elizabeth Wright (Cambridge, MA: Blackwell, 1992), 140.
45. Ilka Quindeau, *Seduction and Desire: The Psychoanalytic Theory of Sexuality since Freud*, trans. John Bendix (London: Karnac, 2013). See, namely, 136–41.
46. David Glover and Cora Kaplan, *Genders*, 2nd ed. (New York: Routledge, 2009 [2000]). See 11–14.
47. Sigmund Freud, "Three Essays on Sexual Theory," in *The Psychology of Love*, trans. Shaun Whiteside (London: Penguin, 2006 [1905]), 206.
48. Sigmund Freud, "Introductory Lectures on Psychoanalysis: New Series," in *An Outline of Psychoanalysis*, trans. Helena Ragg-Kirkby (London: Penguin, 2003 [1933]), 124.
49. See Lynne Segal, "Freud and Feminism: A Century of Contradiction," *Feminism & Psychology* 6, no. 2 (1996): 290–97.
50. Ken Corbett, *Boyhoods: Rethinking Masculinities* (New Haven and London: Yale University Press, 2009), 5.

51. Corbett, *Boyhoods*, 103.
52. Simone de Beauvoir, *Le Deuxième Sexe II* (Paris: Gallimard, 1976 [1949]), 13.
53. Judith Butler, *Gender Trouble*, 2nd ed. (New York: Routledge, 1999 [1990]), 4–5.
54. Ken Corbett, "Gender Now," *Psychoanalytic Dialogues* 18 (2008): 841.
55. Ken Corbett, "More Life: Centrality and Marginality in Human Development," *Psychoanalytic Dialogues* 11, no. 3 (2001): 313–35.
56. Corbett, "Gender Now," 845.
57. Jean Laplanche, *New Foundations for Psychoanalysis*, trans. David Macey (Oxford: Basil Blackwell, 1989).
58. See Quindeau, namely Chapter I (1–71).
59. Stephen Frosh, *For and Against Psychoanalysis*, 2nd ed. (New York: Routledge, 2006 [1997]), 191.
60. Lígia Amâncio, "A(s) Masculinidade(s) em Que-Estão," in *Aprender a ser Homem: Construindo Masculinidades*, ed. Lígia Amâncio (Lisboa: Livros Horizonte, 2004), 13–27.
61. Kimberlé Crenshaw, "Demarginalizing the Intersection of Race and Sex: A Black Feminist Critique of Antidiscrimination Doctrine, Feminist Theory and Antiracist Politics," *The University of Chicago Legal Forum* 140 (1989): 139–67.
62. Leslie McCall, "The Complexity of Intersectionality," *Signs* 30, no. 3 (2005): 1771.
63. Kathy Davis, "Intersectionality as Buzzword: A Sociology of Science Perspective on what Makes a Feminist Theory Successful," *Feminist Theory* 9, no. 1 (2008): 68.
64. Connell, *Gender*, 2nd ed., 9.
65. Scott Coltrane, "Theorizing Masculinities in Contemporary Social Science," in *Theorizing Masculinities*, ed. Harry Brod and Michael Kaufman (London: Sage, 1994), 39–60.
66. David D. Gilmore, *Manhood in the Making: Cultural Concepts of Masculinity* (London: Yale University Press, 1990) and Jeff Hearn and David L. Collinson, "Theorizing Unities and Differences between Men and between Masculinities," in *Theorizing Masculinities*, ed. Harry Brod and Michael Kaufman (London: Sage, 1994), 97–118.
67. See, for instance, Michael Kimmel, *Manhood in America: A Cultural History*, 2nd ed. (Oxford: Oxford University Press, 2006 [1996]).
68. Judith Newton, "Masculinity Studies: The Longed for Profeminist Movement for Academic Men?" in *Masculinity Studies & Feminist Theory: New Directions*, ed. Judith Kegan Gardiner (New York: Columbia University Press, 2002), 176–92.
69. John Beynon, *Masculinities and Culture* (Philadelphia: Open University Press, 2002).
70. Lynne Segal, *Slow Motion: Changing Masculinities, Changing Men*, 3rd ed. (New York: Palgrave Macmillan, 2007 [1990]), 241.
71. The field is interdisciplinary in its nature, with contributions ranging from psychology to sociology and anthropology. Regarding the contributions of literary studies, Daniel Lea and Berthhold Schoene suggest that these are a "late developer." See "Introduction to the Special Section on Literary Masculinities," *Men and Masculinities* 4, no. 4 (2002): 319. Stefan Horlacher, editing a more recent compilation, argues in the same vein, concluding on how "there are obvious deficits in literary studies approaches concerning the analysis of masculinity." See "Charting the Field of Masculinity Studies; Or, Toward a Literary History of Masculinities," in *Constructions of Masculinity in British Literature from the Middle Ages to the Present*, ed. Stefan Horlacher (New York: Palgrave Macmillan, 2011), 12.

72. Antonio Gramsci, *Selections from the Prison Notebooks*, ed. and trans. Quintin Hoare and Geoffrey Nowell Smith (New York: International Publishers, 1971). See, particularly, 245–46.

73. Toby Miller, "Masculinity," in *A Companion to Gender Studies*, ed. Philomena Essed, David Theo Goldberg, and Audrey Kobayashi (Oxford: Blackwell, 2005), 116.

74. R. W. Connell, *Masculinities*, 2nd ed. (Cambridge: Polity Press, 2005 [1995]), 77.

75. Amâncio considers how gay men are subordinated through the connection of the institution of marriage and family with heterosexuality. Corbett's *Boyhoods* considers how boys who identity as "feminine" are deemed as lacking in coherence as gendered beings.

76. Susana Trovão, "Comparing Postcolonial Identity Formations: Legacies of Portuguese and British Colonialisms in East Africa," *Social Identities* 18, no. 3 (2012): 261–80.

77. For the relations between globalisation and masculinities, see: R. W. Connell, "Masculinities and Globalization," *Men and Masculinities* 1, no. 1 (1998): 3–23 and R. W. Connell, "Change among the Gatekeepers: Men, Masculinities, and Gender Equality in the Global Arena," *Signs* 30, no. 3 (2005): 1801–25.

78. See Sandra Harding, *Sciences from Below: Feminisms, Postcolonialities, and Modernities* (Durham and London: Duke University Press, 2008).

79. See Michael S. Kimmel, Jeff Hearn and R. W. Connell, eds., *Handbook of Studies on Men & Masculinities* (Thousand Oaks, CA: Sage Publications, 2005).

80. Homi K. Bhabha, "Are you a Man or a Mouse?" in *Constructing Masculinity*, ed. Maurice Berger, Brian Wallis, and Simon Watson (New York: Routledge, 1995), 57–65.

81. Bhabha, "Man or a Mouse," 57.

82. Niels Sampath, "'Crabs in a Bucket': Reforming Male Identities in Trinidad," in *The Masculinities Reader*, ed. Stephen M. Whitehead and Frank J. Barrett (Cambridge: Polity Press, 2001), 330–40.

83. As Chandra Mohanty argues in her influential essay, constructive criticism assumes the non-monolithic nature of Western feminism, as much as it is aware of the "coherence of *effects* resulting from the implicit assumption of 'the West' (in all its complexities and contradictions) as the primary referent in theory and praxis." "Under Western Eyes: Feminist Scholarship and Colonial Discourses," *Feminist Review* 30 (1988): 61–62.

84. Andrea Cornwall, "Introduction: Perspectives on Gender in Africa," in *Readings in Gender in Africa*, ed. Andrea Cornwall (Oxford: James Currey, 2005), 1.

85. Cornwall, *Readings in Gender in Africa*, 1.

86. Nancy Rose Hunt, "Introduction," *Gender & History* 8, no. 3 (1996): 323–37.

87. Cornwall, *Readings in Gender in Africa*, 1.

88. A tentative notion at the time of its suggestion, which nevertheless espouses the centrality of research on masculinities of this new phase: "Are we now, with these studies of masculinity, of the formation of subjective, social and institutional identities, and of generational, homosocial struggles, and with subtle, cautious 'post-' moves, witnessing the beginning of a third wave in histories of gender in Africa?" See Hunt, "Introduction," 324.

89. Cornwall, *Readings in Gender in Africa*, 1.

90. As argued most persuasively in Robert Morrell, "Of Boys and Men: Masculinity and Gender in Southern African Studies," *Journal of Southern African Studies* 24, no. 4 (1998): 605–30.

91. See Mrinalini Sinha, "Giving Masculinity a History: Some Contributions from the Historiography of Colonial India," Gender & History 11, no. 3 (1999): 448.

92. Philippa Levine, The British Empire: Sunrise to Sunset (Harlow: Pearson Education Limited, 2007). Specifically, see Chapter IX, 142–65.

93. Karen R. Lawrence, "Orlando's Voyage Out," Modern Fiction Studies 38, no. 1 (1992): 253–77.

94. See Mrinalini Sinha, Colonial Masculinity: The "Manly Englishman" and the "Effeminate Bengali" in the Late Nineteenth Century (Manchester and New York: Manchester University Press, 1995).

95. Angela Woollacott, Gender and Empire (New York: Palgrave Macmillan, 2006). See Chapter III (59–80).

96. Graham Dawson, British Adventure, Empire and the Imagining of Masculinities (New York: Routledge, 1994), 282.

97. Martin Green, Dreams of Adventure, Deeds of Empire (New York: Basic Books, 1979), 23.

98. Amal Treacher Kabesh, Postcolonial Masculinities: Emotions, Histories and Ethics (Farnham, Surrey: Ashgate, 2013), 79.

99. Amal Treacher Kabesh, "Injurious Imperialism: Reflecting on my Father," Journal of Postcolonial Writing 45, no. 3 (2009): 341–50.

100. Cornwall, Readings in Gender in Africa, 1.

101. Cornwall, Readings in Gender in Africa, 1–2.

102. Elleke Boehmer and Frances Gouda, "Postcolonial Studies in the Context of the "Diasporic" Netherlands," in The Postcolonial Low Countries: Literature, Colonialism and Multiculturalism, ed. Elleke Boehmer and Sarah de Mul (Lanham: Lexington Books, 2012), 25–44.

103. Nigel Penn, "The Fatal Passion of Brewer Menssink," in Rogues, Rebels and Runaways: Eighteenth-Century Cape Characters (Cape Town: David Philip Publishers, 1999), 11.

104. Nigel Worden, "Demanding Satisfaction: Violence, Masculinity and Honour in Late Eighteenth-Century Cape Town," Kronos 35 (2009): 32–47.

105. Worden, "Demanding Satisfaction," 34.

106. Carl Sagan, Cosmos (New York: Ballantine Books, 2013 [1980]).

107. Benjamin B. Roberts, Sex and Drugs Before Rock 'N' Roll: Youth Culture and Masculinity during Holland's Golden Age (Amsterdam: Amsterdam University Press, 2012), 103.

108. This is also true of the maps of fiction: "To chart the external world is to reveal ourselves—our priorities, our interests, our desires, our fears, our biases. We believe we're mapping our knowledge, but in fact we're mapping what we want—and what we want others—to believe. In this way, every map is a reflection of the individual or group that creates it." Peter Turchi, Maps of the Imagination: The Writer as Cartographer (Texas: Trinity University Press, 2004), 146.

109. Partha Chatterjee, "Whose Imagined Community?" in Empire and Nation: Selected Essays (New York: Columbia University Press, 2010 [1991]), 26.

110. Neil Lazarus, The Postcolonial Unconscious (Cambridge: Cambridge University Press, 2011), 65.

111. Lazarus, The Postcolonial Unconscious, 70.

112. Frantz Fanon, *Les Damnés de la* Terre (Paris: Éditions La Découverte & Syros, 2002 [1961]), 127.
113. Fanon, *Les Damnés*, 138–39.
114. Fanon, *Les Damnés*, 305.
115. Lois A. West, "Nation," in *A Companion to Gender Studies*, ed. Philomena Essed, David Theo Goldberg, and Audrey Kobayashi (Oxford: Blackwell, 2005), 146.
116. Andries Visagie, "White Masculinity and the African Other: *Die werfbobbejaan* by Alexander Strachan," *Alternation* 9, no. 1 (2002): 132.

PART II

MAKING MEN:
PLACES OF MASCULINITIES

· 2 ·

FATHERS OF THE NATION

What has made it impossible for us to live in time like fish in water, like birds in air, like children? It is the fault of Empire! Empire has created the time of history.

J. M. Coetzee, *Waiting for the Barbarians*

The theme of Afrikaner politics is one that animates the trilogy, be it in more subtle ways, such as the episodic, quasi-anthropological style of *Boyhood*, depicting life in post-1948 South Africa, or in more direct, overt ways, such as in Vincent's interview with Sophie in *Summertime*, where the former seeks to uncover Coetzee's relation to Afrikaner identity and the latter eventually demonstrates the multifaceted, complex nature of cultural belonging. It is a nuanced understanding that Coetzee the author has sought to present, stressing the ideological over the cultural aspect of Afrikanerdom, whereby the term "Afrikaner" became a site whose mode of interpellation would be based not only on linguistic but also, and foremost, on "racial, cultural and political criteria."[1]

Such criteria would be incomplete without considering how Afrikaner nationalism was also a gendered project, as Coetzee would recognise elsewhere. In discussing *apartheid* thinking through the figure of Geoffrey Cronjé, one of its influential theorists, Coetzee considers how the Afrikaner nationalist movement held "a patriarchal threat or promise," whereby the Afrikaner woman is held to a set of strict sexual policies, as befits the guarantor of the purity of the Afrikaner line, and thus of the nation.[2] As for the male Afrikaner, he is to assume his place as the rightful patriarch within a family structure that emulates the pre- twentieth-century rural Afrikaner one. The patriarch is the regulator of women's bodies, ascertaining their viability for procreation, and an undemocratic, tyrannical figure overall: "The patriarch is the one who lays down the law… The way of obedience is the only way."[3]

As attested by its marked excesses of violence, South Africa would know and be formed by such virulent enactments of masculinity. It would also harbour forms of masculinity that would serve as paradigmatic examples of ethical possibilities at the gendered level. The trilogy, by occupying different temporalities—from *apartheid* to post-*apartheid* time[4]—necessarily deals with the intense questions of how identity is articulated in, for the most part, a South African context, and how the white, male subject is particularly located in this fraught, difficult situation.

Of Farms and Nations

Good for intro

It was the worst of times, as we can gather from *Boyhood*'s introductory lines: "All the houses on the estate are new and identical. They are set in large plots of red clay earth where nothing grows, separated by wire fences" (B, 1). The bleakness of *apartheid* is portrayed through a constitutive inability to welcome life: this is a closed environment, "a box of a house" (B, 2), where anything stemming from outside its frontiers, even that which is necessary for one's bodily survival, falters and is prevented from thriving: "hens do not flourish" (B, 1), "rainwater, unable to seep away in the clay, stands in pools in the yard" (B, 1). It is also a place of matter-of-fact, daily violence:

> His mother takes the hens between her knees, presses on their jowls till they open their beaks, and with the point of a paring-knife picks at their tongues. The hens shriek and struggle, their eyes bulging…He thinks of her bloody fingers. (B, 1–2)

ie Coetzee chooses to tell us this

The boy also exhibits violent traits: "He plays with the vacuum cleaner…. He holds the pipe over a trail of ants, sucking them up to their death" (B, 2).

Through the description of the crudeness of such context, we are gradually introduced to this family, first the mother, then the "he" of the story, John, his father and the Joycean-esque brother, whom much like Mr. Dedalus's Maurice is largely left uncharacterised.[5] There is a gradation in the presentation of the characters whose importance becomes clearer later on, and the overall absence of the brother indicates an oedipal-like composition, the triangulation of father-mother-boy.

This composition becomes important in allowing for a reading of the first chapter as providing a microcosmic view of gendered organisation in South Africa during *apartheid*-era. It is indicative of the ideological operations of what can be termed Afrikaner masculinity, as considered by the parameters of the nationalist movement. As Adriaan du Pisani summarises, "through the ideological coordination of nation, manhood, and whiteness a 'national manhood' had been established."[6]

To speak of South Africa as a "nation" is to support Ernest Renan's assertion that "nations are not something eternal. They had their beginnings and they will end."[7] "Nation" is a complicated term, of uneasy definition, for "no nation ever makes the mistake of defining itself permanently, in essentialist terms," suggests Robert Young.[8] Homi Bhabha expounds on the ambivalence that can be located at the heart of the concept, and to those who live and write in and of it.[9] This ambivalent status is due to the "conceptual indeterminacy" that characterises it,[10] stemming from the necessary understanding of the multitude of meanings ascribed to the term. It is no accident that Bhabha employs the psychoanalytic-derived term of "ambivalence,"[11] for, as Robert Young suggests, it is this term that is more apt towards making clearer the "oscillations" of the nation[12]: "'Nationness' is a state of constant tension, or oscillation between heterogeneity and homogeneity, between difference and sameness, the past and the future, between processes of mixing, miscegenation, hybridization and those of separation, purity, cleansing."[13] Judith Butler considers that the making of the nation-state demands a negation of its heterogeneity, whereby "periodic expulsion and dispossession of its national minorities" is the continuous process through which the nation-state ensures its legitimacy.[14]

As has been suggested, the house/nation was somber and uninviting. It is also telling that the theme of national identity, and its necessarily gendered aspects, should be present right in the first chapter. For, as the philology of the word "nation" recognises, it is associated with "origin or descent: 'naissance, extraction, rang' to quote a dictionary of ancient French,"[15] thus generally being employed to depict a place of birth. Only in the nineteenth century would the match of nation and state be considered as natural.[16] The introduction of the nuclear, heterosexual family in *Boyhood*'s very first chapter may be read as a national allegory for the standardised fantasies ruling the nation, where the institutionalised power that disadvantages women is demonstrated alongside the male powers that, seeking to prevent women's advancement, come together for such a goal. The question to be answered in the following parenthetical analysis of South African history is how these gender arrangements came to be.

Due to the discovery of diamonds on the Vaal-Hartz river junction in 1867, there was an increase of British participation in the life of the subcontinent from the 1870s onwards, an imperial masculinity being espoused that reflected a public school upbringing centered on notions of "superiority and toughness…, a willingness to resort to force and a belief in the glory of combat."[17] This imperial masculinity would clash with existing masculinities, namely the Afrikaner and African.[18]

In the Afrikaner republics persisted a rural system of production, patriarchal in nature.[19] This land-based system eventually collapsed under the demands of British-favored intense, large-scale commercialisation. As Robert Morrell argues, "the replacement of the old order based on the family … with a new and impersonal modern state, posed a threat which men experienced as an attack on their masculinity."[20]

The 1920s, therefore, saw both an impoverished and landless Afrikaner population, a dire social situation that would be targeted by a sensationalistic nationalist movement:

> Nationalism in the 1920s, 1930s and 1940s brought Afrikaners together. Sports, particularly rugby, were an integral part of this process. The church and, for a period, the schools … were also critical in protecting the position of the Afrikaner men and in bolstering a new Afrikaner masculinity.[21]

The defeat at the hands of the British in the Anglo-Boer War (1899–902) created the need for Afrikaners to rethink their place and identity in South African society. The ensuing Act of Union in 1910, that aggregated the Boer republics of Transvaal and Orange Free State with the British colonies of Natal and the Cape, opened two political paths in terms of the white population. One would be represented by the South African Party, led by L. Botha and J. C. Smuts, espousing a more inclusive South Africanism, allowing for the possibility of collaboration between Afrikaners and English-speaking South Africans. The other political path would be that of an exclusive Afrikaner nationalism, enacted by J. B. M. Hertzog's National Party.

In 1934, both political parties united and formed the United Party. The Afrikaner right wing responded to such a political movement by forming, through the leadership of D. F. Malan, the *"Gesuiwerde" Nasionale Party* (Purified National Party), with claims to be the political home of nationalist Afrikanerdom.

The dominant modes of being a man, seen through the prism of nationalism, would be crystallised in the assumptions that formed, in 1918, the *Afrikaner-Broederbond*, with a series of values characterised as representing the core of the Afrikaner nationalist manly ideal. According to Adriaan du Pisani, the Afrikaner man should be financially independent, white, Afrikaans-speaking, Protestant, adhere to the Calvinist version of Christianity, possess an irreproachable character and be committed to their fatherland, language and culture. These extensive qualities should necessarily be combined with other implicit elements, such as heterosexuality and political conservatism.[22]

The future in nationalist thinking becomes only possible through the organising of the nation. The nation is articulated as an *a priori* necessity: "A man must have a nationality as he must have a nose and two ears; a deficiency in any of these particulars is not inconceivable and does from time to time occur, but only as a result of some disaster, and it is itself a disaster of a kind."[23] More to the point, Benedict Anderson also specifies this need: "in the modern world everyone can, should, will 'have' a nationality, as he or she 'has' a gender."[24] A concise definition of the nation and its relations to nationalism and colonialism is provided by Cynthia Enloe:

> A "nation" is a collection of people who have come to believe that they have been shaped by a common past and are destined to share a common future. That belief is usually nurtured by a common language and a sense of otherness from groups around them. Nationalism is a commitment to fostering those beliefs and promoting policies which permit the nation to control its own destiny. Colonialism is especially fertile ground for nationalist ideas because it gives an otherwise divided people such a potent shared experience of foreign domination. But not all nationalists respect other communities' need for feelings of self-worth and control. Some nationalists have been the victims of racism and colonialism; others have been the perpetrators of racism and colonialism.[25]

Such strict formations could be interpreted as a reaction to a series of events that were initiated in the late nineteenth century with a more incisive intervention of the British in Cape politics.[26]

In the 1920s, due to an accentuated development of British-originated capitalism, "hundreds and thousands of Afrikaners were landless and impoverished."[27] Afrikaner nationalism would base its message on a specific, nostalgic conception of Republican life and masculinity, with farm-based production at its core. This message targeted the central frailty of Afrikaner identity, its constant seeking to secure a firmer place in the southern tip of Africa. As John would say, in *Summertime*:

> Once upon a time he used to think that the men who dreamed up the South African version of public order, who brought into being the vast system of labour reserves and internal passports and satellite townships, had based their vision on a tragic misreading of history. They had misread history because, born in farms or in small towns in the hinterland, and isolated within a language spoken nowhere else in the world, they had no appreciation of the scale of the forces that had since 1945 been sweeping away the old colonial world.... Alone and friendless at the remote tip of a hostile continent, they erected their fortress state and retreated behind its walls. (5)

The republican ideal held the promise of the restoration of the Afrikaner *volk*, emasculated as it had been by British imperialism. Afrikaner hegemonic masculinity in the 1930s and 1940s thus found its grounding in the tensions between rural and urban spaces, whereby the actual urban space, rifled with poverty due to British-induced capitalism, contrasted with a nostalgia for a wealthier rural past:

> As a result of their negative experience of urban life Afrikaners harked back to a romanticised rural past. For many years after the majority of Afrikaner men had ceased to be farmers the puritan image of the simple, honest, steadfast, religious, and hardworking *boer*, who had earned a claim to the land through the cultivation of his farm and his love for the soil of the fatherland, remained the dominant representation of Afrikaner masculinity.[28]

The National Party would rule from 1948 until 1994. At the height of nationalist mobilisation, adherence to Malan's party and its principles were the only way to be confirmed as a man, with alternative conceptions of masculinity largely being silenced or stigmatised.[29]

The nation is thus a place constructed not only in the ambition of territorial definition, articulated by the creation of artificial mythological pasts that seek to bind the collective imagination of its people, but also, at a deep symbolic level, where sexual difference also gains mythic qualities. As Elleke Boehmer considers on this matter:

> Images of women and of men occupy different positions and levels in national iconographies and ideologies. ... The image of the mother invites connotations of origins—birth, hearth, home, roots, the umbilical cord—and rests upon the frequent, and some might say "natural," identification of the mother with the beloved earth,

the national territory and the first-spoken language, the national tongue. In contrast the term fatherland has conventionally lent itself to contexts perhaps more strenuously nationalistic, where the appeal is to *Bruderschaft*, filial duty, the bonds of fraternity and paternity.[30]

As an imagined community,[31] its fraternity-implied basis is organised through the building of a common, mythical past that strengthens the possible envisioning of a shared future, the populations of a nation being "represented in the past or in the future *as if* they formed a natural community, possessing of itself an identity of origins, culture and interests which transcends individuals and social conditions."[32]

The modern nation is then organised according to gendered metaphors, in which the domesticity of women, with its perceived inherent components of frailty and instability, is to be retained and defended through the war-like comradeship that is the due enactment of men. The female figure, while standing for the nation, and thus symbolically above men, "in reality ... is kept below them."[33] A poignant question then arises: "If the structures of nations or nation-states are soldered onto the struts of gender hierarchies, and if the organisation of power in the nation is profoundly informed by those structures, how then is the nation to be imagined outside of gender?"[34]

Sexual difference and its implications in nation-making become clearer as one returns to the first chapter of *Boyhood*. In it, the exhaustive qualities of inaction—life is not advancing, the barrenness of social politics intrudes into the human heart—bore their fruits in the form of resistance of the mother, the Other of nationalism. The mother's desire for actualisation, in the buying of a bicycle, triggers a deep-rooted anxiety regarding the gendered norms of the time:

> She bought the bicycle thinking that riding it would be a simple matter. Now she can find no one to teach her. His father cannot hide his glee. Women do not ride bicycles, he says. His mother remains defiant. I will not be a prisoner in this house, she says. I will be free. (B, 3)

The literal means of mobility from the private sphere are thus denied to the woman, as she finds no possibility of learning how to go beyond her social station. The division between the public and the private spheres are here reified in their gendered meanings—woman as servant to the male heirs of the boer commando. Home is the space of the feminine, providing comfort for the male hero, whereas the public space is the place of male comraderie and autonomy.[35] The influence of the father changes the boy's own glee for the mother's project:

> At first he had thought it splendid that his mother should have her own bicycle. He had even pictured the three of them riding together down Poplar Avenue, she and he and his brother. But now, as he listens to his father's jokes, which his mother can meet only with dogged silence, he begins to waver. Women don't ride bicycles: what if his father is right? (B, 3)

The harmonious, idyllic, image of the family coming together is impeded by the seed of doubt placed by the father, the upholder of traditional ways regarding gender. In imagining his mother having been granted her wish, the boy's construction of such an idyllic image soon meets societal disapproval. The father provides the *locus* of reference for the established social hierarchy. The lack of societal references regarding women's emancipation furthers the boy into agreeing with his father: "If his mother can find no one willing to teach her, if no other housewife in Reunion Park has a bicycle, then perhaps women are indeed not supposed to ride bicycles" (B, 3). The silencing of women's agency transpires through the narrative, ensuring the reproduction of her oppressed status; and yet, this is an enactment of a societal nature, that is to say, women's agency is unrecognised because the context disallows it, both implicitly—it is, as we have seen, part of its founding myth—and explicitly, or in more direct ways, such as the father's correction of what an image of communal pleasure may constitute.

What distinguishes the narrative from a standardised enactment of masculinity is its ability to provide a more nuanced understanding of the ambivalence towards women's social predicaments. It recognises not only that some injustice is being practiced, but also how the power disparity triggers other aspects beyond the immediate glee of righteous privilege. The banding together of the men in the family is portrayed in guilty terms, as the boy feels that he has betrayed his mother, and regrets her being alone.[36] And, if ultimately he belongs with the men, his alliance is not so unilateral as to disallow any thoughts regarding his mother's position in this affair. "He knows she has been defeated, put in her place, and knows that he must bear part of the blame. I will make it up to her one day, he promises himself" (B, 4). Putting her in her place implies an acknowledgement of the power play enacted through his and the other men's actions, a situation that is not met with pride, but with shame. His enactment towards autonomy and male camaraderie then, is understood to bear an afflictive side with it.

These politics of living are an expression of the wider societal nationalist ideology: the woman as the symbolic equivalent of the nation is to be protected by the male constituents of the land, and by being denied any material capacity of relating to that land herself, she is also deprived of her agency as an integral human being with desires of her own, desires that escape imputed symbolic conceptions. Such gendered politics are an approximation of the *volksmoeder* ideology, that is, the Afrikaner woman is perceived as needing to be protected, through male agency and comradeship, from outside perils, represented by, for instance, black men.[37]

Such comradeship is notable for its homosocial component, as women are seldom accounted for as actors in nation-building. Nationalism, Joane Nagel stresses, is a pursuit of "masculine cultural themes", as the "'microculture' of masculinity in everyday life articulates very well with the demands of nationalism, particularly its militaristic side."[38] That is, nation-building creates instances in which aspects recognised as masculine, such as bravery and duty, are heavily promoted.

The boy's betrayal of the mother does not lead, however, to its expected counterpoint, the adoration of the father. "His father likes the United Party, his father likes cricket and rugby, yet he does not like his father. He does not understand this contradiction, but has no interest in understanding it" (B, 43). The consequence is that he is not interested in the very idea of having a father: "Even before he knew his father ... he had decided he was not going to like him. In a sense, therefore, the dislike is an abstract one: he does not want to have a father, or at least does not want a father who stays in the same house" (B, 43). It could be read that, in eschewing the father, John was seeking to attain manhood. However, his manhood, as defined in a nationalistic context, is dependent on the father-figure, especially in the crucial moment of childhood.

To mute the father out of the familial picture is not only to shatter the nationalistic conception of the patriarchal family, but also to enter the feminised world entirely, of which there is no correspondent in the nationalistic fantasy: "In a normal household, he is prepared to accept, the father stands at the head: the house belongs to him, the wife and children live under his sway" (B, 12). His father, alongside his other uncles from his mother's side, are no more than "an appendage, a contributor to the economy as a paying lodger might be" (B, 12).

This is the power of the Macbeth-like sisters—"His father calls the three sister-mothers the three witches" (B, 39)—the comparison serving not only to underline the mystical properties of women whose logic escapes the centripetal movement of nationalism, but perhaps primarily to draw a veiled shadow on men's ambitions to power, as counteracted by women. The comparison is drawn when assessing the attachment of mothers to sons, John's cousins, of which John declares that he is the one most matured from motherly embrace, an infrequent moment of self-assuredness. The supernatural allegory serves to emphasise how feminine logic is outside the paradigm of accepted modes of masculinity, and the underlying threat of the feminine as sabotage to masculine ambitions.

Not only is the specific figure of the father derided, but also his extended family: "his father's family has never taken him to its bosom" (B, 37). The justification given is that the father's family is aware of the "perversion of the natural order," whereby "the family, led by his grandmother, is not blind to the secret of No. 12 Poplar Avenue, which is that the eldest child is first in the household, the second child second, and the man, the husband, the father, last" (B, 38). This insistence on gender—the man, the husband, the father—impresses how the arrangements in the family home are viewed as abnormal according to the norms. There is an economy at play here then, as straying away from norms implicates social exclusion. An economy the cost of which the boy is willing to pay in this particular case, as "he is chilled by the thought of the life he would face if his father ran the household, a life of dull, stupid formulas, of being like everyone else" (B, 79).

This economy plays into the boy's relation to the family farms. Farm stories are the happiest moments for him, due to the "teasing and the laughter that go with them" (B, 22). Time on the farm is when John is understood as being happiest, with family gatherings and "children roaming the veld as free as wild animals" (S, 108). For John, "farms are places of freedom, of life" (B, 22). It is also, at the same time, both a sign of difference from his friends and a sign of entry into a collective past:

> His friends do not come from families with stories like these. That is what sets him apart: the two farms behind him, his mother's farm, his father's farm, and the stories of those farms. Through the farms he is rooted in the past; through the farms he has substance. (B, 22)

The farm is mother-like to John: "He has two mothers. Twice-born: born from woman and born from the farm. Two mothers and no father" (B, 96). Yet it possesses none of the complexity John holds to his human mother:

"Everything that is complicated in his love for his mother is uncomplicated in his love for the farm" (B, 79).

The initial effect of this aura, an illuminative promise that life is to be found there, that community might be established, is the enacting of the mythical return to the land, present in the farm novel (*plaasroman*) of Afrikaans writers in the 1920s and 1930s. The *plaasroman*, seeking to depict farming life, approached the reality of "the insular patriarchal culture of the Boer farm," where nature acted as second mother.[39] Ownership of land activates, and is the sole principle of, "self-realisation—realisation of the self not as individual but ... as the transitory embodiment of a lineage."[40] It is this communal aspect that gives its central meaning to the *plaasroman*, a consciousness based on lineage through which the individual gains a sort of immortality, for the *locus* of living is the farm: "Lineal consciousness brings about a liberation from the sense of being alone in the world and doomed to die: as long as the lineage lasts the self may be thought to last. Conversely, the self may perpetuate itself by perpetuating the lineage."[41] The farm is the fantasised site whereby nostalgia of an idealized rural life is enacted, a lost arcadia whose continued pastoral inscriptions provide a way of affirming white presence in South Africa.

Still, this relation has its edge of pain, and the boy considers that "he will never be more than a guest, an uneasy guest.... The farm and he are traveling different roads, separating, growing not closer but further apart" (B, 79–80). It is a gradual recognition that proceeds throughout *Boyhood*, in which the farm is increasingly seen as losing its alluring effect. A fissure in this fantastic elaboration of the farm is made in terms of the disconnection between the boy and the men, in that the farm as homosocial site both succeeds and fails. John draws pleasure from male company, but it is made clear that entrance into that male world, as contextualised by the farm, is made void by issues pertaining to generational difference. This involves not only the failed comparison in terms of school-based beatings, as an institutionalised way of promoting masculinity (which will be discussed in the following chapter, "Family Outcast"), but also the male-privileged activity of hunting.

The latter activity's biggest reward is not the amount of game killed, but rather its homosocial component: "He never manages to hit anything ... yet never does he lives [*sic*] more intensely than in the early mornings when he and his father set off with his guns" (B, 87). Indeed, the acquisition of game is not the point, as any occurrence in the hunting trip provides "enough of a story to tell the rest of the family" (B, 88).

Gradually, the boy comes to understand the implicit set of rules in the farm:

> He broods on the word *mustn't*. He hears it more often than anywhere else, more often even than in Worcester ... Would that be the price, if he were to give up going to school and plead to live here on the farm: that he would have to stop asking questions, obey all the *mustn'ts*, just do as he was told?... Is there no way of living in the Karoo—the only place where he wants to be—as he wants to live: without belonging to a family? (B, 91)

To live in the farm is not to live in blissful freedom, but rather to accept a series of preconditions that are never really explained in terms of their existence.

Considering the functions of the *plaasroman* (in which the farm is the privileged site of Self-enhancement), the irony is that it is the farm that eventually becomes stifling of any hopes for Self-actualisation. The farm is mired in a structure of subservience, of secret undercurrents that pervert the idyllic notion of the place. Here parallels with animal life serve to portray the violence that mines such a conception of the farm, namely in its literal castrating procedures:

> There is no way of talking about what he has seen. "Why do they have to cut off the lambs' tails?" he asks his mother. "Because otherwise the blowflies would breed under their tails," his mother replies. They are both pretending; both of them know what the question is really about. (B, 99)

As John watches these procedures, "at the end of the operation the lambs stand sore and bleeding by their mothers' side, who have done nothing to protect them" (B, 99). The castration scene makes the implication of identity-making clearer: John's mother, the outsider in the father's farm, Voëlfontein, serves as the model through which John's identity can grow beyond the stiffness of this place. As such, he himself becomes increasingly an outsider.

It is through an anthropomorphic moment that the rigidity and subservient qualities of the farm are indirectly stressed:

> Sometimes when he is among the sheep—when they have been rounded up to be dipped, and are penned tight and cannot get away—he wants to whisper to them, warn them of what lies in store. But then in their yellow eyes he catches a glimpse of something that silences him: a resignation, a foreknowledge not only of what happens to sheep at the hands of Ros behind the shed, but of what awaits them at the end of the long, thirsty ride to Cape Town on the transport lorry. They know it all,

down to the finest detail, and yet they submit. They have calculated the price and
are prepared to pay it – the price of being on earth, the price of being alive. (B, 102)

This is a glimpse of the authoritarian nature of the farm, where no possibility
of disagreement is permitted, and which ultimately leads to death. Not only
bodily death, but as is hinted in the passage, death of the soul, an economy
that, as we have seen, John questions.

It is also more troubling to observe the analogy made between the hap-
penings of the farm and Auschwitz concentration camps. This is a passage
close to the heart of Elizabeth Costello, the Coetzeean alter ego, who also
questions the possibility of the ethical relations between humans and animals,
and vis-à-vis how addressing such relations may promote more ethical thinking between humans themselves. That John is able to establish a degree of
connection with the sheep that escapes the rules of the context in which he
is located may account for some of the deeper messages of the trilogy, those of
an ethics based on the sympathetic imagination.[42]

In the search for a place he can call home, this alien-esque boy considers
the farm one of the more accessible sites he can belong to:

> The secret and sacred word that binds him to the farm is *belong*. Out in the veld by
> himself he can breathe the word aloud: *I belong on the farm*. What he really believes
> but does not utter, what he keeps to himself for fear that the spell will end, is a differ-
> ent form of the word: *I belong to the farm*. (B, 95–96)

As already seen, this is an uneasy identification, whose deeper meaning John
attempts to keep outside himself. The farm's existence is outside his own,
independent, and yet still exerting its powers, as site of one's lineage. It exists
outside of time, eternal and unchangeable: "When they are all dead, when
even the farmhouse has fallen into ruin like kraals on the hillside, the farm
will still be here" (B, 96). This contrasts with an initial understanding that
"one day the farm will be wholly gone, wholly lost; already he is grieving at
that loss" (B, 80).

In this sense, identification with the land is never an entirely resolved
issue, for the farm provides joy, although it also is a site of violence. These
are irremediable features that draw tense identifications. And yet, such identifications are one step further from the strict understanding provided by the
plaasroman, namely in the unveiling of the farm's routine diet of violence,
necessary as it may be in some cases.[43] The terms of women's agency and their
limited acting sphere as ordained by a patriarchal order are considered; nev-

ertheless the identification with the feminine is stronger than with the set of codes and rules understood as masculine.

This is a subversive act in terms of a purported Afrikaner identity. As we shall see, despite John being presented as a little despotic child, the portrayal of identity in the trilogy is dismissive of a "linear consciousness" paradigm appointed by the identity-formulating *plaasroman*, namely the idea that one should bow to one's lineage. Although the attraction to such a mode of consciousness is certainly there, it is itself conflicted, never entirely resolved, open to questioning.

Of Fathers and Strangers

"South Africa is a country without heroes…. Do South Africans have to support other South Africans even if they don't know them?" (B, 108). In terms of national aspirations, a non-heroic South Africa is a betrayal of its fundamental basis, and a dismissal of the nationalist-inflected mythologising of the past. As Anne McClintock suggests:

> Nationalism takes shape through the visible, ritual organization of fetish objects: flags, uniforms, airplane logos, maps, anthems, national flowers, national cuisines and architectures, as well as through the organization of collective fetish spectacle—in team sports, military displays, mass rallies, the myriad forms of popular culture, and so on.[44]

The nationalist movement had as one of its pillars the demi-god like elevation of a gallery of male *volkshelde* (national heroes). This pantheon would be celebrated through monuments and ingrained in education:

> At school they learn, over and over again, year after year, about Jan van Riebeeck and Simon van der Stel and Lord Charles Somerset and Piet Retief…. Although, in examinations, he gives the correct answers to the history questions, he does not know, in a way that satisfies his heart, why Jan van Riebeeck and Simon van der Stel were so good while Lord Charles Somerset was so bad. (B, 65–66)

The VOC established a fort in the Table Bay area in 1652, under the leadership of Jan van Riebeeck. Initially a spot for resupplying the Company's ships with products such as milk and fresh meat, as provided by the Khoikhoi, there was an initial lack of interest in further exploration of the area. Eventually, and as the poor trade deals on the part of the Company would elicit the resistance of the indigenous communities, it saw the need to further its expansion. Led by Riebeeck, a series of wars were enacted with "the aim of driving the Khoikhoi from their land and replacing them with commercial farms run by European settlers and worked by imported slaves."[45] Burghers under the direct command of the VOC, were expected to produce fresh food, sowing and to plant what was sought by the Company, at low prices. Cape burghers would eventually develop their own mythology, internal to their community, that of "defenders of the land". Finding themselves "indispensable to the Cape settlement," this foundational myth would be the "first sign of an emerging political consciousness."[46]

Riebeeck's successor, Simon van der Stel, arrived at the position of Governor of the Cape in 1679, a position he would occupy for the following twenty years, eventually handing it over to his son, Willem Adriaan van der Stel, in 1699. Encouraging agriculture, and the subsequent increasing of settlement, Simon van der Stel would be a driving force behind the establishment of colonialist rule in the ever-expanding Cape.[47] The burghers would act as frontiersmen, expanding the existing frontiers through the cultivation of land increasingly farther from the colony.

British permanent occupation of the colony in 1806 would tip the balance of the ongoing conflict between the settlers and the indigenous populations, namely the Xhosa. Despite shows of strength on the Xhosa part, such as the war of 1834–835, the eventual call for more European troops would prove effective in quelling the rebellion. The British ruling of the colony was, however, increasingly challenged, due to at least three different factors: the farmers who had lost much in these conflicts; the increased displeasure at the emancipation of slaves; and the need to move northward for sheep-farming.[48]

These factors resulted in the movement that would be termed "The Great Trek," undertaken by thousands of the Dutch-speaking people in the colony seeking to escape a "perverse sense of being marginalized" in the British-led Cape.[49] The issue at hand was foremost the seeking of a place the burghers could claim as their home:

> The real issue was the burghers' feeling that they had been marginalized and disempowered where they lived.... This sense of marginalization and disaffection [occurred] within the context of a government that introduced a social revolution at the same time as removing virtually all the local government institutions with which the burghers had identified.[50]

The nationalist movement of the twentieth century considered the golden age of Afrikanerdom the period ranging from the start of the Great Trek, in the 1830s, to the Anglo-Boer war. John exhibits no particular interest in these affairs, even though he is supposed to: "Nor does he like the leaders of the Great Trek as he is supposed to, except perhaps for Piet Retief, who was murdered after Dingaan tricked him into leaving his gun outside the kraal" (B, 66).

Under the military and tactical prowess of King Shaka, the Zulus would come to dominate the East coast of South Africa. By murdering his brother, Dingane would own the military power of the Zulus. Wishing to settle close to the borders of the Zulu state, Retief sought a treaty with Dingane.[51] After killing Retief and his party, Dingane would launch an attack on the remaining trekkers, eventually being defeated in the Blood River battle, a counter-attack led by Andries Pretorius.

This battle would become a central piece of Afrikaner nationalist mythology.[52] In the boy's account, Retief, although meriting a greater degree of recognition over the rest of the Voortrekkers, fails in his assessment as a hero. The childish gloss can, however, be also read as a telling comment on the excesses of nationalistic production.

The Great Trek would, in nationalist times, be revised according to its very generative conditions. The Trek would, in these terms, be considered a purposeful moving away of British laws, a candid assertion of the Afrikaner patriarch against the effeminate British, the fears of Anglicisation becoming one of the flags of Afrikaner nationalism.[53] The centennial commemoration of 1938 produced a narrative that celebrated unity through enacted spectacle, by recreating Voortrekker wagons that represented "the whip-wielding white patriarch prancing on horseback, black servants toiling alongside, white mother and children sequestered in the wagon."[54] Notwithstanding their shared sense of marginality, the trekkers were largely "loyal subjects" and the Trek would be marked by constant "conflict, cooperation and complex interaction" with African polities, a reading in contrast with the nationalist narrative that interprets the Trek as the steady incursion of the proud *volk*.[55]

Tellingly, the boy meets a modern day version of Retief, who in this incarnation is a contractor who drives the family back to Cape Town: "Retief's van feels like Noah's Ark, saving the sticks and stones of their old life" (B, 134). This homonymous version of the nationalist Afrikaner hero is more benign, apparently lacking the nationalist-contoured excesses. In recapturing the dominant narrative of the Trek as searching for home, it is this modern day Retief who finally provides the means through which John can do so. That Cape Town eventually disillusions him, and provides no longer a valid answer to what "home" may be, is in tandem with the concept, within the trilogy, being posited as frustratingly unstable in its meaning.

As has been advanced, national communities are organised through a wide array of forms, such as flags, foods and costumes.[56] Such is also the case with the national anthem that figures in *Boyhood*: "'Uit die blou can onse hemel,' they sing in their deep voices, standing to attention, gazing sternly ahead: the national anthem, *their* national anthem" (B, 24). *Die Stem an Suid-Afrika* [*The Call of South Africa*], instituted by the National Party in 1957, was the South African anthem in *apartheid* times, taking the place of *God Save the Queen*, and promoting Afrikaner superiority.

Joining in the anthem is a chore, necessitating outside motivation, for there appears to be little within oneself: "The teacher tries to uplift them, encourage them.... At last it is over." (B, 24). "The boys file out of the hall. A fist strikes him in the kidneys, a short, quick jab, invisible. '*Jood!*' a voice whispers" (B, 24). The corrective is administered not only due to the purported lack of feeling in John's singing, that marks him as outsider to Afrikaner culture, but also to his confused dealings with religion.

John decides to become Roman Catholic on a "spur of the moment" decision (B, 18), a comic portrayal of a decision that had clear consequences, in a society dominated by a group with strong ties to the Dutch Reformed Church. Yet, the purportedly thoughtless decision is based on his parents not holding religious convictions; equally, it serves as a foreshadowing of his future staying at a Catholic school in Cape Town. His choice of religion stems from a romanticised idea based on the impossible odds of Horatius Cocle,[57] that is soon to give way to a more concrete understanding of what sporting such an identity entails, not only in terms of its rituals, but also in acknowledging the violence that other groups draw upon him.

To become Roman Catholic, is to unnerve the Afrikaans boys, who mete out their violence in due form:

> One day during the lunch break two Afrikaans boys corner him and drag him to the farthest corner of the rugby field.... He pleads with them.... The more he gabbles, the more the fat boy smiles. This is evidently what he likes: the pleading, the abasement. (B, 19–20)

This is one of the many instances when male Afrikaners are characterised as basing their interactions on force and violence: "angry and obdurate and full of menaces and talk about God" (B, 66). The Afrikaners, with their rage, are depicted as menacing, with an overall aura of threat: "a manner that Afrikaners have in common too—a surliness, an intransigence, and, not far behind it, a threat of physical force … that he does not share and in fact shrinks from" (B, 124).

Violent youth in South Africa springs to mind the *tsotsi*, a style adopted by young black men in the townships, based on violence and theft, and that would constitute, among other aspects, a response to *apartheid* politics. The life of the *tsotsi*, and the internal struggles that characterised it, would best be captured by Athol Fugard:

> When he thought of himself inwardly, Tsotsi thought of darkness. Inwardly there was darkness, something like the midnight hour, only more obscure. At night when he lay on his bed it was almost one continuum of obscurity, as dark without as within, the separation being his flesh. … He never dreamed. … He lived according to a set of tried and tested rules. … If he failed to observe them the trouble started.[58]

The rigidity of this particular enactment of masculinity, so impoverishing at the psychic, intra/interpersonal level, also tells of social arrangements necessarily wider than the individual, but that result on individual quests towards enacting these "rules" and ensuring their maintenance.

And yet, one could also make allusion to the *Ducktails*, a white hedonistic subculture, composed mostly by young males, whose origins can be traced back to the late 1940s, and whose activities, in their more aggressive bent, included "gate crashing, vandalism, the temporary theft of cars for the purposes of joy-riding, the assault of innocent bystanders, inter-gang street fighting, petty crime, involvement in the illicit liquor and *dagga* trade, the molesting of girls and women and assaulting African and homosexual men."[59]

It is the violence of white Afrikaner boys that is directly addressed in *Boyhood*, on the already mentioned aspects of extreme physicality that seems to be the most obvious external marker of Afrikaner youth coming into manhood: "On the streets it is best to avoid groups of them; even singly they have a truculent, menacing air" (B, 124–25). Thus violence is recognised as a bastion of power of those who rule.

To be a Roman Catholic is also to spend more time in the playground with boys who identify as Jews. To be a Jew is to be an easy target for the Afrikaner boys' violent actions. Unlike boys belonging to other religious groups, "Jews do not judge…. The Jews wear shoes too. In a minor way he feels comfortable with the Jews. The Jews are not so bad" (B, 21). However, the Jews have a darker side: "For the Jews are everywhere, the Jews are taking over the country. He hears this on all sides, but particularly from his uncles, his mother's two bachelor uncles, when they visit" (B, 21).

This supposed "hears this on all sides" is a note on how anti-Semitism would become part of the nationalistic formula, with the Jewish man being regarded as "morally weak, unmanly, and effeminate," and the "Jewish question" being used as political fodder by the National Party, starting in 1938 and until the 1948 elections.[60] John's uncles' anti-Semitic paranoia is understood by the allegiance of at least one of them, Norman, to the Ossewabrandwag, a nationalist, anti-British, pro-German organisation, formed in 1939 by Afrikaners who objected to South Africa's involvement in World War II. It is not strange that John's father is the most vocal in deriding Norman, for he is the employee of Standard Canners, a Jewish-owned canning factory, and a soldier in the war. His defense also foreshadows his coming to work for another Jewish firm, as seen in *Summertime*.

In an indication of the veiled desire of Afrikaners for Jewish identity, we are told the following by Julia the interviewee:

> White South Africans in those days liked to think of themselves as the Jews of Africa, or at least the Israelis of Africa: cunning, unscrupulous, resilient, running close to the ground, hated and envied by the tribes they ruled over. All false. All nonsense. It takes a Jew to know a Jew, as it takes a woman to know a man. Those people were not tough, they were not even cunning, or cunning enough. And they were certainly not Jews. In fact they were babes in the wood. That is how I think of them now: a tribe of babies looked after by slaves. (S, 54)

This formulation is akin to Coetzee's reading of Cronjé's eventual desire for the racialised Other. In this reading, the Jews are derided due to the inherent weaknesses of the immature Afrikaner.

English identity seems to John to be more appealing, a consideration based on its propagated myths of bravery and courage, whereas the Afrikaner identity is deemed lower in esteem:

> He cannot understand why it is that so many people around him dislike England. England is Dunkirk and the Battle of Britain. England is doing one's duty and accepting one's fate in a quiet, unfussy way. England is the boy at the battle of Jutland, who stood by his guns while the deck was burning under him. England is Sir Lancelot of the Lake and Richard the Lionheart and Robin Hood with his longbow of yew and his suit of Lincoln green. What do the Afrikaners have to compare? Dirkie Uys, who rode his horse till it died. Piet Retief, who was made a fool of by Dingaan. And then

the Voortrekkers getting their revenge by shooting thousands of Zulus who didn't have guns, and being proud of it. (B, 128–29)

The overall dislike for the English is true to the era of the 1940s and 1950s, when foreign public opinion on *apartheid* was largely one of unison against it.[61] By aligning himself with the English, the boy is siding with an anti-*apartheid* stance. Particularly, it should be noted that the above passage withdraws masculine power from Afrikaner nationalism, the Afrikaner heroes paling in comparison to the British.

But the trilogy never settles for an easy translation of any identity as fundamentally good or bad, worthwhile or not. The English would also stifle John, "with their good manners, their well-bred reserve. He preferred people who were ready to give more of themselves; then sometimes he would pluck up the courage to give a little of himself in return" (S, 54–55).

John's confabulation over the English is that they, unlike the Afrikaners, "have not fallen into a rage because they live behind walls and guard their hearts well" (B, 73). The following episode that the narrative provides is one that figures as the "fly in the ointment" of such a theory, describing as Trevelyan, a lodger who is "English through and through" (B, 73) provides punishment to Eddie, an apprentice. This violent moment shatters the linearity of the either/or mode of identity, introducing once again complexity in the matter.

Thus far, we have suggested that Afrikaner identity, in what pertains to its characteristics formed by nationalistic advances, is shunned through a series of sympathetic identifications with its Others, such as the feminine, the English or the Jew. As a conclusion, it remains to be seen how these politics can be read in the renewed South Africa.

Of Newness

In 1897, Enoch Sontonga, a school teacher in Johannesburg, would compose *Nkosi Sikelel' iAfrika* [*God Bless Africa*]. It would be recorded by Sol Plaatje in 1923 and adopted as the official hymn of the ANC (African National Congress) in 1925.[62] The hymn "offers a message of unity and uplift and an exhortation to act morally and spiritually on behalf of the African continent."[63]

Both *Nkosi* and *Die Stem* would, in hybrid form, fashion the anthem of democratic South Africa, transmitting the ideal of a united community.

Much like the anthem, the ANC's message of unity—"One Nation, Many Cultures"—implies the recognition of the country's cultural diversity.

The first democratically-held elections of South Africa, on 27 April 1994, that would proclaim Nelson Mandela as its first black President, were, in Dickensian terms, the best and worst of times. There was fear in the air over possible security breaches and attempts at Nelson Mandela's life. Yet, in a necessarily retrospective glance, accounts of the historical event stress the purported coming together of a nation, the starting point of a healing process that would prove more necessary, and eventually more long-term, than was initially thought. Archbishop Desmond Tutu recalls the event as follows:

> Those long hours helped us South Africans to find one another. People shared newspapers, sandwiches, umbrellas, and the scales began to fall from their eyes. South Africans found fellow South Africans—they realized what we had been at such pains to tell them, that they shared a common humanity; that race, ethnicity, skin colour were really irrelevancies. They discovered not a Coloured, a black, an Indian, a white. No, they found a fellow human being. What a profound scientific discovery for the whites, that blacks, Coloureds (usually people of mixed race), and Indians were in fact human beings, who had the same concerns and anxieties and aspirations as they did.[64]

The South African democratic turn represented the hope of ending the racist structures of *apartheid*, a system whose governing body promoted the nation's exclusionary impetus in exemplary fashion. The newly-installed democratic government sought to create a new kind of political body that would be attentive to the needs of those whose voices had been silenced: "The day has been captured for me," writes Nadine Gordimer, "by the men and women who couldn't read or write, but underwrote it, at last, with their kind of signature."[65]

The men and women who gained a new political voice in a democratic South Africa would have been the same "children of iron" who endured decades of *apartheid*: "The age of iron. After which comes the age of bronze. How long, how long before the softer ages return in their cycle, the age of clay, the age of earth? A Spartan matron, iron-hearted, bearing warrior sons for the nation."[66]

A common past now needed to be forged, identities to be reshaped. The white minority, once in power, was now grappling with its more precarious political situation, and repositioning itself regarding what was now seen as the criminal times of the past decades. Autobiography and confession played a role of paramount importance in the shaping of post-*apartheid* South African society. Reconciliation would be key to a nation that was recreating itself to become a model of democratic living, eschewing the terrors of its colonial past.[67]

We can establish a connection the trilogy draws in terms of the ambitions of this new South Africa. John's passion for the Russians met its highest point in 1947, the beginning of the Cold War. This serves not only to emphasise his connection to his mother—her name Vera sounds Russian—but also to further underscore his status as outsider, as his close community are pro-American.

His liking of the Russians, impeded as it is by a degree of ignorance—"He does not know what the Russians do when they are not making war" (B, 28)—may serve as a foreshadowing of Coetzee's enjoyment of Russian literature, his encyclopaedic knowledge of Dostoyevsky,[68] and his novel *Master of Petersburg*.[69] Particularly important is the possible link we could establish between Russia and the efforts of national liberation led by the ANC.

Communism is derided in school, though John understands that his teachers must be incorrect, that their positions may have a counterproposal: "He is troubled. He knows that his teachers' stories must be lies, but he has no means of proving it. He is discontented about having to sit captive listening to them, but too canny to protest or even demur" (B, 141). John's distaste for the unilateral presentation of politics by his teachers goes against the general compromise of dismissing socialist efforts, as they were too closely linked with the ANC. It would be through the support of the Soviet Union that the ANC would find its identity, its leadership considering the Soviet Union as "the embodiment of progress and justice, a symbol of the bright future of humanity and the model for a future South Africa—South Africa after the ANC's victory."[70] In this, a connection is established to the efforts of a collective that would be represented by one of the foremost fathers of the nation.

Eventually, after decades of struggle, South Africa would meet democracy and be led by a man who would be understood as the cultural antithesis of the formations of masculinity promoted by Afrikaner nationalism. Recognised by Coetzee as a "great man ... he may well be the last of the great men,"[71] Nelson Mandela would, through his consummate ability to rethink and refashion himself,[72] become the father of a nation, through an ethics that both inspires in its necessity, and frustrates in its possible betrayal.

From an early belief in armed struggle to humanist reconciliation,[73] Nelson Mandela's long walk to freedom has provided a fitting allegory for South Africa's tortuous path towards democratic politics. If Mandela has come to be understood as the living embodiment of the democratic nation that is now South Africa, he has also been understood as the purveyor of new formations of masculinities.[74]

In his autobiography, when reflecting on the transition to manhood through the ritual of circumcision, Mandela provides the reader with an understanding of the tensions and contradictions surrounding such an event:

> We were clad only in our blankets and as the ceremony began, with drums pounding, we were ordered to sit on a blanket on the ground with our legs spread out in front of us. I was tense and anxious, uncertain of how I would react when the critical moment came. Flinching or crying out was a sign of weakness and stigmatized one's manhood. I was determined not to disgrace myself, the group or my guardian. Circumcision is a trial of bravery and stoicism; no anaesthetic is used; a man must suffer in silence ... Suddenly I heard the first boy cry out, "*Ndiyindoda!*" ("I am a man!"), which we had been trained to say at the moment of circumcision ... I looked down and saw a perfect cut, clean and round like a ring. But I felt ashamed because the other boys seemed much stronger and firmer than I had been; they had called out more promptly than I had. I was distressed that I had been disabled, however briefly, by the pain, and I did my best to hide my agony. A boy may cry; a man conceals his pain.[75]

Mandela's understanding of the range of contradictions experienced in achieving manhood is one of the salient aspects of his autobiography. Alongside his admission of the important role of women in the *apartheid* struggle, such aspects are regarded as instrumental in the making of new masculinities. In Liz Walker's study on this particular theme, an illuminating example is provided, by drawing a distinction between a society where men achieve their manhood through a mix of force and pain, and the Mandela era, where such codes are no longer of use: "But you can't be a man now by force. You need to make yourself understood and not by forcing things. This is the society of Madiba [Mandela]."[76]

In a country plagued by alarming rates of violence, rape and HIV, Madiba's society came to mean a period of acute attention to matters of human rights. The new Constitution instituted in 1996 would recognise the equality of all people in the country, also being progressive in terms of women's rights and sexual orientation issues. Policies were put in place that prevented discrimination. Marital rape was made illegal in 1993; domestic violence, contraception and abortion, among other aspects directly related to gender matters, were addressed.[77]

The golden age of gender equity could only be dreamed up through Mandela's able positioning of himself as a reachable character. Indeed, Mandela was "*the* famous man…with the Atlas-like weight of our future borne on his erect shoulders,"[78] the necessary hero of a country healing its wounds. The new masculinity that he presented was, as suggested by Elaine Unterhalter, a "heroic masculinity," one which understood that personal and social change are interconnected: "Heroic masculinity entails giving oneself to the struggle and reforming oneself in that process; the self is not held apart from the work."[79] Political work, with its sights in social change, also implies personal change as part of it. If this golden age would be maintained through Thabo Mbeki's act as President, after Mandela's retirement in 1999, a bleaker note would be introduced with Jacob Zuma's rape scandal, the outcome of which would highlight the pervading force of traditional thinking in terms of masculinity.[80] Mandela's background as member of an elite, in contrast with Zuma's humble origins, made the latter more easily approachable to the public—the ordinary man.

Heroic masculinity is formulated as a response to violent masculinity, the latter reaching its apogee—and logical conclusion—in the form of *apartheid*. To outline the conditions necessary for validating heroism was, thus, a political demand following the country's liberation in 1994. South Africa's past was also kept in focus, the reconciliatory tone of the new polity privileging the workings of the TRC: "Government efforts led by the African National Congress to invoke a new national past rooted in the black struggle against oppression have focused primarily on the twentieth century."[81] However, current South African historiography is still interested in reformulating its pre-colonial and colonial past, arguing for counter-narratives of its institutionalised history, by illuminating the complexities in the tensions between its various groups.

As others would later comment, the truth that the TRC was supposed to present about the nation was never really achieved; instead, a more anxious, less accommodating aspect would reveal itself, the permanence of the Self's artificial construction.[82] While the crystallised Self offers security, through its element of stability, it is also pathological in nature, for it bears no attempt at renewal, providing no surprise. And yet, it would also help in making the point clearer, that violence was oftentimes drawn by male bodies, or by a masculinist ideology, a variation of which Antjie Krog names "the second narrative":

> For six months the Truth Commission has listened to the voices of victims. Focused and clear, the first narrative cut into the country.… Yet something is amiss. We prick up our ears. Waiting for the Other. The Counter. The Perpetrator. More and more

we want the second narrative.... After six months or so, at last the second narrative breaks into relief from its background of silence—unfocused, splintered in intention and degrees of desperation. But it is there. And it is white. And male.[83]

"South Africa is faintly embarrassing, and therefore not talked about, since not everyone who lives in South Africa is a South African, or not a proper South African" (B, 18). The alienated John is in constant search for a place he can call home, a space that can offer him the affective bearings he feels to be lacking. In this, as we have seen, he fails. Much like the bleak eucalyptuses (B, 2) that line the road providing access to the house's nearest commerce, John resembles this foreign flora, known for its invasive properties, and introduced through the mechanisms of colonialism. Allegorical in nature, such flora and its roots convey the fantasies that inhabit nationalism, namely who belongs, or not within the strictly defined borders of the nation.[84]

John does not belong, cannot belong in a true, definitive sense. But his search for home also carries another message. We have seen that Cape Town acts as the Promised Land for the better part of *Boyhood*, though inevitably it falls short of such magnanimous fantasies. And yet, the reading that may be more important is what Cape Town represents. The city has been mythologised in South African historiography as the one with the least amount of racial segregation during *apartheid*.[85] Myth exaggerates,[86] but the promise of togetherness is a submerged pattern in depictions of the city: as Señor C, in *Diary of a Bad Year*, suggests: "During the years Cape Town was my home, I thought of it as "my" city not just because I had been born there but above all because I knew the history of the place deeply enough to see its past as palimpsest beneath its present."[87]

The city as palimpsest implies a variety of accounts that do not form a simple, inescapable, meaning. Reminiscing on this particular topic, Damon Galgut suggests:

> Different spirits and histories do not add up. In the end your own face is just one more in the crowd: another element in the dissonant harmony. And while you search in vain for a single story to unite all these characters, you may experience again that sensation of transience, of restless not-quite belonging, which may be the only unifying story we have.[88]

The city will also provide John with one of the biggest tests of his life. He must care for his father in sickness, he must become his nurse. Or, he may escape. "One or the other: there is no third way" (S, 266). That we are not provided with the situation's outcome, with its inherent promises and pitfalls, just as we were not provided with the answer to whether John had managed to keep his promises to his mother, attests to the difficulties of masculinity, even in the throes of the "rainbow nation".

Notes

1. J. M. Coetzee, *Doubling the Point*, ed. David Attwell (Cambridge, MA: Harvard University Press, 1992 [1986]), 342.
2. J. M. Coetzee, "The Mind of *Apartheid*: Geoffrey Cronjé (1907–)," *Social Dynamics* 17, no. 1 (1991): 7.
3. Coetzee, "The Mind of *Apartheid*," 17.
4. Alternatively, Derek Hook employs the concept of "(post)*apartheid*" as signalling that the "current South African period might be read both as a definitive break from, and yet also as a sub-category of, the *apartheid* past." *(Post)Apartheid Conditions* (Cape Town: HSRC Press, 2014), 15.
5. See James Joyce, *A Portrait of the Artist as a Young Man* (Oxford: Oxford University Press, 2000 [1916]). The absence of this brother is noted in Julia's interview in *Summertime*; while speaking with John's father, she learns that he is not a single child. "'No, no, he has a brother, a younger brother.' He seemed surprised I did not know. 'That's curious,' I said, 'because John has the air of an only child.' Which I meant critically. I meant that he was preoccupied with himself, did not seem to make allowances for people around him" (*S*, 46).
6. Jacobus Adriaan du Pisani, "Hegemonic Masculinity in Afrikaner Nationalist Mobilisation, 1934–48," in *Masculinities in Politics and War: Gendering Modern History*, ed. Stefan Dudink, Karen Hagemann, and John Tosh (Manchester: Manchester University Press, 2004), 172.
7. Ernest Renan, "What is a Nation?," in *Nation and Narration*, ed. Homi K. Bhabha, trans. Martin Thom (London: Routledge, 1990 [1882]), 20.
8. Robert J. C. Young, *Torn Halves: Political Conflict in Literary and Cultural Theory* (Manchester: Manchester University Press, 1996), 148.
9. Homi K. Bhabha, "Introduction: Narrating the Nation," in *Nation and Narration*, ed. Homi K. Bhabha (New York: Routledge, 1990), 1–7.
10. Bhabha, "Narrating the Nation," 2.
11. In considering ambivalence—wanting one thing and wanting its opposite—Bhabha famously argues that "colonial presence is always ambivalent, split between its appearance as original and authoritative and its articulation as repetition and difference." *The Location of Culture* (New York: Routledge, 1994), 153.
12. Young, *Torn Halves*, 150.
13. Young, *Torn Halves*, 149–50.
14. See Judith Butler's consideration of these aspects in Judith Butler and Gayatri Chakravorty Spivak, *Who Sings the Nation-State?* (Calcutta: Seagull Books, 2007), 33.

15. See Eric Hobsbawm, *Nations and Nationalism Since 1780: Programme, Myth, Reality*, 2nd ed. (Cambridge: Cambridge University Press, 2012 [1990]), 15.

16. See Pierre Renouvin and Jean Baptiste Renouvelle, "El Sentimiento Nacional," in *Introducción a la Historia de Las Relaciones Internacionales*, trans. Abdiel Macías Arvizu (Mexico: Fondo de Cultura Económica, 2000 [1991]), 171–209.

17. See Robert Morrell, "Of Boys and Men: Masculinity and Gender in Southern African Studies," *Journal of Southern African Studies* 24, no. 4 (1998): 616.

18. In terms of the latter, an important effect of such interventionist politics was that the Zulu kingdom would eventually be destroyed in the 1879 war. The 1964 movie *Zulu*, directed by Cy Endfield, is a popular rendition of the conflict between British and Zulu. Ensuing South African capitalisation guaranteed changes in terms of work, whereby "migrant work came to define the lives of most nonelite African men … migration to the cities rose, and towns grew outside of cities where worker residences became more permanent." See Thembisa Waetjen, *Workers and Warriors: Masculinity and the Struggle for Nation in South Africa* (Urbana and Chicago: University of Illinois Press, 2004), 42–43.

19. Boer (the Afrikaans word for farmer) family life operated under male leadership, present in both domestic life and in the militaristic commando life, a system whose origins can be traced to the early days of the Cape settlement, originating as the armed force of the settlers, whose function was to recover stolen cattle, eventually developing into the force that was summoned to protect the land frontier. See Herman Giliomee, *The Afrikaners: Biography of a People* (London: C. Hurst & Co, 2011), particularly 22–57. A boer acceded to the male figure as representing authority, in charge of the laws and all community decisions, especially military. See Sandra Swart, "A Boer and His Gun and His Wife Are Three Things Always Together: Republican Masculinity and the 1914 Rebellion," *Journal of Southern African Studies* 24, no. 4 (1998), 737–51.

20. Morrell, "Of Boys and Men," 617.

21. Morrell, "Of Boys and Men," 617.

22. Adriaan du Pisani, *Masculinities in Politics and War*, 159.

23. Ernest Gellner, *Nations and Nationalism* (Oxford: Basil Blackwell Publisher Limited, 1983), 6.

24. Benedict Anderson, *Imagined Communities* (London: Verso, 2006 [1983]), 5.

25. Cynthia Enloe, *Bananas, Beaches and Bases: Making Feminist Sense of International Politics*, rev. ed. (Berkeley and Los Angeles: University of California Press, 2001 [1989]), 45.

26. As Nigel Worden suggests, this British "aggressive thrust into the whole sub-continent" (24) has been explained in differing ways. Prior to the 1970s, historians tended to argue that this renewed British enterprise was either for humanitarian reasons—concern over the treatment of Africans in the Trekker republics—or a part of the scramble for empire, anticipating the other rival European powers. Contemporary interpretations tend to underline the 1867 discovery of diamonds in the South African interior. The then-existing polities were considered to not be sufficiently equipped for a due exploration of these resources. See *The Making of Modern South Africa*, 5th ed. (Malden: Wiley-Blackwell, 2012 [1994]).

27. Morrell, "Of Boys and Men," 617.

28. Adriaan du Pisani, *Masculinities in Politics and War*, 167.

29. See Kobus du Pisani, "Puritanism Transformed: Afrikaner Masculinities in the *Apartheid* and Post-*Apartheid* Period," in *Changing Men in Southern Africa*, ed. Robert Morrell (London: Zed Books, 2001), 157–75.

30. See Elleke Boehmer, *Stories of Women: Gender and Narrative in the Postcolonial Nation* (Manchester: Manchester University Press, 2005), 27.

31. The nation "is an imagined political community—and imagined as both inherently limited and sovereign." See Benedict Anderson, *Imagined Communities*, 6. According to Anderson, the limit of the nation resides in its finitude (echoing Renan's view), whereas its sovereignty is an indicator of its ambition towards authoritative status. Anderson sums up his argument by stating that to imagine the nation as a community is to recognise that "the nation is always conceived as a deep, horizontal comradeship" (7), based on the bonds erected by fraternity.

32. Etienne Balibar and Immanuel Wallerstein, *Race, Nation, Class: Ambiguous Identities*, trans. Etienne Balibar and Chris Turner (London: Verso, 1991 [1988]), 96.

33. Boehmer, *Stories of Women*, 29.

34. Boehmer, *Stories of Women*, 29.

35. See Elaine Unterhalter, "The Work of the Nation: Heroic Masculinity in South African Autobiographical Writing of the Anti-*Apartheid* Struggle," *The European Journal of Development Research* 12, no. 2 (2000), 167.

36. Shame and guilt are operative terms in Coetzee's work, which shall be addressed in the following chapters.

37. An example of nationalist propaganda employing gendered aspects is given by Adriaan du Pisani: "On the eve of the 1948 election a cartoon appeared … which showed a white woman standing on a small island surrounded by a black ocean threatening to engulf her…. Her two small children were clinging to her dress on which was written 'South Africa'." See Adriaan du Pisani, *Masculinities in Politics and War*, 166.

38. Joane Nagel, "Masculinity and Nationalism: Gender and Sexuality in the Making of Nations," *Ethnic and Racial Studies* 21, no. 2 (1998): 251–52.

39. J. M. Coetzee, *White Writing: On the Culture of Letters in South Africa* (Braamfontein: Pentz Publishers, 2007 [1988]), 65.

40. Coetzee, *White Writing*, 90.

41. Coetzee, *White Writing*, 113.

42. "I return to the death camps. The particular horror of the camps, the horror that convinces us that what went on there was a crime against humanity, is not that despite a humanity shared with their victims, the killers treated them like lice. That is too abstract. The horror is that the killers refused to think themselves into the place of their victims, as did everyone else." J. M. Coetzee, *The Lives of Animals*, 34.

43. As Coetzee has already shown, particularly in *In the Heart of the Country* (London: Vintage, 2004 [1977]), or *Disgrace* (London: Vintage, 2000 [1999]).

44. Anne McClintock, "Family Feuds: Gender, Nationalism and the Family," *Feminist Review* 44 (1993): 71.

45. Lynn Meskell and Lindsay Weiss, "Coetzee on South Africa's Past: Remembering in the Time of Forgetting," *American Anthropologist* 108, no. 1 (2006): 89.

46. Giliomee, *The Afrikaners: Biography of a People*, 6–7.

47. M. Whiting Spilhaus, "The Story of Simon van der Stel," in *Company's Men*, ed. M. Whiting Spilhaus (Cape Town: John Malherbe Pty Ltd, 1973), 93–171.

48. Robert Ross, *A Concise History of South Africa*, 2nd ed. (Cambridge: Cambridge University Press, 2008 [1999]), 42.

49. Giliomee, *The Afrikaners: Biography of a People*, 144.

50. Giliomee, *The Afrikaners: Biography of a People*, 150.

51. "Retief arrived at Dingane's kraal with seventy white trekkers and thirty servants, expecting the Zulu king to sign a treaty for the cession of land. On 6 February 1838, just before the signing ceremony, Dingane persuaded Retief to instruct his men to leave their arms outside the chief's village, whereupon the Zulu king's men seized all the unarmed trekkers and their servants and clubbed them to death one by one. Retief was killed at the end after watching all his men being clubbed down." See Giliomee, *The Afrikaners: Biography of a People*, 165.

52. The killing of Retief and his party by Dingane has, within the strict Boer account of events, allowed not only Dingane to be marked as a traitor but, by extension, black people as a whole. As Adam Kuper argues, this narrative would serve as the validating basis of the "Afrikaner conquest of Black South Africa. God had elected the Boers as His Chosen People in South Africa. The execution of Piet Retief took on something of the aura of a martyrdom." "The Death of Piet Retief," *Social Anthropology* 4, no. 2 (1996): 136. Kuper's political interpretation of the event provides an understanding of the various possible reasons for Dingane's actions, thus going beyond the traditionally accepted Boer account. When cognisant of the multiple factors that may, or may not have interfered in Dingane's resolution, the readily accepted image of Dingane as a barbarian can, probably in more accurate fashion, be replaced by the image of a leader who "had an accurate strategic appreciation of the threat posed by the Boers, the British, and Zulu refugees in Natal" (142). For Jackie Grobler, the interpretation of the event as "a well-planned pre-emptive attack by the Zulus on the Voortrekkers," goes against the earliest tendencies of South African historiography. See "The Retief Massacre of 6 February 1838 Revisited," *Historia* 56, no. 2 (2011): 131.

53. Hence why Lord Charles Somerset, Cape governor between 1814 and 1826, who sought to anglicise the Cape, is derided through the school system.

54. McClintock, "Family Feuds," 69.

55. Nigel Worden, "Demanding Satisfaction: Violence, Masculinity and Honour in Late Eighteenth-Century Cape Town," *Kronos* 35 (2009): 16–17.

56. See Anthony D. Smith, *Myths and Memories of the Nation* (Oxford: Oxford University Press, 1999), 16.

57. See Livy, *The Rise of Rome*, Books 1–5, trans. T. J. Luce (Oxford: Oxford University Press, 1998). The purported emulation of Horatius's heroic deeds is an expression of John's English education.

58. Athol Fugard, *Tsotsi* (Edinburgh: Canongate Books, 2009 [1979]), 34–35.

59. Katie Mooney, "'Ducktails, Flick-Knives and Pugnacity': Subcultural and Hegemonic Masculinities in South Africa, 1948–1960," *Journal of Southern African Studies* 24, no. 4 (1998): 754.

60. Adriaan du Pisani, *Masculinities in Politics and War*, 163.

61. "In the 1940s and 1950s, the British press reports steadily reinforced the impression that *apartheid* was an ideology antithetical to British values and ideals, one that threatened to be a thoroughly disruptive force in the British empire and Commonwealth." See Ronald Hyam and Peter Henshaw, *The Lion and the Springbok: Britain and South Africa since the Boer War* (Cambridge: Cambridge University Press, 2003), 308.

62. See Bennetta Jules-Rosette and David B. Coplan, "'Nkosi Sikelel' iAfrika': From Independent Spirit to Political Mobilization," *Cahier d'Études Africaines* XLIV, no. 1–2 (2004): 343–67.

63. Jules-Rosette and Coplan, "Nkosi Sikelel' iAfrika", 344.

64. Desmond Tutu, *No Future Without Forgiveness* (London: Random House, 1999), 4. The term "Coloured" refers to ex-slaves and Khoisan. See Ross, *A Concise History of South Africa*, 52.

65. Nadine Gordimer, *Living in Hope and History* (London: Bloomsbury Publishing, 1999), 157.

66. J. M. Coetzee, *Age of Iron* (London: Penguin, 2010 [1990]), 50.

67. Albie Sachs recounts how the Truth and Reconciliation Commission (TRC) would be instituted by the ANC, in order to provide response to two main aspects. The first was an internal report in the ANC regarding violations of human rights committed by some of its members in Angola during the liberation struggle. The second, security forces had been promised amnesty by President De Klerk, raising a difficult political situation in terms of the recognition of the newly elected party. The solution found, Sachs argues, was "to link amnesty to a truth commission: there would be no blanket amnesty, but each individual who came forward and acknowledged what he or she had done, would receive indemnity to that extent. This suggestion was followed, and in this way the Truth Commission and the amnesty process were linked on an individualized basis. That turned out to be the foundation of the South African Truth Commission and the basis for its unprecedented success. It meant that the perpetrators of violations of human rights, the torturers, the killers, had a motive to come forward and reveal what they had done. In exchange, the country would learn the truth." See Albie Sachs, *The Strange Alchemy of Life and Law* (Oxford: Oxford University Press, 2009), 71. A different reading of the success of the TRC is given in Mahmood Mamdani, "Amnesty or Impunity? A Preliminary Critique of the Report of the Truth and Reconciliation Commission of South Africa (TRC)," *Diacritics* 32, no. 3–4 (2002): 33–59.

68. J. M. Coetzee, "Dostoyevsky: The Miraculous Years," in *Stranger Shores: Essays 1986–1999*, ed. J. M. Coetzee (London: Vintage, 2001), 134–48.

69. An imaginative recounting of Dostoyevsky's life. See J. M. Coetzee, *Master of Petersburg* (London: Vintage, 2004 [1994]).

70. See Irina Filatova, "The Lasting Legacy: The Soviet Theory of the National-Democratic Revolution and South Africa," *South African Historical Journal* 64, no. 3 (2012): 508.

71. J. M. Coetzee, "On Nelson Mandela (1918–2013)," *New York Review of Books*, January 9, 2014, http://www.nybooks.com/articles/archives/2014/jan/09/nelson-mandela-1918-2013/ [accessed 23 March 2014] (para. 7 of 7).

72. See Elleke Boehmer, *Nelson Mandela: A Very Short Introduction* (Oxford: Oxford University Press, 2008) for a reading of Mandela as holding the capacity to represent himself in

different ways by employing his masculinity. Following Boehmer, Brenna Munro would summarise how Mandela's "authoritative, yet emotive masculinity made very different kinds of people feel included in his adoptive embrace." See "Nelson, Winnie, and the Politics of Gender," in *The Cambridge Companion to Nelson Mandela*, ed. Rita Barnard (Cambridge: Cambridge University Press, 2014), 92.

73. Elleke Boehmer provides a comprehensive chronology of such political trajectories. See "Postcolonial Terrorist: The Example of Nelson Mandela," *Parallax* 11, no. 4 (2005): 46–55.

74. Per Elaine Unterhalter: "Nelson Mandela has embodied the democratic nation of South Africa. ... Mandela has come to stand for a distinctive formation of masculinity in South Africa" (158).

75. Nelson Mandela, *Long Walk to Freedom* (London: Abacus, 1995 [1994]), 32–33.

76. See Liz Walker, "Men Behaving Differently: South African Men since 1994," *Culture, Health & Sexuality: An International Journal for Research, Intervention and Care* 7, no. 3 (2005): 232.

77. For a review of the changes in terms of gender equity in the post-1994 South African society, see Robert Morrell, Rachel Jewkes, and Graham Lindegger, "Hegemonic Masculinity/ Masculinities in South Africa: Culture, Power, and Gender Politics," *Men and Masculinities* 15, no. 1 (2012): 11–30.

78. Gordimer, *Living in Hope and History*, 150–51.

79. Unterhalter, "The Work of the Nation," 165.

80. Regarding Jacob Zuma's rape trial and its implications in traditional thinking regarding black masculinity, see Dobrota Pucherova, "'Land of my Sons': The Politics of Gender in Black Consciousness Poetry," *Journal of Postcolonial Writing* 45, no. 3 (2009): 331–40. The gendered aspects of both pre- and post-*apartheid* South Africa, alongside Zuma's involvement in such politics, is further addressed in the sixth chapter.

81. Carolyn Hamilton, Bernard K. Mbenga, and Robert Ross, "The Production of Preindustrial South African History," in *The Cambridge History of South Africa, Volume 1: From Early Times to 1885*, ed. Robert Ross, Anne Kelk Mager, and Bill Nasson (Cambridge: Cambridge University Press, 2010), 1.

82. As Sarah Nuttall concludes: "To see that one has not located the truth about the past, but only an ongoing narrative of self—to see the subjectivity of the versions of the past one has offered to oneself, binaries, perhaps, which have been able to hold the weight of one's sorrow, to guard against a void of meaning and understanding which one most fears—can be newly painful ... [b]ut it can highlight in a newly self-conscious way the complexity of memory's meanings and motives." "Telling 'Free' Stories? Memory and Democracy in South African Autobiography since 1994," in *Negotiating the Past: The Making of Memory in South Africa*, ed. Sarah Nuttall and Carli Coetzee (Cape Town: Oxford University Press, 1998), 85.

83. See Antjie Krog, *Country of my Skull* (London: Jonathan Cape, 1998), 56.

84. See Jean Comaroff and John L. Comaroff, "Naturing the Nation: Aliens, Apocalypse and the Postcolonial State," *Journal of Southern African Studies* 27, no. 3 (2001): 627–51. The sense of alienness, in the more obvious allusion to the figure of the extraterrestrial, has

been employed to great success in the movie *District 9*, by Neill Blomkamp (TriStar Pictures, 2009).

85. See Paul Maylam, "Explaining the *Apartheid* City: 20 Years of South African Urban Historiography," *Journal of Southern African Studies* 21, no. 1 (1995): 19–38.

86. See Vivian Beckford-Smith, "South African Urban History, Racial Segregation and the Unique Case of Cape Town?" *Journal of Southern African Studies* 21, no. 1 (1995): 63–78.

87. J. M. Coetzee, *Diary of a Bad Year* (London: Vintage, 2008 [2007]), 56.

88. Damon Galgut, "My Version of Home," in *A City Imagined*, ed. Stephen Watson (Johannesburg: Penguin, 2006), 19–20.

· 3 ·

FAMILY OUTCAST

I had a regular white South African boyhood; my life outside the classroom was dominated by sport, particularly by cricket.

J. M. Coetzee, *Doubling the Point*

"That is what he would like to be: a hero" (B, 25). One of the great ambitions of the boy in *Boyhood* seems a contradiction in a country in which, as we have seen, there are, according to his own assessment, no heroes. The presumed extinction of heroism in South Africa is linked to *apartheid* regulation: "He has not forgotten Dr. Malan's first act in 1948: to ban all Captain Marvel and Superman comics, allowing only comics with animal characters, comics intended to keep one a baby, to pass through the Customs" (B, 70). The country's apparent lack of heroes contrasts with the abundance stemming from the classical world, English heroes, and North American superheroes. The recurring theme of Afrikaner culture as a site of arrested development is counter posed to English culture as one providing such space for growth.

Looking for Heroes

Heroes achieve recognition by dealing with obstacles, whether ordinary or extraordinary, "with uncommon courage and grace, setting them apart from most others."[1] Coetzee places the hero as the seeker of quest:

> Captain America is a great flag-wrapped phallus striding out, like all heroes of adventure since Achilles, in quest of a foe worthy of all that bulging, displaced potency. And striding out of the shadows somewhere, eternally, is the figure of the super-villain, monstrously musclebound or cranially overdeveloped, come to measure his endowment against Captain America's.[2]

For Coetzee, then, the model of the hero is to be found in the Homeric epic, living an endless, eternal cycle of measuring his prowess, with sexual overtones, against a villain. Achilles's is the idealised figure of the hero, showing the arc of the hero as the youth's escape from his mother and Self-involvement towards an understanding of one's own mortality,[3] his prowess to be found in his performance as a fighter.

Masculinity as understood in this ideological framing is, therefore, based on action, generally violence, and an outward appearance that evidences toughness and denies any sign of emotion. This armor-like appearance, sometimes literal through the use of a costume, sustains the very identity of the traditional hero as a man in a mission:

> When Steve Rogers becomes Captain America, it is to hold himself together. For now he is defined and confined by his icon. The line bounding him is hard and unwavering. The colors that block him out are elementary and never wash over the line. His emblem proclaims the truth. Contained and maintained at three levels of being—by the muscular exoskeleton, by the mask and costume, by the bounding line—Captain America is the image of the stable ego.[4]

The hero is enacted in a series of compromises over several lines, articulating his relation to authority and law, while purporting the immediate validity of Truth and Being. Following this, the traditional hero and villain are a representation of excess, of extremes of virtue and ignobility, enacted through the logic of a clear dichotomous line.

These extremes serve an educational and inspirational purpose, by dealing with individual and cultural aspects. According to such a perspective, the hero's quest is a possibility for the reader to learn about life and both its pleasures and dangers. In a feminist analysis, the journey gains a double meaning, as it is not only a physical journey, but a symbolic path erected at the individual and cultural level of one's gradual immersion and ultimate acceptance in the adult world, a man's world. The journey is then an alluring event, as it responds to individual desires to be recognised for one's outstanding feat, summarily, to be a hero.

As many masculinity theorists have noted, however, this "heroic masculinity" harbours a self-destructive contradiction, as it unhealthily conflates "a man's desire for outstanding individual autonomy with the emasculating imperative to succumb without objection to the remote control of patriarchal law."[5] The Achillean hero, embodiment of strength and invincibility, is the epic representation of militaristic pursuits, and yet also harbours mortal flaws that prevent him from reaching omnipotent status.

Such extremes while acting at a representational level, elude the strategies that come into constructing the very identities that are represented. As already seen, in his escape from strict nationalist Afrikaner identity, John understands such events as "Dunkirk" to be one of the examples of the epitome of heroic pursuit (B, 128). The collapse of the Allied defence implicated the series of movements that culminated in what is known as "Dunkirk," whereby between 26 May and 4 June 1940, hundreds of thousands of British, French and Belgian troops were evacuated from the beaches of Dunkirk in northern France. Within the scope of Second World War Britain, this event would inform a sense of national masculinity that "combined the young, fit, heroic man with the ordinary, home-loving, emotionally reserved, good-humoured and sportsman-like team player,"[6] the amalgamation of what was considered as masculine and feminine traits a desired outcome so as to better distinguish British military culture from its Nazi Germany opposite.

The Imperial Hero

In Victorian England, a shift occurred from a model of education largely based in home tuition towards private school-based for boys of the middle and upper classes. As the number of public schools rose, soon the codes of masculinity—of being a man—would be enacted largely through the school system. It was thought that schooling would furnish the necessary peer experience for upper middle and middle class boys in guiding them towards manhood, while ensuring, through a series of activities, that such bonding would result in the creation of certain identities that would praise and reproduce a sense of English.[7]

The deeply gendered nature of imperialism—"from the moment of colonial conquest by a workforce of men (soldiers, sailors, administrators, priests) to the stabilization of colonial societies with their racial hierarchies and institutions of plantation labour and domestic service"[8]—implied that there was a need to create specific forms of masculinity in order to ensure the success and subsequent stability of the imperialist system, with the design of power structures based on the notions of the coloniser as the heroic braver of unknown lands serving the nation and the colonised as the subservient, thus feminine, subject.[9]

A way of promoting such gendered formation was through children's literature, with its educational quality playing a large role in the shaping of boys' mentalities and bodies. From the 1840s onwards, North American literature written for children became popular in Britain, raising concerns over what "ideals" British children were being taught. Conservative nationalist rhetoric soon emerged, preoccupied with a perceived "disintegration" of national texts, thus demanding an upholding of purported traditional values. The island would soon become a cultural trope, acting as a microcosm of society in depicting its anxieties. Islands as geographically-sealed units, Bristow argues, allowed for "the possibility of representing colonialist dreams and fears in miniature."[10] The island, thus, becomes politically invested with imperialistic norms regarding masculinity. As Diana Loxley considers, the island territory is a veritable laboratory engaged with the promotion of a "perfect masculinity": "the image of the ideal healthy male body informs the anxious quest for a total dominion,"[11] thus conflating "perfect masculinity" with omnipotence.

In the mid-1850s, public schools largely became institutions concerned with the shaping of bodies for war. To this end, the boy who would fight for the nation would need to be moulded both in body and spirit. A cult of athleticism arose that commended physical exercise, and team games in particular, as "highly effective means of inculcating valuable instrumental and expressive goals—physical and moral courage, loyalty and cooperation and the ability both to command and obbey."[12] Children's literature then became imbued with a notion of "natural morality," whereby the hero should uphold a series of moral codes translated into actions of conquest and expansion that every boy should try to emulate. Ethics would then be largely dismissed, as this newfound morality would be self-evident, allowing for the underlying war ideology[13] found in literature to provide new gusto to a nation regarding its empire. This increased violence would, however, incorporate traits of the gentlemanly British subject; hence, this new kind of heroic masculinity is an amalgamation of its "raffish forebears" with the older, "more honourable ideal of the polite gentleman who based his very being in what the middle classes most admired: respect."[14]

This newfound kind of masculinity was largely organised as a response to a wide array of anxieties concerning men's positions in late Victorian society. As Margaret Walters argues, "it was not until the second half of the nineteenth century that anything like a true women's 'movement' began to emerge in England."[15] With demands at the level of employment and education, and with a long struggle for the right to vote, these were the seeds of a social revolution that would ultimately reshape, to the point of non-recognition, the power relations that existed between the sexes. Domesticity, albeit with different formulations according to one's class, was fiercely upheld with Queen Victoria's ascension to the throne, with the idea of home as central to the configuration of the Victorian man and woman. From the 1880s onwards, however, and after two or three generations deeply invested in this idea, there was a general flight from domesticity, whereas a new generation of men dismissed this notion altogether, conflating it with burdening aspects of femininity. With the wider popularity of writers such as Henry Rider Haggard and Robert Louis Stevenson, whose heroes are largely defined by adventure in exotic places, where motion is the keyword in narrative terms and familial bonds are mentioned only in passing,[16] men became largely discontented with domesticity, either refusing, or postponing marriage, as is the case of Lord Robert Baden-Powell, as it will be seen.

These strategies, as historian John Tosh argues, heavily depended on young men finding occupations which ruled out marriage, such as teaching careers in the proliferating boarding schools, or celibacy. The imperial project and its aspirations provided, however, a rather more appealing escape route: the aforementioned occupations "paled into insignificance beside colonial careers, which included administration, the armed services, commerce and missionary work in most quarters of the globe. The empire was run by bachelors; in the public mind it represented devotion to duty, or profit (and sometimes pleasure), undistracted by feminine ties."[17] To ensure that these bachelors would provide a good service to the imperial cause, a new kind of institution needed to be created, one that would understand and capture young men's fantasies. The basis for such an institution would spring from the mind of a British officer in the midst of one of the most memorable acts of warfare of the British Empire's history, eventually resulting in the creation of the Scout's movement.

Enter the Scout

The boy's entrance into the Scout's movement signals one of the established steps in acquiring manhood:

> For his inauguration as a Scout he prepares himself punctiliously. With his mother he goes to the outfitter's to buy the uniform: stiff olive-brown felt hat and silver hat-badge, khaki shirt and shorts and stockings, leather belt with Boy Scout clasp, green shoulder-tabs, green stocking-flashes. He cuts a five-foot stave from a poplar tree, peels off the bark, and spends an afternoon with a heated screwdriver burning into the white woodflesh the entire Morse and semaphore codes. He goes off to his first Scout meeting with this stave slung over his shoulder with a green cord that he has himself triple-braided. Taking the oath with a two-finger salute, he is by far the most impeccably outfitted of the new boys, the "tenderfeet." (B, 14)

The rituals and dress code composing the Scout movement were idealised, in a first instance, by its founder, Lord Robert Baden-Powell. Its creation would prove the necessary catalyst for a renewed hope in the public eye of the continued possibility of the British Empire after the Boer War.

Riebeeck's dreams of gold and riches in the "mythical interior" of the southern part of Africa would be exacerbated and put into practice by the British, through the imaginings of writers such as H. Rider Haggard, or the ambitions of Cecil John Rhodes.[18] In the 1870s the British would adopt a more interventionist stance towards expansion of their powers in the interior of the land, due to the discovery of diamonds on the Vaal-Hartz river junction in 1867. Robert Morrell argues that this aggressive expansionist phase, represented in cultural terms by the supposed superiority of the British over others, was a process "led by white British men, many of whom had a public school upbringing," the school being the place where such notions of superiority were taught: "A willingness to resort to force and a belief in the glory of combat were features of imperial masculinity and the colonial process."[19]

The Jameson Raid led by Cecil Rhodes against the Transvaal only aggravated the already existing tensions between Boers and *uitlanders*, resulting in the declaration of war by the Kruger government on the British in 1899, with the invasion of Natal and the northern Cape. Baden-Powell would command the defense of Mafeking, a small border town.[20] It was the success in mounting the town's defenses, that would, particularly due to the depressing turnout of the war, make his name equivalent with renewed hope in the Empire's success. His skilled approach of combining tactical mastery with a sense for the needs of the community, would make his morale boosters famous. These comprised various competitions, games and assorted entertainment.[21] "It was this same mix of imperial fortification with fun, or of service and smiles, which would prove the winning formula of Baden-Powell's so-called 'boyology,' his understanding of boys, in *Scouting for Boys*."[22] This defining work, a manual that would instruct young boys throughout the Empire on how best to serve it, would materialise in 1908.

The boy, then, by acquiring and presenting himself in Scout uniform, is following the rules of the founder himself: "If you already belong to a corps which has a uniform, you dress in that uniform; but on passing the tests for a scout given here you wear the scout badge, if your commanding officer allows it, in addition to any of your corps' badges that you may have won."[23] The boy's assertion that "Boy Scouts, he discovers, consists, like school, of passing examinations" (B, 14), underscores the rewards that continuous training brings in terms of hierarchical climbing. Boys' bodies should be modelled according to strict rules that promote, among others, cleanliness and muscular strength. The scout's mission, with its central purpose of providing support to the Empire, consisted of spying and tracking. Such activities would be largely present in the realm of fiction, and Baden-Powell would employ such examples to draw the boys' imagination to his cause.[24]

The attention to the body, and the success of Powell's message, would only be possible through the understanding of the body-as-machine logic that permeated the modern era. The body, by the early twentieth century, was understood in the optimal sense of "efficiency," whereby a machine culture "dreamed of bodies without fatigue."[25] It was such a logic that allowed for the rapid proliferation of messages by groups such as the Scouts.

Among other logics, however, was a great anxiety at the turn of the century over what was seen as women's rapid social progression. Gender anxieties would be at the core of the formation of a muscular Christianity, with Michael Kimmel arguing that the image of Jesus would be "transformed from a beatific, delicate, soft-spoken champion of the poor into a muscle-bound he-man whose message encouraged the strong to dominate the weak."[26] Muscular Christianity embodied the precepts of public school morality: "physical fitness, conformity to the needs of the team, and discipline."[27] It would first appear in the works of Charles Kingsley and Thomas Hughes, being most successfully epitomised in the latter's *Tom Brown's Schooldays*.[28] The book would help in solidifying Thomas Arnold's school reform, and in advancing the notion that games were the privileged means towards "strengthening the body,"[29] by placing the Brown family as a metonym for all of the British Nation: "Wherever the fleets and armies of England have won renown, there stalwart sons of the Browns have done yeomen's work."[30] The Brown family could only more readily serve the Nation and the Empire if allowed the joys of public schooling, where games, with its aesthetics and philosophy of war, would serve to better prepare boys for future ordeals.

Escaping the Family

The initial success of Baden-Powell's *Scouting for Boys* is thus a combination of various factors: "his delight in play-acting..., his belief in the games ethic of the Victorian public school and the bourgeois principle of individual self-advancement."[31] According to Cynthia Enloe, Baden-Powell's "original intention was to restore manly self-control in white boys: in their hands lay the future of the empire."[32] As the Brown family was scattered across the Empire,[33] the ideals of public schools would be exported to the colonies:

> Military and colonial administrators, and the human flood of missionaries, educators, traders, engineers, merchants and British colonists more generally, were vitally important elements of the varied judicial, educational, economic and religious strands of wider imperial domination, and this aided their role in the spread of sport. They not only played sports amongst themselves but shared an ethnocentric, self-confident certainty that the rest of the world should be converted to their beliefs and sporting institutions.... Cricket, soccer and rugby could be employed as moral tools which aided the propagation of British civilization, culture and imperial power. Even some of the conquered were won over and came to admire them.[34]

Alongside sports, the notion of physical punishment associated with muscular Christianity would also be exported. Beatings would be met, for the most part, as a necessary aspect in proving one's masculinity: "Most boys preferred a beating to other non-physical forms of punishment. There was a macho bravado that accompanied beatings. They challenged one another to 'races' to see who would get the most strokes over a stipulated period of time."[35]

In *Boyhood*, the beatings at the boy's school seem to provide a mettle for masculinity: "Every teacher at his school, man or woman, has a cane and is at liberty to use it.... In a spirit of knowing connoisseurship the boys weigh up the characters of the canes and the quality of pain they give" (B, 6). This homosocial gathering over the quality and amount of beatings as a marker of masculinity is something the boy misses for his never having experienced it, as seen in this interaction (or lack thereof) with his father and uncles:

> They reminisce about their schoolmasters and their schoolmasters' canes; they recall cold winter mornings when the cane would raise blue weals on their buttocks and the sting would linger for days in the memory of the flesh. In their words there is a note of nostalgia and pleasurable fear. He listens avidly but makes himself as inconspicuous as possible. He does not want them to turn to him, in some pause in the conversation, and ask about the place of the cane in his own life. He has never been beaten and is deeply ashamed of it. He cannot talk about canes in the easy, knowing way of these men. He has a sense that he is damaged. (B, 9)

What distinguishes him is his fear of public shame, of not being able to endure the beating. This implies, in the boy's logic, a non normalcy that he blames the mother for. The father is deemed normal, normality here being equated with the possibility of violence, the "occasional blue-eyed rages and threats" (B, 8), with the mention of rage evoking the general understanding of Afrikaner men as fueled by such sentiment. Tellingly, the beatings also provide a bond among the male members of the family. Only John seems to escape this world of manhood-proving.

What the beatings acquire in the colonies is a more overt aspect in terms of group tensions. A teacher's flogging of a student is the site to alleviate tensions between Afrikaner and English: "When he lets it slip that Rob Hart is being flogged by Miss Oosthuizen, his parents seem at once to know why. Miss Oosthuizen is one of the Oosthuizen clan, who are Nationalists; Rob Hart's father, who owns a hardware store, was a United Party town councillor until the elections of 1948" (B, 67).

In not being able to partake in these conversations, the boy finds a lack in himself, as if he is broken. In such an account, we may discern not only the anguish over being left out of such groups, but also perhaps a certain pleasure in it. Ken Corbett suggests that, while norms "compel compliance and conformity," configuring "that which lies outside the customary as socially unintelligible and psychically incoherent," "there is always distinction between humans, and multiplicity within any given human. Static norms impede our capacities to appreciate variance, to reflect justly, and to respond with empathy, even pleasure."[36] In gendered terms, one could question whether normative definitions of masculinity are indeed achievable for the great majority of men, as we are usefully reminded by Connell that "the number of men rigor-ously practicing the hegemonic pattern in its entirety may be quite small."[37]

Again, as Richard Holt and many others have argued, the most readily available marker of masculinity would, however, be sports. Cricket would be introduced in South Africa by the British settlers, but the initial doubt of the British regarding the Boers' capacities in sportsmanship would eventually result in that the game would always remain "an expression of Anglo-Saxon separateness and superiority in the eyes of Afrikaner farming people."[38]

If the hero is the one that sacrifices himself while enmeshed in battle, the boy can only hope to become a hero through practices such as cricket:

> This is cricket. It is called a game, but it feels to him more real than home, more real even than school. In this game there is no pretending, no mercy, no second chance. These other boys, whose names he does not know, are all against him. They are of one mind only: to cut short his pleasure. They will feel not one speck of remorse when he is out. In the middle of this huge arena he is on trial, one against eleven, with no one to protect him. (B, 53)

The "enemy" is both anonymous and amorphous, as it is subsumed in the gen-eralisation of other boys. The boy can only be great, can only proceed in his true path, through a violent dismissal of the others. Cricket is a test between bowler and batsman, the encounter between two male subjectivities bent on the other's destruction. For the boy, cricket "is the truth of life" (B, 54), with no apparent way to dodge such test. That is, in gendered terms, there seems to be no available route for boys to explore alternative ways of becoming men, of foregoing the institutionalised ways of becoming men.

Diary of a Bad Year's Señor C, while reminiscing on his childhood in South Africa, provides a telling account of cricket's constitutive aspects and how these relate to subjectivity-making:

> In childhood, almost as soon as I learned to throw a ball, cricket took a grip on me, not just as a game, but as a ritual. That grip does not seem to have relaxed, even now. But one question baffled me from the beginning: how a creature of the kind I seemed to be—reserved, quiet, solitary—could ever become good at a game in which quite another character-type seemed to excel: matter-of-fact, unreflective, pugnacious.[39]

What Señor C alludes to is not only the institutionalised nature of cricket, but also how it is manufactured to tailor a certain kind of masculine personality.

Tellingly, in the boy's first foray on a "proper cricket field," the boy is car-rying "his father's bat" (B, 52). Masculinity could be seen here as passing from father to son, were it not for the indications in the text that draw us to other possible readings. The father's bat is too heavy for the boy, suggesting an uneasiness and difficulty in performing masculinity. Also, the field is seen as contrary to the fantasies of heroism: "a great and lonely place: the spectators are so far away that they might as well not exist" (B, 53). Normative masculinity, or the places where one learns such performances, is here depicted as barren.

The sterility of the proper cricket field is also contrasted with the imagination of children's play, where a division is made between real and imaginary cricket. Whereas proper cricket is depicted through accounts of suffering—"stony ground where you bloody your hands and knees every time you fall" (B, 29)—the boy devises other ways of playing the game, his imaginary cricket, thus subverting the rules and goals of proper cricket that seeks to promote leadership skills and, as seen above, furious competition. Such subversive acts, while destabilising certain institutionalised meanings, may also reproduce social prejudice: "The spectacle is too shameful, too easily seen from the street: a mother playing cricket with her son" (B, 29). If the boy wishes his mother "would be normal" (B, 38), there are instances, such as the case above, when such desire for normality is enacted in order to preserve one's masculine façade towards the outer community.

Cultural interpretation of what a boy, or a man, should be is produced and reproduced through a strict policing by close groups and the wider community. Thus, the ideal of hegemonic masculinity arises, with its attached fantasies of "ascendancy achieved through culture, institutions, and persuasion."[40] Such cultural stories result in a widespread fear of retaliation for not succeeding in achieving such an ideal: "he has failed the test, he has been found out, there is nothing to do but hide his tears, cover his face, trudge back to the commiserating, politely schooled applause of the other boys" (B, 54). The boy has been found wanting in his expression of masculine prowess, with the inevitable feeling of shame arising from such lack. The passage, however, indicates that another narrative may be constructed, as the "politely schooled applause of the other boys" may be read as emerging not only from an instance of civilised sympathy for a teammate, but perhaps also because they themselves have felt the sting of failure. The constant pressure to succeed results in an anxiety of defeat: "to be tested again and again and again, until he fails" (B, 53). The very understanding of such cultural mechanisms may suggest that, at some level, there is an awareness of the illusion embedded in the quest for heroism. As the real Coetzee suggests in a letter to Paul Auster regarding the relation of heroism and sports:

> You don't work to become a hero. That is to say, what you do in preparation for the heroic contest is not "work", does not belong to the round of production and consumption. The Spartans at Thermopylae fought together and died together; they were heroes all of them, but they were not a "team" of heroes. A team of heroes is an oxymoron.[41]

The above passage indicates the somewhat supernatural character of heroism, which cannot be emulated or trained merely through work. And yet, displays of strength, physical prowess or breaking records are dependent on strenuous training.[42] This is the contradiction at the core of hegemonic models of masculinity particularly dependent on body prowess, that it demands so much previous training and testing before the final act, deemed to be natural.

Indeed, in *Summertime*, the dead John is depicted as an example of extreme failure in tending to hegemonic masculinity's saving graces, the relentless enactment of how he continuously failed in aspects of his life providing a mockery of hegemonic masculinity's incessant beckoning.

Avoiding cricket, the Afrikaners would, however, not eschew all of British sports. Rugby would be introduced in South Africa "in the late nineteenth century through the English-speaking private church schools."[43] The game would prove popular with many groups, particularly with the black elite, but it would achieve its greatest popularity with the Afrikaners. "Rugby became a means (as cricket never did) for the economically disadvantaged Afrikaner to assert himself magically over the Englishman."[44] Robert Ross suggests that a country diet had allowed many Afrikaners the physique required for the game and that, "at a more local level, rugby provided an opportunity for the manifestation of a rawness and brutality which was central to the self-image of many white South African males as males."[45] Rugby, as defined by Coetzee himself, is a game where "two teams of unarmed men struggle for possession of an object that they try to carry home with them,"[46] with an inherent violence being acknowledged.

Sports prove the surviving link between father and son in *Summertime*: "He goes with his father to Newlands because sport—rugby in winter, cricket in summer—is the strongest surviving bond between them" (*S*, 245). Male bonding occurs through sports, providing an opportunity for meeting and creating community. As an event focused on ritualised physical showing, it allows for mutual understanding without greater emotional overture. The perceived dwindling importance of rugby in the context of the country may be equated with the reshaping of masculine Afrikaner identity, no longer employing so much public power as before, and thus necessarily inviting a reworking of men's rituals and places in wider society. The immediate violence that rugby offers seems to be sedated by an increasing technological world—*Summertime* alludes to the coming of television—and the breaking up of community. This suggests that as the trilogy closes, there is an attempt at reconciliation with the debilitated father figure that represents the protagonist's Afrikaner herit-age. There is an acknowledgement of the frailty of the father, and an ambig-uous relation with him, based on the perceived lack of contact and ability on both parts to communicate their feelings and wishes.

That we can perceive this instance of seeking reconciliation must be ac-companied by a final suggestion on the politics regarding sports portrayed in the trilogy. We have assumed that, by locating himself in a more feminine position, the boy seeks to forego more violent displays of masculinity, thus breaking with imperial codes of manhood. What seems more interesting is the ability to locate certain aspects within the whole enterprise of violent sports that provide pleasure and to appropriate them for oneself, necessarily changing their core rules. A good example may be the division between real and imaginary cricket, where some of these old rules may even be entirely dismissed, thus doing away with their initial colonial purpose.

While here one could still acknowledge the preponderance of institution-alised rules, as the real cricket still maintains a modicum of power, imaginary cricket is found more pleasurable in its non aggressiveness and overall pos-sibility of advancing one's growth as an imaginative subject. Coetzee asserts a fundamental difference between sports and play that may be instrumental in understanding what is at stake here. Sports, understood as "a game played according to a well-defined code of rules," is someone else's idea. The individ-ual, then, who plays sports is playing according to someone else's rules, within the scope of institutionalised settings, namely schools, that seek to form one's character. Play differs in this account, due to its lack of previously established rules, and as such is frowned upon by authority. As Coetzee further argues:

The child who submits to the code and plays the game is therefore reenacting a profoundly important moment of culture: the moment at which the Oedipal com-promise is made, the moment at which the knee is bent to government. This is the moment at which sport and the arts, the two most complex forms of play, part ways. In the creative arts, the artist both composes his game and plays it. He thus asserts an omnipotence that the player of sports yields up. This helps to explain why sports are so easily captured and used by political authority, while the arts remain slippery, resistant, undependable as moral training grounds for the young.[47]

It is in this act of mimicking the game and creating one's own experience and version of it, that a different kind of experience of education, straying from its mainstream form, may be achieved. Violent masculinity is derided, in its stead appearing an agreeable and enjoyable version of physical and mental activity, focused on play and hinting at the possibility of community building across racial lines. Thus John eludes the Brown family, foregoing the illusions of legendary status.

Notes

1. According to Scott T. Allison and George R. Goethals, *Heroes: What they Do and Why We Need Them* (Oxford: Oxford University Press, 2011), 29.
2. J. M. Coetzee, "Captain America in American Mythology," in *Doubling the Point*, ed. David Attwell (Cambridge, MA: Harvard University Press, 1992 [1986]), 107.
3. Thomas Van Nortwick, *Imagining Men: Ideals of Masculinity in Ancient Greek Culture* (London: Praeger, 2008). On the topic of mortality see 1–23.
4. Coetzee, *Doubling the Point*, 108.
5. Berthold Schoene-Harwood, *Writing Men: Literary Masculinities from Frankenstein to the New Man* (Edinburgh: Edinburgh University Press, 2000), 15.
6. See Sonya O. Rose, "Temperate Heroes: Concepts of Masculinity in Second World War Britain," in *Masculinities in Politics and War: Gendering Modern History*, ed. Stefan Dudink, Karen Hagemann, and John Tosh (Manchester: Manchester University Press, 2004), 186. For the multiple representations of Dunkirk in popular culture, see Penny Summerfield, "Dunkirk and the Popular Memory of Britain at War, 1940–58," *Journal of Contemporary History* 45, no. 4 (2010): 788–811.
7. See John Tosh, *A Man's Place: Masculinity and the Middle-Class Home in Victorian England* (New Haven and London: Yale University Press, 2007), in particular 102–22.
8. See Raewyn Connell, *Gender: In World Perspective*, 2nd ed. (Cambridge: Polity Press, 2009), 92.
9. Namely in the case of British occupation of India, Steven Patterson argues that the British colonisers created an aura of invincibility, claiming their natural right to become the lords of India, whereas the Indians were depicted as inherently lazy, dirty and unable to guide a country to success. See "Postcards from the Raj," *Patterns of Prejudice* 40, no. 2 (2006): 142–58. For the classic and nuanced portrayal of the dimensions of gender employed in the distinctions between coloniser and colonised, see Mrinalini Sinha, *Colonial Masculinity: The "Manly Englishman" and the "Effeminate Bengali" in the Late Nineteenth Century* (Manchester and New York: Manchester University Press, 1995).
10. Joseph Bristow, *Empire Boys: Adventures in a Man's World* (London: Harper Collins Academic, 1991), 94.
11. Diana Loxley, *Problematic Shores: The Literature of Islands* (London: Macmillan Press, 1990), 117.

12. See J. A. Mangan, *"Manufactured Masculinity"*: *Making Imperial Manliness, Morality and Militarism* (New York: Routledge, 2012), 60.

13. Militarism would also be confounded with the increased addresses towards "citizenship," with its inevitable imperialist and gender politics: "[T]he association between militarism, empire and citizenship lent a decidedly masculinist tone to the language of citizenship. This was evident in magazines for middle-class boys that equated citizenship with patriotism, while similar themes coloured children's books and magazines." See Keith Mcclelland and Sonya Rose, "Citizenship and Empire, 1867–1928," in *At Home with the Empire: Metropolitan Culture and the Imperial World*, ed. Catherine Hall and Sonya O. Rose (Cambridge: Cambridge University Press, 2006), 285.

14. Bristow, *Empire Boys: Adventures in a Man's World*, 58.

15. Margaret Walters, *Feminism: A Very Short Introduction* (Oxford: Oxford University Press, 2005), 56.

16. As Nicholas Ruddick considers, the fact that the great majority of important fantastic fiction of the *fin-de-siècle* is penned by male authors suggests "that the period was characterized by intense desires and anxieties of a specifically masculine kind. Men feared emasculation, or supersession by the rising generation of well-educated, free-thinking, assertive New Women, but their fears were often modified into ambivalence by erotic excitement." "The Fantastic Fiction of the *Fin de Siècle*," in *The Cambridge Companion to the Fin de Siècle*, ed. Gail Marshall (Cambridge: Cambridge University Press, 2007), 192.

17. Tosh, *A Man's Place*, 175.

18. Michael Chapman, *Southern African Literatures* (Scottsville: University of Natal Press, 2003), 77.

19. Robert Morrell, "Of Boys and Men: Masculinity and Gender in Southern African Studies," *Journal of Southern African Studies* 24, no. 4 (1998): 616.

20. Malcolm Flower-Smith and Edmund Yorke, *Mafeking! The Story of a Siege* (Weltevredenpark: Covos-Day Books, 2000). See, particularly, 46–69 for an understanding of the campaign.

21. Tim Jeal, *Baden-Powell*, rev. ed. (New Haven and London: Yale University Press, 2001 [1989]).

22. Elleke Boehmer, "Introduction," in Robert Baden-Powell, *Scouting for Boys*, ed. Elleke Boehmer (Oxford: Oxford University Press, 2004 [1908]), xvii.

23. Robert Baden-Powell, *Scouting for Boys*, ed. Elleke Boehmer (Oxford: Oxford University Press, 2004 [1908]), 38.

24. Most notably, Kipling's *Kim* is considered by Baden-Powell to be one of the finest examples of the possible achievements of a Boy Scout. See Baden-Powell, *Scouting for Boys*, 14.

25. Christopher E. Forth, *Masculinity in the Modern West: Gender, Civilization and the Body* (New York: Palgrave Macmillan, 2008), 171.

26. Michael S. Kimmel, *The History of Men: Essays on the History of American and British Masculinities* (New York: State University of New York Press, 2005), 65.

27. Jan Graydon, "'But it's More than a Game. It's an Institution': Feminist Perspectives on Sport," *Feminist Review* 13 (1983): 5.

28. Thomas Hughes, *Tom Brown's Schooldays* (Oxford: Oxford University Press, 1989).

29. William E. Winn, "Tom Brown's Schooldays and the Development of 'Muscular Christianity,'" Church History 29, no. 1 (1960): 70.

30. Hughes, Tom Brown's Schooldays, 2.

31. Boehmer, "Introduction," in Scouting for Boys, xvii.

32. Cynthia Enloe, Bananas, Beaches and Bases: Making Feminist Sense of International Politics, rev. ed. (Berkeley and Los Angeles: University of California Press, 2001 [1989]), 50.

33. "[T]he great army of Browns, who are scattered over the whole empire on which the sun never sets, and whose general diffusion I take to be the chief cause of that empire's stability." See Hughes, Tom Brown's Schooldays, 5.

34. Mike Huggins, The Victorians and Sport (London and New York: Hambledon and London, 2004), 220.

35. Robert Morrell, From Boys to Gentlemen: Settler Masculinity in Colonial Natal 1880–1920 (Pretoria: University of South Africa, 2001), 61.

36. Ken Corbett, "Gender Now," Psychoanalytic Dialogues 18 (2008): 838–39.

37. R. W. Connell, Masculinities, 2nd ed. (Cambridge: Polity Press, 2005 [1995]), 79.

38. Richard Holt, Sport and the British: A Modern History (Oxford: Clarendon Press, 1989), 227.

39. J. M. Coetzee, Diary of a Bad Year (London: Vintage, 2008 [2007]), 170.

40. R. W. Connell and James Messerschmidt, "Hegemonic Masculinity: Rethinking the Concept," Gender & Society 19 (2005): 832.

41. Paul Auster and J. M. Coetzee, Here and Now: Letters 2008–2011 (New York: Viking, 2013), 40.

42. Connell, Masculinities, particularly 63–64.

43. Robert Ross, A Concise History of South Africa, 2nd ed. (Cambridge: Cambridge University Press, 2008 [1999]), 178.

44. Coetzee, Doubling the Point, 122.

45. Ross, A Concise History of South Africa, 179.

46. See Coetzee, "Notes on Rugby," in Doubling the Point, 121.

47. Coetzee, Doubling the Point, 125.

· 4 ·

ART OF ONE

And it was now that I resolved to abandon the shipwrecked island and all on it, and
to seek my chieftainship in that real world from which, like my father, I had been cut
off. The decision brought its solace. Everything about me became temporary and unimportant; I was consciously holding myself back for the reality which lay elsewhere.

V. S. Naipaul, *The Mimic Men*

Imagining History

What might have happened, wonders Coetzee, if Samuel Beckett had been
offered a lectureship at the University of Cape Town in 1937? Perhaps, he
fantasises, a meeting between the two would have been possible in 1957, as
Coetzee enrolled at the university as an undergraduate. Inevitably, it seems,
Coetzee would have gone to the USA, via England, but in this alternate universe, he would not have written his doctoral dissertation on Beckett's prose
style; and yet, Beckett's influence would probably have remained in his work,
Coetzee suggests.[1]

Coetzee had read *Waiting for Godot* in the 1950s, but it would be his encounter with *Watt*[2] that would produce in him a "sensuous delight."[3] In *Youth*, reading
Watt creates one of the few sparks of what is purported to be genuine joy:

> *Watt* is quite unlike Beckett's plays. There is no clash, no conflict, just the flow of a voice telling a story, a flow continually checked by doubts and scruples, its pace fitted exactly to the pace of his own mind. *Watt* is also funny, so funny that he rolls about laughing. When he comes to the end he starts again at the beginning. (*Y*, 155)

It is through the rummaging of John's room, provided by Julia, the first inter-viewee in *Summertime*, that we understand this relation of fictioneers to be an intimate one: "John's room, where I had slept, was larger and better lit. A bookshelf: dictionaries, phrasebooks, teach yourself this, teach yourself that. Beckett. Kafka. On the table, a mess of papers. A filing cabinet" (*S*, 79–80).

The above passage underlines, thus, how such a relation is indicative of both a sense of intimacy and paternity. This may be further expounded on if we are to read Coetzee's own words on the subject of his literary parentage. In 1993, in an "Homage" to several writers—including Rilke, Musil, Pound, Faulkner, Ford and Beckett—Coetzee would write: "This is about some of the writers without whom I would not be the person I am, writers without whom I would, in a certain sense, not exist. An acknowledgement, therefore, of liter-ary paternity."[4]

Beckett's postmodern style would provide Coetzee the possibility of en-countering new worlds of interpretation, and necessarily of fashioning the Self. Both are interested in questioning their assumptions on reality,[5] just as both are translingual writers, Coetzee preferring English to Afrikaans and Beckett pre-ferring French to English.[6] The father-son connection also holds, however, its own limitations. In an earlier essay, Coetzee comments that "the art of Samuel Beckett has become an art of zero, as we all know. We also know that an art of zero is impossible."[7] According to Coetzee, the very act of writing is already an affirmation. In this logic, Coetzee's sense of being alienated concurs with the need to "write about the pressing ethical questions of South Africa in the *apartheid* era,"[8] whereby the very act of literature is explored in its dimensions of incorporating texts originating from different political landscapes.[9]

As *Youth*'s epigraph shows—"Wer den Dichter will verstehen/muß in Di-chters Lande gehen"[10]—Coetzee can never truly abandon the project that is South Africa, for the coordinates to understand the writer are necessarily there. Another passage provides additional proof of his continuous engage-ment with South Africa, as John inadvertently writes a short story on it:

> Though the story he has written is minor (no doubt about that), it is not bad. Nev-ertheless, he sees no point in trying to publish it. The English will not understand it. For the beach in the story they will summon up an English idea of a beach, a few

pebbles lapped by wavelets. They will not see a dazzling space of sand at the foot of rocky cliffs pounded by breakers, with gulls and cormorants screaming overhead as they battle the wind. (Y, 62)

Beckett's project is equally infused with national callings, his elusive style being the possible means to reconnect with his Irish heritage. In his attempt to commune with the dead, particularly with his father, "*Watt* pushes the genre's sense-making capacity to the limit,"[11] an appreciation already advanced by Coetzee: "*Watt* is an uneven and somewhat anarchic work.... Its fragmentary Addenda ... have caused considerable unease to me and perhaps to other of Beckett's commentators."[12]

From Beckett, Coetzee would then draw an "aesthetic of impotence and failure,"[13] a possibility of going beyond the demands of rationality that was his guarantor as a man educated according to Western principles. As Chris Ackerley further comments, *Youth* may be seen as an analysis of the modernist tradition and how it relates to John's status as a provincial, eventually devolving into "a portrait of the artist manqué, destined to be unexceptional, heartless, pretentious, shortsighted,"[14] if not for the surprise that constitutes the encounter with Beckett's work.

John, in his endless quest for oneness, the motion of going back to the womb, may be the example of the frustration inherent in this platonic endeavour, of living according to a perceived totality. The association with Beckett, a literary father, allows, on the contrary, for the illustration of the perilous outcomes of an incessant belief in the sole attributes of rationality. This would be a welcomed lesson, for in *Youth* the lines between the confessional and the political connect in the act of bearing witness to the downfall of the major political players and the shifting struggles of international power.[15] By this token, *Youth* explores the vulnerable states that ensue from such a position, equally capturing the demands of what would be called "The Sixties," a time when refashioning oneself would be mandatory.

Angry Men

The 1950s would witness the "pathological silencing" of women in the political sphere,[16] as new forms of masculinity developed, generally centered in the figure of the family man. With men now back from the battlefield, their new role was to learn the pleasures of domestic life. This new arrangement would prove to hold its own hardships:

> Men and women were trapped together as unequals, occupying segregated domestic
> roles and living largely separate lives, albeit under the same roof. If women desired
> solid, dependable breadwinners, men wanted homemakers and housekeepers. Child-
> care was solely the province of women.... For most families across the United King-
> dom there was tension, isolation, boredom and a desperate longing for something
> better, more exciting, more meaningful, an escape from the mutual entrapment of
> men-as-breadwinners and women-as-mothers.[17]

Man as the breadwinner, and the correlate of woman as housekeeper, was a
sign of societal arrangement considered the sign of maturity. This was a keyword in the psychology of the 1950s, that assumed the "ingredients of wisdom,
responsibility, empathy, (mature) heterosexuality and a 'sense of function,' or,
as a sociologist would have put it, acceptance of adult sex roles."[18] Anxieties
over homosexuality and the perceived feminisation of society would claim
the 1950s as a period of crisis in masculinity, even as Alfred Kinsey's research
would shed a different light on gender identity.[19]

Wider political shifts would also have an impact on gender relations, not
only in terms of the post-war management of the men who returned from the
front, but also of the increasing recognition of the British Empire's ruin and
the subsequent search for what type of role Britain would play in a new, oftentimes tense, international plateau.

"All you need is love," sang the Beatles in 1967, close to the end of a decade that would be generally known for its optimism and youthful ideals. As
the race for space would prove the mettle for the earthly powers of Cold War's
major players, times were indeed changing, in multiple ways. The sixties, with
their utopian bent, created a society that was agitated in its search for new
references in terms of identity.[20] Attempts at refashioning Selves would imply a continuous back-and-forth between tradition and modernity. As Sheila
Rowbotham comments:

> Sixties culture oscillated between dramatic lunges towards modernity and nostalgic
> flirtations with the old which embraced the earthed simplicity of arts and crafts and
> the exotic coils of *fin de siècle* degeneracy.... We looked backwards and forwards,
> forwards and backwards as the world spun round. Our sense of crisis, our intensity,
> our conviction that time was running out, these did not simply derive from a youthful
> self-importance. We faced the very real problem that capitalism was changing much
> faster than we were.[21]

The outcome of the *Lady Chatterley's Lover* trial in 1960 would assert the
changing social mores on sexuality,[22] further confirmed by the rise of women's

liberation movements and the decriminalisation of homosexuality. Still, changes in legislation and increased freedom in terms of sexual expression co-habitated with virulent notions of masculinity as portrayed in popular culture.

John Osborne's 1956 play *Look Back in Anger* is one of the most represent-ative works in terms of capturing the tensions of the period.[23] Osborne's hero Jimmy Porter is the eponymous angry man in at least three different sites. The first, in the portrayal of anger due to the status of class, enacted by targeting his wife's affluent friends and ex-colonial family.

Secondly, anger also transpires over the apparent lack of direction of con-temporary politics, namely the crisis in international affairs.[24] Events such as the 1955 Bandung Conference, in its appeals and demands for greater non-Western representation in international politics, would settle the climate of change in the post-war world. Additionally, the Suez crisis would reveal to Britain how the tactics of this new world were changing. With Anthony Eden emerging defeated from his political clash with Gamal Abdel Nasser, the Suez Crisis would come to be understood as marking "the confrontation between the old ambitions of British imperialism and the new realities of post-imperial retrenchment.... It was a reflection of Britain's changed role in the world, partly as a result of two ruinously expensive global wars."[25]

On this particular topic, Randall Stevenson further comments how Os-borne's play would reach popular success in its 1956 autumn revival: "Men-aced by international crises and the Big Bang, and bereft of obvious strategies for dealing with either, the mid-1950s found its anxieties compellingly ex-pressed in the impotent urgency of Jimmy's monologues."[26]

Thirdly, *Look Back in Anger* would target women as a men-devouring menace, blameworthy as they were of stifling the male ego. One of Jimmy's angry tirades proves revelatory:

> Oh, my dear wife, you've got so much to learn. I only hope you learn it one day.... If you could have a child, and it would die. Let it grow, let a recognizable human face emerge from that little mass of indiarubber and wrinkles.... I wonder if you might even become a recognizable human being yourself. But I doubt it.... She has the pas-sion of a python. She just devours me whole every time, as if I were some over-large rabbit. That's me. That bulge around her navel—if you're wondering what it is—it's me. Me, buried alive down there, and going mad, smothered in that peaceful looking coil.... She'll go on sleeping and devouring until there's nothing left of me.[27]

The angry men would be further popularised, with most success, through film adaptations, such as *Saturday Night and Sunday Morning* (1960),[28] or *The*

Loneliness of the Long Distance Runner (1962).[29] Both would be based on Alan Sillitoe's eponymous written work, portraying anarchic working-class young men who seek to escape the authority of their jobs and what seems like the inevitable marriages that attend them. In the more strict sexual sphere, the objectification of women would be more intently observed in *Alfie* (1966),[30] with the gallant hero referring to women as "it".

These being the dominant modes of masculinity generated in these so-cietal contexts, it will be seen that those from outside the center of empire would find it difficult to emulate such performances, as their experiences were of a different kind.

Provincial Life

"He is proving something: that each man is an island; that you don't need parents" (Y, 3). *Youth* begins with a depiction of the protagonist's daily life, centered on the making of his independency. His multiple jobs provide him with a comfortable living, in spite of his young age, his economic endeavours a pointed way of escaping his parents' authority: "He may only be nineteen but he is on his own two feet, dependent on no one" (Y, 2). These assertions of independence are quickly, however, acknowledged to be lacking: "There is something essential he lacks, some definition of feature. Something of the baby still lingers in him. How long before he will cease to be a baby? What will cure him of babyhood, make him into a man?" (Y, 3).

Youth's overall tone is one of confusion, stagnation and sadness, the op-timism of the sixties seemingly absent. These hopeful, changing times, clash with the isolated voice of a contemplating bystander, torn between fantasies of artistry and the demands of the nascent corporate world.[31]

These politics of pessimism are first addressed in a strict colonial sense, for the reasoning of exile is due to the political turmoil in South Africa. In addressing these politics, Coetzee is also making visible a more worldly under-standing of the decade, not subsumed to its westernised history, indeed, often blind to historical events outside its borders.

"After the carnage of Sharpeville nothing is as it was before" (Y, 37). The first decade of *apartheid* would introduce a series of legislative movements to-wards ensuring its ultimate goal of racial division. As Nigel Worden considers:

The prohibition of "mixed marriages" (1949) and the Immorality Act (1950) extend-ed the existing ban on sex between whites and Africans outside marriage to prohibit all sexual contact between whites and other South Africans, including Indians and coloreds. Racial division in the future was the goal. And the Population Registration Act of the same year enforced the classification of people into four racial categories: white, colored, "Asiatic" (Indian) and "Native" (later "Bantu" or African).[32]

Other legislative action, such as the Group Areas Act (1950) implied a urban restructuring according to imposed governmental racial lines; the Natives Re-settlement Act (1954) provided the government with the power to forcibly evacuate Africans to separate townships; the Reservation of Separate Amen-ities Act (1953) enforced social segregation in public spaces; the Suppression of Communism Act (1950) and the Criminal Law Amendment Act (1953) provided the necessary legal background from which to ban all oppositional forces to government.

These and other legislative actions would be the target of various acts of resistance throughout the 1950s, with the general support of the ANC, though "limited financial and administrative resources and heightened state repression" and "conscious alienation of its [ANC] leaders from popular or working-class interests"[33] would not result in changing the segregationist di-rection of the state.

Resulting political rifts would see the emergence of the PAC (Pan Afri-canist Congress) in 1959, "under the presidency of Robert Sobukwe, with the slogan of 'Africa for the Africans.'"[34] The PAC was met with anxious hope in the political scene, the outcome of a generation restless with frustration:

> Pan-Africanist leaders ... tended to recruit disproportionately from young men, often unemployed school leavers, who were more likely than their elders to be predisposed in favour of aggressively assertive kinds of political action. Again and again, both in the recollections of PAC leaders and in their claims at the time, they emphasized their success in mobilizing "the youth."[35]

Distancing itself from the ANC by calling for "a more sustained campaign, in-volving refusal to carry passes and mass presentation at police stations to de-mand arrest,"[36] the stage was set for the demonstrations of 21 March 1960. The inexperienced policemen in the Sharpeville police station, alarmed by its size, would open fire on the crowd, resulting in sixty-nine dead and 180 wounded. In-ternational uproar over the massacre would mark Sharpeville as the emblematic start of a global anti-*apartheid* movement, led in part by South African exiles:

> Networks of organized activity in four countries constituted the core dynamics of global public opposition to *apartheid*. The movement was wider ... but these national

networks were the most enduring and the best organized. These networks were located in the United Kingdom, Sweden, the Netherlands, and the United States. In each of these countries anti-*apartheid* movements would succeed in enlisting public sympathy and popular activism on a large scale and from time to time they would help to shape official decision making.[37]

Throughout the decade, such networks would build the necessary political gusto for resistance regarding warfare and the demand for peace. Commenting on such arrangements, Sheila Rowbotham clarifies that, in part inspired by anti-colonial movements, the internationalism of peace protests "was much more than an abstract political idea, because the students who came from South Africa, Rhodesia, Latin America, the United States, Greece, Italy and Ireland brought information and radical ideas from their own milieux."[38] Despite the collapse of the British Empire, London would remain in its role as "a centre of international finance,"[39] and post-war London would experience a surge of migratory currents from the ex-colonies, who would shape the city into the multicultural hub of the 1970s.[40]

Contrary to such movements, in *Youth* the young man eludes political activity, as he seeks to erase his colonial past:

> He would prefer to leave his South African self behind as he has left South Africa itself behind. South Africa was a bad start, a handicap. An undistinguished, rural family, bad schooling, the Afrikaans language: from each of these component handicaps he has, more or less, escaped. He is in the great world earning his own living and not doing too badly, or at least not failing, not obviously. He does not need to be reminded of South Africa. If a tidal wave were to sweep in from the Atlantic tomorrow and wash away the southern tip of the African continent, he will not shed a tear. He will be among the saved. (Y, 62)

Disdaining his past, seeking to build this new Self, he seeks to reproduce the cultural traits he fantasises as being British. As has been noted previously, the young man of *Youth* is already articulated with an identity suffused with the culture of the British Empire.[41]

"Life … at its fullest intensity" can only be experienced in three places in the world: "London, Paris, perhaps Vienna." The choice among these three imperial hubs is left, in large part, to the young man's educational background: to go to Paris would imply a strong education in French, and the dismissal of Vienna, with its "logical positivism" and psychoanalysis may foreshadow the overall intent of countering rationality and science as the definite ways of being and understanding human relations. London is the logical place as the destination for exile, "where South Africans do not need to carry papers and where people speak English" (Y, 41).

The use, or claim of art as defining one's Self is, thus, not only a possible vocation, but apparently also a necessary aspect of the so-called provincial's survival in the metropolis. As Elleke Boehmer places it, drawing on the work of V. S. Naipaul, "colonials who migrate to the capital do not escape alienation, though their condition is manifested in a different way.... They must learn to overcome the fracture which divides their lived experience from their fantasy of metropolitan life."[42]

Such fracture is of impossible tones, if we read Jean Rhys's heroine Anna's overwhelming sensory attack that constitutes the difference of the metropolis:

> It was as if a curtain had fallen.... It was like being born again.... The feeling things gave you right down inside yourself was different.... But a difference in the way I was frightened and the way I was happy.[43]

Anna, not enjoying England at first, sought to "pretend" by drawing from her memory and emotional repertoire, aspects of her original home, and to infuse some of those affective bearings in a landscape that felt hostile and too different to accommodate familiarity.

Tellingly, in Naipaul's *Mimic Men*, fantasy is the antidote to dealing with the "difficult emotions" of one's colonial childhood, laden as they were with shame.[44] Per Amal Treacher's definition, shame is:

> An intensely painful experience and emotion and it evokes and is provoked by other emotions—humiliation, retaliation, mortification, helplessness and ridicule. Humiliation is precisely one of the tropes of colonization—colonized, taken over and made to feel as if they cannot and should not rule.[45]

Both Naipaul and Treacher, when addressing the issue of shame, place it squarely within the side of the colonised. However, shame also belongs to the autobiographical moment, particularly as it is enacted through the confessional mode, whereby it "accompanies each stage in the interminable process of skeptical self-examination, as the revelation of a further truth shamefully exposes the inadequacy of what has been revealed so far."[46] According to Timothy Bewes, Coetzee's work is one that creates a spiraling of shame, for Coetzee understands, as we have discussed within the particular scope of his relation with Beckett, both the need and the impossibility of writing about matters such as *apartheid* or other widespread unjust phenomena.[47] Namely, and in what pertains to gender politics, one can draw the attention to the relations of John with women, marked as they are by betrayal and the despotic use of these for his own purposes.[48]

The first lines in *Youth*: "He lives in a one-room flat near Mowbray railway" (Y, 1), recall the geographical barrenness, and its emotional correlate, present in *Boyhood*. The depiction of London is of a more mixed nature: "London may be stony, labyrinthine, and cold, but behind its forbidding walls men and women are at work writing books, painting paintings, composing music" (Y, 41). The metropolis is the *locus* of the projected anxieties of the young man, with its perceived lack of human connection and confusing structure, whereas the private sphere, both inside the city but outside its representational field, the private space of human connection, is where art resides.

This creates a series of dispositions. The first, is that the dichotomy of public and private sphere is reinforced in its gendered terms, with man as the master of the first and woman a poorer master of the second; the second, is that art is apparently absent from public life, and such life is, thus, to be ruled according to other logics other than fantasy; thirdly, art implies a sort of relation regarding human connection: to be an artist is an outcome that may be achieved only in connection to another, be it a muse, or a fellow creator.

The role of women becomes of central importance in the mediation between this "stony, labyrinthine, and cold" reality and transcendental art, "the secret flame burning in him" (Y, 5). He "must wait for the aid of some force from outside, a force that used to be called the Muse" (Y, 166–67). In this train of thought, the young man is alluding to Goethe's influences, for it was instrumental in the work of the Weimar giant that women serve the artistic tendencies of men:

> Goethe's sense of masculinity and his role as a male was an integral part of his aesthetics. The "other" (the female) was of little interest to him unless she could be absorbed into his own work and be subsumed under his masculine creativity.... For Goethe and his age, literary women were to serve as muses, not to write as independently creative individuals.[49]

Women are the stirrers of the artistry that resides in men, for they themselves do not possess such qualities: "It is in quest of the fire they lack, the fire of love, that women pursue artists and give themselves to them" (Y, 66). The lack of definition of his character, that prevents him from making the desired jump from boyhood to manhood, is to be erased through the transformative power of love: "The beloved, the destined one, will see at once through the odd and even dull exterior he presents to the fire that burns within him" (Y, 3). His depth will, thus, be reached by the knowing will and gaze of a woman, and his determination to become an artist to finally be achieved.

The sexual act would be akin to a transaction, through which the artist would be enhanced by his work, and the woman transfigured, though the inexperience of the young man in sexual matters and the lack of canonical work that further explores what such transfiguration implied to women underscores that we are still in the place of overwhelming silence regarding feminine sexuality.

Another feature that informs the style of *Youth* and owes its debt to Goethe is the emotional excess that so famously characterises Werther: "Alas, this void! This dreadful void that I feel in my breast!—I often think: If you could press her to your heart just once, just once, the entire void would be filled."[50]

Correspondingly, the young man oscillates between states of euphoria and melancholy:

> As for himself, he suspects that if Jacqueline has come to treat him more as a confidant than as a lover, that is because he is not a good enough lover, not fiery enough, not passionate. He suspects that if he were more of a lover she would very soon find her missing self and her missing desire. (Y, 14)

> The faraway cries of children, the birdsong, the whirr of insects gather force and come together in a paean of joy. His heart swells. *At last!* he thinks. At last it has come, the moment of ecstatic unity with the All! Fearful that the moment will slip away, he tries to put a halt to the clatter of thoughts, tries simply to be a conduit for the great universal force that has no name. (Y, 117)

Such emotions, experienced as confusing, seem to be the litmus test for the provincial person, for it is through these and how they are accounted for, that the path towards being legitimised and recognised as a non-outsider is paved: "He journeyed to the great dark city to be tested and transformed.... If he has not utterly been transfigured, then at least he has been blessed with a hint that he belongs on this earth" (Y, 117).

In its depictions of gender relations, we have advanced that *Youth* presents women as the necessary element in an equation formulated towards producing the man-artist. Again, the mistress is the necessary ingredient in this transfigurative event of becoming an artist: "If he had a beautiful, worldly-wise mistress who smoked with a cigarette-holder and spoke French, he would soon be transformed, even transfigured, he is sure" (Y, 4).

In addressing the issues of lack in terms of sexuality and the encounter with the transforming woman, the novel is engaging in its dependence to

James Joyce's works and, necessarily, the modernist tradition. These are then allusions to Stephen Dedalus's inquiry on the aesthetics of life, with their penchant towards achieving manhood:

> He did not want to play. He wanted to meet in the real world the unsubstantial image which his soul so constantly beheld. He did not know where to seek it or how: but a premonition which led him on told him that this image would, without any overt act of his, encounter him.... They would be alone, surrounded by darkness and silence: and in that moment of supreme tenderness he would be transfigured.... Weakness and timidity and inexperience would fall from him in that magic moment.[51]

Much like Joyce, whose modernist tendencies would, in the vein of constant allusion, imply a necessary connection with a wide array of past texts and authors, so does *Youth* imply a consideration of how various sexual mores, drawn from different cultural sources, inform the young artist's attempt at organising his life.

"Out of the passion that flares up anew with each new mistress, [these] are reborn into everlasting art. That is how it is done" (Y, 11). Tendentiously, the mistresses of Tolstoyan extraction and the Lawrentian nymphomaniacs clash in their representations and purposes with the women who mother, though the links between these different representations of women run deeper.

The way of things as presented in its naturalness evokes Tolstoy's "tightly corseted view of appropriate roles for women,"[52] whose natural duties were focused on being childbearers, though his views would, despite his conservative stance, eventually undergo changes throughout his works. Anna Karenina would provide the template for the conflict between society and sexual desire. Torn between her familial duties and the pleasures of a lover, these are the plateaus where her conflict resides, even as her actions as a mistress are eventually condemned.

As the young man suggests, regarding the influence of Lawrentian fiction in daily sexual mores: "From Lawrence they were learning to smash the brittle shell of civilized convention and let the secret core of their being emerge" (Y, 67). Lawrentian fiction represents a more savage approach to society's sexual mores, and yet its women are understood as barbaric and threatening: "The women in Lawrence's books made him uneasy; he imagined them as remorseless female insects, spiders or mantises.... With some of them he would have liked to go to bed, that he could not deny ... but he was too scared. Their ecstasies would be volcanic; he would be too puny to survive them" (Y, 68).

Lawrentian women would prove too excessive in their sexuality, whereas the more controlled, because thought of as more natural, Tolstoyan mistresses would prove difficult to decipher in their ways. The eroticisation of marginality proves to be too demanding, and yet alternatives to such arrangements are yet to be found. "Must it all be so cruel?," inquires the young man, "Surely there is a form of cohabitation in which man and woman eat together, sleep together, live together, yet remain immersed in their respective inward explorations" (Y, 11).

This attempt at mediating overwhelming passion with the rationality that must be construed in order to create a *milieu* of "inward exploration" leads him, in frustration, to inquire regarding his own sexuality: "Is it possible that he was not made to love women, that in truth he is a homosexual?" (Y, 78–79). The subsequent anonymous sexual encounter with a man inclines him towards dismissing the idea, and offering the notion that it is "a game for losers." (Y, 79). The irony contained in this tournament of sexual preferences is that homosexuality, in its still clouded understanding in social terms, is the possible target of his own anxieties over himself not being a part of the big league. The chapter in question starts as follows:

> In England girls pay no attention to him, perhaps because there still lingers about his person an air of colonial gaucherie.... The young men he sees in the trains and the streets, in contrast, wear narrow black trousers, pointed shoes, tight, boxlike jackets with many buttons. They also wear their hair long, hanging over their foreheads and ears, while he still has the short back and sides and the neat parting impressed on him in his childhood by country-town barbers and approved of by IBM. In the trains the eyes of girls slide over him or glaze with disdain. (Y, 71)

Branded as an outsider for his fashion and way of being, and recognising in himself aspects of childhood that he, notwithstanding his long search, cannot erase through the idealised, and hence unattainable, transfigured sexual encounter, his solution is to seek to reinforce his heterosexuality by denying his own sexual shortcomings. The tragic aspect of such denial is met in the revelatory ending, with the full force of such repressed truths creating the possibility of inquiring on the desirability of his quest for transcendence. But what could be the origin of this tragedy?

In his essay *What is a Classic?*,[53] Coetzee comments on T. S. Eliot's enterprise of fashioning himself as an insider to the English identity: "This man had targeted London as the metropolis of the English-speaking world, and with a diffidence concealing ruthless singleness of purpose had made himself

into the deliberately magisterial voice of that metropolis."[54] His American
roots notwithstanding, the fact that Eliot lived in London would, according
to Coetzee, motivate him to claim this new identity. Eliot's early poetry is, in
Coetzee's reading, preoccupied with "the feeling of being out of date, of having been born into too late an epoch, or of surviving unnaturally beyond one's
term." Of particular importance is Coetzee's understanding that "this is a not
uncommon sense of the self among colonials—whom Eliot subsumes under
what he calls provincials—particularly young colonials struggling to match
their inherited culture to their daily experience."[55] Here we must be remindful
that the youth's ambition is "to read everything worth reading before he goes
overseas, so that he will not arrive in Europe a provincial bumpkin" (Y, 25).

According to these coordinates, the trilogy's subtitle, "Scenes from Provincial Life,"—and its title in compiled form – may be read as an engagement
and response to Eliot's notion of the "provincials," that is, the young colonials for whom "the high culture of the metropolis may arrive in the form of
powerful experiences which cannot, however, be embedded in their lives in
any obvious way, and which seem therefore to have their existence in some
transcendent realm."[56]

We have seen Naipaul's and Rhys's replies to this experiential factor: the
need is felt to make room for accommodations to the different space. While
there is a demand for acceding to a protocol of language and behaviour, such
inscription is never entirely performed in those terms, as something always remains amiss. Colonial mimicry, in Bhabha's understanding, reflects "a subject
of a difference that is almost the same, but not quite."[57] As we have seen, the
mimicking of masculinity's emotional abnegations through the posturing of
a hollow man is the expected reply in a society formulated according to the
gendered politics that we have taken account of earlier. The mimicking act,
however, is subversive in itself. In seeking to enact what the culture believes
to be the correct way of being masculine, John comes to understand the inherent flaw in the demands of hegemonic masculinity, that is, the impossibility of
holding a truer connection with another.

The ending of Youth provides the more readily available instances of emotional breakdown of the young man. In his hurriedness, the constant search
for oneness with a transcendental power, and the constant frustration that
stems from such a quest, finally takes its toll. The search for perfect unity, the
idolised Muse, or the moment that invites transfiguration, are all revealed in
their succession of delayed action:

He may pull faces at the poems he reads in *Ambit* and *Agenda*, but at least they are there, in print, in the world. How is he to know that the men who wrote them did not spend years squirming as fastidiously as he in front of the blank page? They squirmed, but then finally they pulled themselves together and wrote as best they could what had to be written, and mailed it out, and suffered the humiliation of rejection or the equal humiliation of seeing their effusions in cold print, in all their poverty. (*Y*, 167)

We may assume this is a man coming to terms with his own tendency to hide, and the suffering that accompanies it. In trying to stifle it, he simply creates more situations that augment the issue, and eventually result in his paralysis—the parallelism with Beckett's own psychosomatic disorder is clear. It may now be fruitful to return to the father/son literary connection, and Coetzee's suggestion that he would in all probability not do his doctorate on Beckett's style had he had the chance of meeting him in Cape Town. This is a suggestion that goes to the core of the reason/emotion dualism, with Coetzee's early engagement of Beckett's work through the site of reason, emphasising control and objectivity, being the only path available in a society that purported this route to be the desirable one. Such relation, however, by eschewing the delights of non-reason, and with the sought after elements of intimacy and emotional bonding being derided, would eventually be reshaped in terms of finding itself infused with more affective coordinates.[58]

The possibility of reshaping the relation to one's cultural background, with its tense formulations in terms of rules, mandates and an array of varied influences, is presented in *Youth*'s ending. In finally breaking down the pretense of the masculine mask, a necessary construct to live in society yet whose cost has proven too high, he occupies a position of vulnerability and comes to inhabit the place of the gendered Other, not in all its purported allure, as magnified by masculinist desire, but its confusion and disenfranchisement.

Notes

1. See J. M. Coetzee, "Samuel Beckett in Cape Town—An Imaginary History," in *Beckett Remembering, Remembering Beckett: A Centenary Celebration*, ed. James Knowlson and Elizabeth Knowlson (London: Bloomsbury, 2006), 74–77.
2. Samuel Beckett, *Watt*, ed. C. J. Ackerley (London: Faber and Faber, 2009 [1953]).
3. J. M. Coetzee, *Doubling the Point*, ed. David Attwell (Cambridge, MA: Harvard University Press, 1992 [1986]), 20.
4. J. M. Coetzee, "Homage," *The Threepenny Review* 53 (1993): 5.
5. Paul A. Cantor, "Happy Days in the Veld: Beckett and Coetzee's *In the Heart of the Country*," *South Atlantic Quarterly* 93, no. 1 (1994): 83–110.

6. Steven G. Kellman, "J. M. Coetzee and Samuel Beckett: The Translingual Link," *Comparative Literature Studies* 33, no. 2 (1996): 161–72.

7. J. M. Coetzee, "Samuel Beckett and the Temptations of Style," in *Doubling the Point*, 43.

8. Gilbert Yeoh, "J. M. Coetzee and Samuel Beckett: Nothingness, Minimalism and Indeterminacy," *ARIEL: A Review of International English Literature* 31, no. 4 (2000): 123–24.

9. Pieter Vermeulen, "Wordsworth's Disgrace: The Insistence of South Africa in J. M. Coetzee's *Boyhood* and *Youth*," *Journal of Literary Studies* 23, no. 3 (2007): 197.

10. Johann Wolfgang von Goethe, *Le Divan Occidental-Oriental*, trans. Henri Lichtenberger (Paris: Éditions Aubier Montaigne, 1950 [1819]).

11. Jennifer M. Jeffers, *Beckett's Masculinity* (New York: Palgrave, 2009), 59.

12. J. M. Coetzee, "The Manuscript Revisions of Beckett's *Watt*," in *Doubling the Point*, 39.

13. Chris Ackerley, "Style: Coetzee and Beckett," in *A Companion to the Works of J. M. Coetzee*, ed. Tim Mehigan (New York: Camden House, 2011), 26.

14. Ackerley, *A Companion to the Works of J. M. Coetzee*, 25.

15. For more on the connections between the confessional and the political see J. M. Coetzee, "Storm over Young Goethe," *New York of Books* 59, no. 7 (2012), http://www.nybooks.com/articles/archives/2012/apr/26/storm-over-young-goethe/ [accessed 15 September 2013].

16. Lynne Segal, *Slow Motion: Changing Masculinities, Changing Men*, 3rd ed. (New York: Palgrave Macmillan, 2007 [1990]), 2.

17. John Beynon, *Masculinities and Culture* (Philadelphia: Open University Press, 2002), 69.

18. See Barbara Ehrenreich, *The Hearts of Men: American Dreams and the Flight from Commitment* (New York: Random House, 1983), 16.

19. See James Gilbert, *Men in the Middle: Searching for Masculinity in the 1950s* (Chicago: University of Chicago Press, 2005). For more on the Kinsey report, see specifically 81–105.

20. In acknowledging the importance of political events in shaping what is now understood as "The Sixties," Dominic Brook suggests that the cultural revolution begun in 1956: "The year of the Suez Crisis, the film *Rock Around the Clock*, the play *Look Back in Anger*, and so on. It was in the mid-fifties … that rationing and austerity came to an end, consumer activity began rapidly escalating, the first commercial television channel was established, and the retreat from empire began in earnest." See *Never Had it so Good: A History of Britain from Suez to the Beatles, 1956–1963* (London: Little, Brown, 2005), xx.

21. Sheila Rowbotham, *Promise of a Dream: Remembering the Sixties* (London: Allen Lane, 2000), xiv.

22. See Randall Stevenson, *The Oxford English Literary History Volume 12. 1960–2000: The Last of England?* (Oxford: Oxford University Press, 2004), namely Chapter IX (273–300). Coetzee would question the politics of both the novel and the trial; see "The Taint of the Pornographic: Defending (Against) *Lady Chatterley*," in *Doubling the Point*, 302–14.

23. John Osborne, *Look Back in Anger* (London: Faber, 1960 [1956]).

24. Pedro Aires de Oliveira, *Os Despojos da Aliança. A Grã-Bretanha e a Questão Colonial Portuguesa, 1945–1975* (Lisboa: Tinta da China, 2007).

25. Brook, *Never Had it so Good*, 25.

26. Stevenson, *The Oxford English Literary History Volume 12. 1960–2000*, 278.

27. Osborne, *Look Back in Anger*, 36.

28. *Saturday Night and Sunday Morning*, directed by Tony Richardson (Woodfall Film Productions, 1960).

29. *The Loneliness of the Long Distance Runner*, directed by Tony Richardson (Woodfall Film Productions, 1962).

30. *Alfie*, directed by Lewis Gilbert (Paramount Pictures, 1966).

31. Stuart Hall, "The Neo-Liberal Revolution," *Cultural Studies* 25, no. 6 (2011), 705–28.

32. Nigel Worden, *The Making of Modern South Africa*, 5th ed. (Malden: Wiley-Blackwell, 2012 [1994]), 104–05.

33. Worden, *Modern South Africa*, 113.

34. Worden, *Modern South Africa*, 116.

35. See Tom Lodge, *Sharpeville: An Apartheid Massacre and its Consequences* (Oxford: Oxford University Press, 2011), 65.

36. Worden, *Modern South Africa*, 116.

37. Lodge, *Sharpeville*, 234.

38. Rowbotham, *Promise of a Dream: Remembering the Sixties*, 172.

39. David Harvey, *A Brief History of Neoliberalism* (Oxford: Oxford University Press, 2007), 56.

40. See Sukhdev Sandhu, *London Calling: How Black and Asian Writers Imagined a City* (London: Harper, 2004), namely 183–223.

41. See "Family Outcast".

42. See Elleke Boehmer, *Colonial and Postcolonial Literature: Migrant Metaphors*, 2nd ed. (Oxford: Oxford University Press, 2005 [1995]), 169.

43. Jean Rhys, *Voyage in the Dark* (London: Penguin, 2000 [1934]), 7.

44. V. S. Naipaul, *The Mimic Men* (London: Picador, 2011 [1967]), vii.

45. Amal Treacher, "Postcolonial Subjectivity: Masculinity, Shame, and Memory," *Ethnic and Racial Studies* 30, no. 2 (2007): 287. The relation of shame with guilt will be explored in further detail in the following chapters.

46. Derek Attridge, *J. M. Coetzee and the Ethics of Reading* (Chicago and London: University of Chicago Press, 2004), 147.

47. Timothy Bewes, "The Event of Shame in J. M. Coetzee," in *The Event of Postcolonial Shame* (Princeton: Princeton University Press, 2010), 137–63.

48. For further exploration on this particular topic, see "Shades and Shadows of Life".

49. Barbara Becker-Cantarino, "Goethe and Gender," in *The Cambridge Companion to Goethe*, ed. Lesley Sharpe (Cambridge: Cambridge University Press, 2002), 183.

50. Johann Wolfgang von Goethe, *The Sufferings of Young Werther*, trans. and ed. Stanley Corngold (New York: W. W. Norton & Company, 2012), 64.

51. James Joyce, *A Portrait of the Artist as a Young Man* (Oxford: Oxford University Press, 2000 [1916]), 54.

52. Edwina Cruise, "Women, Sexuality, and the Family in Tolstoy," in *The Cambridge Companion to Tolstoy*, ed. Donna Tussing Orwin (Cambridge: Cambridge University Press, 2002), 192.

53. J. M. Coetzee, "What is a Classic?" in *Stranger Shores: Essays 1986–1999* (London: Vintage, 2001), 1–19.

54. Coetzee, *What is a Classic?*, in *Stranger Shores*, 1–2.

55. Coetzee, *What is a Classic?*, in *Stranger Shores*, 7.

56. Coetzee, *What is a Classic?*, in *Stranger Shores*, 7.

57. Homi K. Bhabha, *The Location of Culture* (New York: Routledge, 1994), 122. For Bhabha, mimicry is a paramount strategy in terms of colonial power, as it takes advantage of the gaps found in communication, thus forming "a discourse at the crossroads of what is known and permissible and that which though known must be kept concealed; a discourse uttered between the lines and as such both against the rules and within them" (128).

58. N. C. T. Meihuizen, "Beckett and Coetzee: Alternative Identities," *Literator* 32, no. 1 (2011): 1–19.

PART III

MAKING THE OTHER:
ALTERNATIVES TO HEGEMONY

· 5 ·

RACE AND MASCULINITIES

Through the blood I saw the sun come up, a great eye slaughtered on the horizon. In the farthest distance—but perhaps it was my imagination—the great sea-birds were sailing off proudly and beautifully to wherever they had come from.

André Brink, *The First Life of Adamastor*

In the second half of the fifteenth century, the Portuguese, "oceanic frontiersmen of European expansion,"[1] seeking a route to India, rounded the Cape of Storms ("Cabo das Tormentas"),[2] so named by Bartolomeu Dias, in 1488.[3] Henceforth, the region of southern Africa "came to be exposed to a whole new set of influences and, eventually, to European conquest and settlement."[4] Initially, the place would be largely neglected by European explorers, as the Portuguese would establish their outposts in the Mozambiquean coast, while also being avoided for its stories of shipwreck and the assassination of viceroy Francisco de Almeida in 1510.[5] Such stories of terror would confirm "an already-existing European iconography in which the inhabitants of Africa were depicted in stages of wild primitiveness,"[6] as early modern Europe would establish a rigid distinction—though not without resistance—between the "civilised" and the "savage."[7]

The anxieties encapsulated in the "civilised"/"savage" dichotomy are not, however, to be understood as initiating only in the aforementioned

historical period. As can be read in Homer's *Odyssey*: "My friends, let the
rest of you stay here. I myself with my own ship's crew will go and find
what manner of men live yonder. Are they barbarous, arrogant and lawless?
Are they hospitable and godfearing?"[8] More *apropos*, though, another passage of the *Odyssey* provides what Van Wyk Smith considers to be "one of
the great ethnogeographic templates of classical, medieval and even early
Renaissance talk about Africa"[9]: "But now Poseidon had gone to visit the
Ethiopians, those distant Ethiopians whose nation is parted within itself, so
that some are near the setting and some near the rising sun, but all alike are
at the world's end."[10]

Herodotus would equally elaborate on the presence of people in the south
of Africa:

> But then the land of the farmers west of the River Triton is very hilly and thickly
> wooded, and teems with wildlife. There are enormous snakes there, and also lions,
> elephants, bears, asps, donkeys with horns, dog-headed creatures, headless creatures
> with eyes in their chests (at least, that is what the Libyans say), wild men and wild
> women, and a large number of other creatures whose existence is not merely the stuff
> of fables.[11]

The rounding of the southern part of the continent by the Portuguese was,
thus, a moment that can be defined not only in economic terms, but also in
terms of the tensions of the Encounter with an Other that was thought of as
"intrinsically hostile to Mediterranean civilisation."[12]

Historical and cultural tensions would also be present in Rousseau's representation of Hottentot life as emblematic of savage life, considering that
such a living was largely one of idleness, preoccupied as the savage man was in
conserving energy for the basic tasks of survival.[13] Coetzee's reading of Rousseau's work stresses idleness as the basis for the separation of the savage from
the civilised man, considering how cultural difference was thought of as an attempt at destroying the cohesion of the Self. To this end, Coetzee introduces
the notion of the "Discourse of the Cape" as indicative of the largely homo-
geneised colonial discourse that was central in constructing the Cape Colony with its hierarchy of racialised powers.[14] The eurocentric discourse of the
black Other as impure and savage would validate the necessary mechanisms
that saw the interior of the Cape Colony as unoccupied, hence legitimating
colonial expansion.[15]

The Work of Adamastor

Africa would thus be defined in terms of the Other of Europe, "peopled by na‑
tives whose way of life occasioned curiosity or disgust but never admiration,"[16]
through the definitions provided by men of science based on traveller's reports.[17]
William Burchell, serving the purpose of advancing the prospects of the Age
of Reason, travelled from England to the Cape Colony and presented various
images of not only the colony but also the places outside its borders, particularly
of its inhabitants: "The sight of the Hottentots, and all their movements, fixed
my attention. ... They seemed now to have recovered their natural manners,
having left behind them the constraints of Cape Town. It was easy to perceive,
that this was the mode of life which suited them, and that they felt quite at
home amongst the bushes."[18]

It should be noted that Burchell's journals would also provide the con‑
scious means towards attaining a very precise political goal, that of ensuring
the British control over the Cape. As he writes in 1819: "As a British colony,
it must end in speaking the English language, and in adopting English customs
and laws."[19] Tellingly, in *Youth* the reader is provided with a glimpse of the fas‑
cination that Burchell's travels spark in John, whose writings he reads at the
British Library: "But even more than by accounts of old Cape Town is he cap‑
tivated by stories of ventures into the interior, reconnaissances by ox‑wagon
into the desert of the Great Karoo, where a traveller could trek for days on
end without clapping eyes on a living soul" (*Y*, 137). That is, John is already
immersed in the narrative that constitutes the "Discourse of the Cape."

According to such a cultural framework, masculinity would largely be
associated with whiteness, as racialised Others would find themselves "van‑
quished by the ideal of white masculinity."[20] Central to such a formulation is
how difference was considered. Racist imaginary is "constructed out of repu‑
diated elements of the personality that are experienced as deeply threatening.
Projecting them into the other means they no longer damage the subject from
within, but it also creates a persecutory and threatening outside world which
has to be defended against."[21]

Taking into consideration the reality of *apartheid* as being established
through racist imaginary, with the constitutive presupposition of white mas‑
culinity as dominant, the following situation in *Boyhood*, where John cele‑
brates his birthday, may serve as a telling statement on how daily life repro‑
duces such cultural coordinates:

> On his birthday, instead of a party, he is given ten shillings to take his friends for a treat. He invites his three best friends to the Globe Café; they sit at a marble-topped table and order banana splits or chocolate fudge sundaes. He feels princely, dispensing pleasure like this; the occasion would be a marvellous success, were it not spoiled by the ragged Coloured children standing at the window looking in on them. (B, 72)

The little prince, dispensing courtesy to his guests, is disarranged in his intents for a blissful time by a set of other children, quite different from the ones that attend the birthday party. The passage alludes to a certain "us" *versus* "them" mentality, as the mirrored space becomes the metaphor for very different social conditions and spaces of living.

Young John already exhibits an internalised sense of the differing social spaces of *apartheid*: "There are white people and Coloured people and Natives, of whom the Natives are the lowest and most derided" (B, 65). The hierarchical placement is well learnt, though tellingly conflated with John's anxieties over his own identity. These are demonstrated in two ways. The first concerns the purported "lore that all Afrikaans boys seem to share" over rituals of initiation into their community at school (B, 69), regarding which John expresses an accentuated disgust. A second form of possible exclusion from a continuous sense of identity is over the prevalent issue of language, with government-mandated transferrals of "schoolchildren with Afrikaans surnames … to Afrikaans classes…. It will be up to the school inspectors, he learns, to remove false English boys from the English classes" (B, 69).

Hierarchies as translating the idiom of belonging are then established not only for Others, but also found in the place of the Self. It is this growing awareness, and its added restlessness, its panic as we are told (B, 69), that can be read as providing some empathic understanding of the culturally disadvantaged place of the Other. These cultural politics gain expression as the boy expresses the precariousness of his identity: "They are of course South Africans, but even South Africanness is faintly embarrassing, and therefore not talked about, since not everyone who lives in South Africa is a South African, or not a proper South African" (B, 18).

After setting the mirrored Encounter between the boys at the party and the Coloured children outside, close but yet clearly separated, the following passage may be read:

> If he were someone else, he would ask the Portuguese with the Brilliantined hair who owns the Globe to chase them away. It is quite normal to chase beggar children away. You have only to contort your face into a scowl and wave your arms and shout … and then turn to whoever is watching, friend or stranger, and explain. (B, 73)

As a white child, John is quite aware of his powers of persuading others to chase other children away, those who are undesirable. He could reccur to the handy services of the Portuguese man—now not an oceanic frontiersman, but still a figure of authority over Others—, in order to guarantee the permanence of a possible version of Eden.

To exert power over Others, with but very little consideration or difficulty, is the hallmark of such privileged positioning within a very specific system of power. Coetzee, quite aware of the mechanisms of colonialist racism, gave answer to such a situation in creating Jacobus Coetzee, the protagonist of *Dusklands*'s second *novella* – *The Narrative of Jacobus Coetzee*—and his alleged ancestor.[22] The self-acclaimed "hunter, a domesticator of the wilderness, a hero of enumeration,"[23] espouses what David Attwell terms as a "metaphysics of the gun."[24]

Indeed, the gun serves as "mediator with the world and therefore our saviour."[25] Such mediation is the only possibility of reaching alterity and maintaining a tenous grasp on sanity:

> The gun saves us from the fear that all life is within us. It does so by laying at our feet all the evidence we need of a dying and therefore a living world. I move through the wilderness with my gun at the shoulder of my eye and slay elephants, hippopotami, rhinoceres, buffalo, lions, leopards, dogs, giraffes, antelope and buck of all descriptions, hares, and snakes; I leave behind me a mountain of skin, bones, inedible gristle, and excrement. All this is my dispersed pyramid to life. It is my life's work, my incessant proclamation of the otherness of the dead and therefore the otherness of life.... The death of the hare is my metaphysical meat, just as the flesh of the hare is the meat of my dogs. The hare dies to keep my soul from merging with the world. All honour to the hare. Nor is he an easy shot.[26]

The play between inside and outside is reflected, however, at yet another level, between the tension of realising whether an outside world exists, or is the fabrication of one's mind, this only apparently being resolved through an onslaught of death that permits one to get a bearing on being alive. Jacobus enacts a kind of masculinity based on a validation of the explorer's path: "I am an explorer. My essence is to open what is closed, to bring light to what is dark,"[27] not necessarily to be changed by the surprise of the meeting with others, but rather with the firm intent of transplanting one's reality to such "darkness". Thus Jacobus, in the ideological framework of European-led colonialism, resembles the idealised image of the coloniser,[28] undercut by fantastical enactments regarding one's place and purpose in the world. Such subjectivity can never be understood, however, in strict psychological ways, as it were, bearing the need to provide a cultural and ideological background to the formation of such a masculinity.[29]

This masculine formation, directly dependent on the enterprise of colonialism, is bent on the destruction of others, not only of animals, but foremost of other human beings. Emblematic of such an understanding is the account of Jacobus's raid of a Hottentot camp: "Through their deaths I, who after they had expelled me had wandered the desert like a pallid symbol, again asserted my reality."[30]

Through the enactment of revenge and hatred, one's reality is maintained. This reality is modelled on omnipotent ways: "I become a spherical reflecting eye moving through the wilderness and ingesting it. Destroyer of the wilderness, I move through the land cutting a devouring path from horizon to horizon. There is nothing from which my eye turns, I am all that I see. Such loneliness!... What is there that is not me?"[31]

Nothing escapes the all-seeing eye of the coloniser. In omnipotent fashion, the coloniser holds reality in its full grasp, moulding it according to his own will, exemplifying the undifferentiation between Self and Other that forms the core of omnipotence.[32] And yet, Coetzee introduces a twist in the portrayal of the coloniser, showcasing its ambivalent nature, as evidenced by the acknowledgement of the loneliness that such a subjective state—always, in the coloniser's lingo, meant to be objective—implies in the psychological makeup of the explorer. To seek mastery over reality is, we read, to necessarily assume a position of centredness that eclipses others and, eventually, destroys oneself psychically, if not physically. Additionally, omnipotence demands watchful domination and paranoid restlessness regarding Others:

> From the fringes of the horizon he approaches, growing to manhood beneath my eyes until he reaches the verge of that precarious zone in which, invulnerable to his weapons, I command his life. Across this annulus I behold him approach bearing the wilderness in his heart. On the far side he is nothing to me and I probably nothing to him. On the near side mutual fear will drive us to our little comedies of man and man, prospector and guide, benefactor and beneficiary, victim and assassin, teacher and pupil, father and child. He crosses it, however, in none of these characters but as representative of that out there which my eye once enfolded and ingested and which now promises to enfold, ingest, and project me through itself as a speck on a field which we may call annihilation or alternatively history. He threatens to have a history in which I shall be a term. Such is the material basis of the malady of the master's soul.[33]

The master's soul will inevitably arise through the enactment of the "little comedies" performed through rigid dichotomic power relations, the passage alluding to the Hegelian master-slave dialectic.[34] In Hegel's framework the subject seeks affirmation of one's pre-conceived reality through the Encounter with an-Other: "Self-consciousness exists in and for itself when, and by the fact that, it so exists for another; that is, it exists only in being acknowledged."[35] Hegelian philosophy implies that the meeting of two selves in the movement for mutual recognition eventually leads to a conflict whose tensions must be surpassed in order to acquire higher forms of consciousness. The Self uses the Other in order to validate a pre-conceived, pre-understood notion of his own inner life, of his composition—the object must never be changed for, in changing it, it is no longer the initial object. The Hegelian subject is one that does not escape social relations, for it needs those to sustain itself; yet, the quality of such relations is the crux of the matter, as an-Other's subjectivity is denied and enslaved in the contribution of the permanence of the omnipotent, auto-regulating Self.

The maintenance of the omnipotent Self has been the concern of postcolonial scholarship, as the Other has historically been understood as the non-European, non-white person.[36] For his part, Frantz Fanon considered how the Hegelian Encounter would present his limitations in a colonised world: "Toute ontologie est rendue irréalisable dans une société colonisée et civilisée."[37] In Fanon's understanding, Hegel's notion of recognition would be subsumed under the prevalent societally induced desire of the black man's appeal towards emulating whiteness: as Fanon accords, the black man would hold no ontological resistance to the appeals of the white man.[38]

Apartheid legislation, a summary of which was presented in the chapter "Art of One," would constitute a form of dealing with desire for the Other. In his reading of Geoffrey Cronjé's works, Coetzee underscores the obsessiveness of such measures. Legislative proceedings "flower[ed] out of self-interest and greed, but it also flowered out of desire and out of the hatred of desire."[39] Fears of racial undifferentiation, coupled with the worrying financial situation of Afrikaners in the 1940s and closer living with people of other races due to changes in urban planning, played an integral part in going from a place of feeling equal (*gelykvoeling*) to social separateness (*gelykstaling*).

Apartheid's rigid view, in seeking to do truth to its namesake would, nevertheless, find it difficult to expel the excess of the Other. The Other as excess of the Self indicates a radical alterity, with a possible Encounter not resulting in assimilation but in a constant reshaping of both what was thought to be true to oneself and the dimensions of such meeting.[40] As Jessica Benjamin argues on this particular espousal of the moment of recognition, "true independence means sustaining the essential tension of these contradictory impulses; that is, both asserting the self and recognizing the other."[41]

Returning to *Boyhood*'s birthday scene, the little prince soon emerges from his private Eden, becoming a little philosopher through an understanding that despite holding the power to evict the Other, the Other has already touched him: "Whatever happens, whether they are chased away or not, it is too late, his heart is already hurt" (*B*, 73).

Here the boy employs the vocabulary of Coetzee. At the core of *apartheid* is a question of deformation of spirit, as Coetzee himself would explain, departing from the theological understanding of *apartheid* as sin:

> Theology has called *apartheid* a sin not because it is a crime of huge dimensions (crimes are defined by the victors, and *apartheid* has not been a victor) but because it set for itself the task of reforming (by which we should understand deforming) the human heart.[42]

In a racist system, deforming the human heart implies a process in which the "vitality and polymorphism of the world becomes flattened and narrowed into a rigid mode of reasoning a single narrative of experience; this means that much that is real is excluded, and returns to haunt the subject as a frightening, because potentially uncontrollable, irrationality."[43]

What may pertain to the realm of the irrational and thus threaten the notion of the Self as an organisation felt as stable and continuous in experience is thrown outside. Commenting on the history of the monster in Western thought, Margrit Shildrick argues that the monstrous figure is a way to consider the always anxious aspect of bodily limits. The monster "reminds us always of what must be abjected from the self's clean and proper body."[44]

In considering the powerful depiction of Otherness as monstrous, it may be useful to further contemplate the event of the rounding of the Cape. As already mentioned, this felicitous event in European expansion necessarily held its anxieties, congealed on a character of *Os Lusíadas*:

> Não acabava, quando hũa figura
> Se nos mostra no ar, robusta e válida,
> De disforme e grandíssima estatura;
> O rosto carregado, a barba esquálida,
> Os olhos encovados, e a postura
> Medonha e má, e a cor terrena e pálida;
> Cheios de terra e crespos os cabelos,
> A boca negra, os dentes amarelos.[45]

The giant Adamastor can be understood, within the scope of Camões's epic poem, as a figure of resistance to the advancement of colonial conquest. Depicted in inhuman form, outside the realm of the civilised, Camões's demigod casts its curse on the Portuguese, drawing on heavily sexualised anxieties enacted towards the inhabitants of Africa: "Verão os Cafres, ásperos e avaros/ Tirar à linda dama seus vestidos."[46]

It is the defeat of Adamastor by Vasco da Gama that opens the doors to India, a new world already showing its promises even in the African coast: "A gente que esta terra possuía/Posto que todos *Etiopes* eram/Mais humana no trato parecia/Que os outros que tão mal nos receberam."[47] The Adamastor would be, in Camões's poem, "not just the barbaric spirit of the Cape but the barbarian himself."[48] As such, his defeat would imply the victory of the Portuguese, and of the colonialist enterprise overall.

The figure of the giant would undergo a series of transformations over the centuries, representing at times colonial resistance by the natives, at times the overpowering force of colonialism. Notwithstanding such transformations— or perhaps because of them—the Adamastor would gain "the status of national legend,"[49] and would come to register the "ambivalence of white South Africans about the European-African antinomies in their heritage and commitments."[50]

The Encounter of the boy with the Coloured children indicates another approach to the violence enacted by the colonialist enterprise. The gaze of the children on the other side of the mirror demands his attention: "On the faces of these children he sees none of the hatred which, he is prepared to acknowledge, he and his friends deserve for having so much money while they are penniless" (B, 72). The white child then acknowledges a sense of embarassment over his privilege, losing innocence in the process. His is also the vocabulary of hatred, that he does not see in the Coloured children's faces, yet one which he is ready to admit as reasonable and expected. Additionally, there is an understanding of how hatred as negation of the Other is simply too easy to enact through his own privileged position, by an appeal to adults who may be overeager to uphold social respectability by removing undesired children and allowing for the possibility of the continuation of the clean, white child, the guarantor of the Self of *apartheid*.

The acknowledgement of his privileged position is an indicator of a certain understanding of the past and how the struggles of history have favoured him. His is the role to play of the civilised child, in the process of becoming a civilised man. Yet, his own precarious sense of belonging aludes to the possibility of his shortcoming, of being found by a higher power to be false and unworthy. Entitlement to omnipotence, and the ability to act on it, are unwarranted by the acknowledgement of one's precarious positioning. That is, through reflexive understanding of one's suffering, one can go outside the narrative of the all-seeing, masterful Self, and enact a different relation to an Other.

The tradition of the coloniser is thus interrupted to a certain degree. The Other serves not as a tool for the Self's purposes, but exists outside such colonising impetus. "If he were someone else" (B, 72), implies not only the easiness of subjugating others, but also how he himself can create a narrative in which such actions may be derided. That is, there is no preconceived notion of absolute determination on one's action: he holds the agency to do otherwise, to be someone else rather than the purported white child of *apartheid*, upholding its norms and cleanliness.

Contrary, thus, to masculinity perceived as totalising the force of the Self, by way of destroying an outside subjectivity, young John derides this tradition, by acknowledging the force of the Other in his motivations and his attempts to prevent suffering on others. Unlike Jacobus Coetzee, with his omnipotent gaze, or Robinson Crusoe, with his penchant for territorial occupation, young John is not a Master of himself.[51]

The centrality of the Other in one's life may be agreed upon by the consideration of unconscious functioning.[52] As a possible means for an alternate conceptualisation of the individual in relation to society,[53] Julia Kristeva argues that Freud's notion of the unconscious justifies an ethics whereby the strangeness of the Other is not to be found solely in the outside world but, perhaps primarily, inside oneself:

> L'inquiétante étrangeté serait ainsi la voie royale (mais au sens de la cour, non pas du roi) par laquelle Freud introduit le rejet fasciné de l'autre au coeur de ce «nous-même» sûr de soi et opaque, qui précisément n'existe plus depuis Freud et qui se révèle comme un étrange pays de frontières et d'altérités sans cesse construites et déconstruites....Délicatement, analytiquement, Freud ne parle pas des étrangers: il nous apprend à détecter l'étrangeté en nous. C'est peut-être la seule manière de ne pas la traquer dehors. Au cosmopolitisme stoïcien, à l' intégration universaliste religieuse, succède chez Freud le courage de nous dire désintégrés pour ne pas intégrer les étrangers et encore moins les poursuivre, mais pour les accueillir dans cette inquiétante étrangeté qui est autant la leur que la nôtre.[54]

Unconscious mechanisms, Kristeva argues, allowed Freud to draw attention to how strangeness inhabits the very core of each of us. This acknowledgement would allow the dispensation of considering such strange and odd feelings as a sort of contamination stemming from an external Other; in this framework, strangeness inhabits the Self, is part of the Self.

Masterful domination over others then is eclipsed, and the suffering of others enters one's heart, uninvited, yet undeterred, by the strongest of social arrangements that sought otherwise. What is outside, already projected as the most horrid, monstrous-like, gains a human face, is represented outside the strict imperialist vocabulary. Adamastor makes his presence known in such moments of poignancy.

"We've Long Been in Hell": Past and Future Presences

Martin's interview in *Summertime* illustrates the clear feeling of unbelonging prevailing among certain white South Africans: "Our attitude was that, to put it briefly, our presence there was legal but illegitimate. We had an abstract right to be there, a birthright, but the basis of that right was fraudulent. Our presence was grounded in a crime, namely colonial conquest, perpetuated by *apartheid*" (S, 209).

The *apartheid* system would prove emasculating for non-white men, as indicated by Mtutuzeli Matshoba's 1979 banned short story *Call me not a Man*[55]:

> By dodging, lying, resisting where it is possible, bolting when I'm already cornered, parting with invaluable money, sometimes calling my sisters into the game to get amorous with my captors, allowing myself to be slapped on the mouth in front of my womenfolk and getting sworn at with my mother's private parts, that component of me which is man has died countless times in one lifetime.[56]

Matshoba's short story is a reminder of the constant assault on one's sense of pride and agency as a black man under the duress of a tyrannical political system. Black men would see their adulthood denied, and necessarily the possibility of intervening in society in more direct ways, through the employment of shameful designations:

> A whole arsenal of negative attributes were associated with blacks in Afrikaner thinking: they were regarded as dirty, contaminated by disease, ugly, dim-witted, lazy, brutal, etc. These negative physical and spiritual attributes were the antithesis of the Afrikaner ideal of masculinity.[57]

Societal norms allowed for the use of the Other, with very little account for alternative ways of behaving:

> It means that if his mother were to call out "Boy!" and wave, as she is quite capable of doing, this boy would have to stop in his tracks and come and do whatever she might tell him (carry her shopping basket, for instance), and at the end of it get a tickey in his cupped hands and be grateful for it. (B, 61)

"Boy" as a derogatory term appears as the enunciation of mastery over the Other's status. As Robert Morrell indicates, "the use of the word 'boy' by whites (men and women, boys and girls) to refer to black men reflected a workplace reality in which African men did the menial work, requiring strong, energetic and powerful bodies."[58] Summoning the Other must be met with obedience; the Other is to abandon his life and accede to the demands required of him.

This is further addressed in the following passage in *Boyhood*: "He is not sure whether Freek counts as a man or a boy, whether he is making a fool of himself when he treats Freek as a man. With Coloured people in general, and with the people of the Karoo in particular, he simply does not know when they cease to be children and become men and women. It seems to happen so early and so suddenly: one day they are playing with toys, the next day they are out with men, working, or in someone's kitchen, washing dishes" (B, 86).

This is of an unreflexive nature. Were the boy to demand another course of action, the mother's probable reply is telling: "She would simply smile and say, 'But they are used to it!'" (B, 61). Thus the relation to the racialised Other, embedded in the social fabric, is permeated by historical violence, and the desired aspects of physical masculinity projected in African men to be found useful in multiple sites of production, such as farms or mines.[59] As a trope of colonisation, humiliation is understood by Amal Treacher Kabesh as "an act of subjugation in which power relations are continually involved. Unlike shame, which is a more internal process and involved feelings about the self, humiliation is largely external, as it is always about the other person."[60]

John necessarily partakes in this societal discourse. Colonial discourse has formed him, as we have already noticed how his imagination is informed by reading Burchell's travel reports, through the inculcation of the Discourse of the Cape. This distortion is also present in *Boyhood*, when the boy understands the Natives as "invaders from the North" (B, 61). The myth of the unoccupied land serves the purpose of sustaining childish play, depositing on the Native Other the blame for conscious mischievousness. This is exemplified by John and his brother's blaming of Josias, first presented as "the delivery boy"

(B, 63), soon rectified as "in fact not a boy at all but a grown man" (B, 64). Tellingly, such mischievousness does not have the racialised Other as sole target, as other Afrikaans children are also its recipients.

In *Summertime*, a particularly poignant event is described that encourages a notion of how white masculinity is derided in its dominant position, through a series of ironic displacements of such power. Margot is stranded with her cousin on their way to Voëlfontein, due to a malfunction in the truck. John is unprepared to deal with such a situation, as Margot tactfully withholds commentary: "She knows enough about men never to question their competence with machines" (S, 109). Clumsily, John is eventually unable to do the repairing. His excuse is the lack of proper training, a sign of his being in a country where one makes "other people do our work for us while we sit in the shade and watch" (S, 111).

White people, John argues, avoid manual labour for fear of being unclean. The argument, although with its merits, as it unveils an interest in broadening one's field of action, is also flawed, as Margot, sensing a possible underlying prejudice in her cousin, suggests taking the truck to a white repairman: "I am not suggesting that you take your car to a Native" (S, 111). This is met with what may be understood as a political reply: "'I do the garden work. I do repairs around the house. I am at present re-laying the drainage. It may seem funny to you but to me it is not a joke. I am making a gesture'" (S, 112). Such gesture goes to the extent of acknowledging one's embeddedness in a racist society and an attempt at exacting some degree of change.

Viewing her cousin as sexless, interested in devoiding her future children of "their Coetzee inheritance" (S, 117), Margot considers him a failed man: "Failed runaway, failed car mechanic too, for whose failure she is at this moment having to suffer. Failed son" (S, 120). In its characteristic portrayal of John as the excessively redundant man, the passage further derides any possibility of a sexual liaision with him: "He looks a mess, with his unkempt hair and beard sticking out at all angles. *Thank God I don't have to wake up with you in my bed every morning*, she thinks. *Not enough of a man. A real man would do better than this*" (S, 121).

Strikingly, help arrives in the form of Hendrik, a servant from the farm. This frail stranger—"the slightest physical effort makes him wheeze" (S, 122)—, unassuming in his presentation, outside the scope of the physical masculinity assumed in the racialised Other, is however the one who rescues the well-intentioned yet clueless white man.

As Hendrik enters the scene, we are reminded of another Hendrik in Coetzee's *oeuvre*, the also farm servant of *In the Heart of the Country*. This Hendrik, himself a Coloured man, occupies not only the place of the servant, but the more tantalising, for necessarily indeterminate, place of the stranger: "For soon Hendrik is going to open the back door, and while it is true that the essence of servanthood is the servant's intimacy with his master's dirt ... Hendrik is not only essence but substance, not only servant but stranger" (15). In *Summertime*, John's insistence on dirtying his own hands may, through the logic provided in the aforementioned passage, underscore once again his attempt at shifting the discourse of the master and slave.

Hendrik, in being presented as a Coloured servant of the Afrikaner farm, recalls the already enunciated hierarchical placement of racial categorisation that the young boy elaborates, but the desirability of which he is unsure of (B, 65). In such racialised categories of *apartheid*, it is important to consider the personal understanding of the positioning of Coloured people. To the boy, "not only do they come with the land, the land comes with them, is theirs, has always been" (B, 62). This right to the land betrays the affective bonds with Coloured people in his life who are, tellingly, shaped by the *milieu* of the Afrikaner farm.

The Afrikaans that is spoken in the father's farm is actualised to the possibilities of diversity, revealing its creolised nature. Not only is it enmeshed with English—"Greedily he drinks in the atmosphere, drinks in the happy, slapdash mixture of English and Afrikaans that is their common tongue when they get together" (B, 81)—, this "lighter, airier" Afrikaans is different from the one taught at school, "weighed down with idioms that are supposed to come from the *volksmond*, the people's mouth, but seem to come only from the Great Trek, lumpish, nonsensical idioms about wagons and cattle and cattle-harness" (B, 81).

In this derision of an idiom that seeks to maintain timeless codes that are reproduced half-heartedly, the past is a country to be explored, out of which the figure of his grandfather emerges.

The grandfather is portrayed in specifically masculine imagery. Margo, in *Summertime*, solidifies the image of the entrepreneur, "a man with plenty of ... *spunk*, more spunk probably than all his children put together. But perhaps that is the fate of the children of strong fathers: to be left with less than a full share of spunk." Equally, the image is of someone who induces fear: "After the midday meal, she remembers, the whole house would freeze into silence: Grandpa was having his nap. Even at that age she was surprised to see how fear of the old man could make grown people creep about like mice" (S, 106).

Described as a "gentleman farmer" (B, 82), and responsible for immersing his progeny in the English language, from which the boy draws such joy—and confusion regarding his loyalties—, the story of the Coetzees is also one of decay after the man's death: "Then, after his grandfather's death, the barnyard began to dwindle, till nothing was left but sheep" (B, 82).

However, the farm holds another patriarchal figure, a Coloured man:

> Outa Jaap was on the farm before his grandfather; he himself remembers Outa Jaap only as a very old man with milky-white, sightless eyeballs and toothless gums and knotted hands, sitting on a bench in the sun, to whom he was taken before he died, perhaps in order to be blessed, he is not sure. Though Outa Jaap is gone now, his name is still mentioned with deference. (B, 84)

The reverence contained in the passage is for a wise man, with the power to bring forth the validation of life through the act of blessing. This spiritual, shaman-like guide, is the Adam-esque figure of property of the farm: "Outa Jaap was part of the farm; though his grandfather may have been its purchaser and legal owner, Outa Jaap came with it, knew more about it, about sheep, veld, weather, than the newcomer would ever know" (B, 84).

The grandfather's entitlement to the farm then, is of an economic nature, whereas Jaap's bond to the farm is deeper, rooted in an acute understanding of its nature. There is a cyclical aspect also to this idea: John's certainty that Coloured people come with the farm, have always been of the farm, suggests that the legacy of colonialism, in its economic dimension, will eventually fade and give place to the legitimacy of those who, in turn, possess the intricate knowledge of the land.

Those who have obtained privilege from their relation to a tradition of colonisation are, then, doomed to a sense of transience, a precarious attachment to a place that is falsely theirs: "In the world of South Africa he is no more than a ghost, a wisp of smoke fast dwindling away, soon to have vanished for good" (Y, 130–31).

The Coetzees are equated to migratory birds, their vacation-like stance towards the farm inadequate to the business of running it:

> It seems to him that Freek belongs here more securely than the Coetzees do—if not to Voëlfontein, then to the Karoo. The Karoo is Freek's country, his home; the Coetzees, drinking tea and gossiping on the farmhouse stoep, are like swallows, seasonal, here today, gone tomorrow, or even like sparrows, chirping, light-footed, short-lived. (B, 87)

An additionally telling passage is the one concerning the arrangements of
the two graveyards that hold the remains of those connected with the farm.
Whereas one of them holds his grandfather's tombstone, "the only Coetzee
there" (B, 97), the other, without a fence, holds what can be understood as
the true masters of the land:

> On the other side of the road is a second graveyard, without a fence, where some of
> the grave- mounds are so weathered that they have been reabsorbed into the earth.
> Here lie the servants and hirelings of the farm, stretching back to Outa Jaap and far
> beyond. What few gravestones still stand are without names or dates. Yet here he
> feels more awe than among the generations of Botes clustering around his grandfa-
> ther. It has nothing to do with spirits.... Whatever dies here dies firmly and finally:
> its flesh is picked off by the ants, its bones are bleached by the sun, and that is that.
> Yet among these graves he treads nervously. From the earth comes a deep silence, so
> deep that it could almost be a hum. (B, 97)

The denial of mystical qualities in the Encounter with the second graveyard
serves only to underline the importance of the excess of such an Encounter.
John is among those who share a rapport to the land the dimensions of which
are to be envied or emulated by the Coetzees, a process flawed from its very
beginning. Here, the notion of the mystical may be understood as underlining
the inability to fully grasp the dimensions of those whose comprehension of
the land is deemed superior; as such, the mystical becomes the mode of considering how knowledge of the Other's life is always situated. Knowledge of
the Other does not imply writing the Other; knowledge of the Other recognises the fundamental impossibility of writing the Other solely by the means
of one's linguistic codes.[61]

As Neil Lazarus argues, "it is important to problematise representation
and the issues around it where the writer's desire to speak *for* others—to en-
dow 'them' with consciousness and voice—shades over into ventriquilisation,
into speaking *instead* of 'them'".[62] The deep silence emanating from the earth,
should it be put into words, would be denied in its Otherness.[63]

Silence as metaphor has been employed by Coetzee to underline the tensions between white writing and black speech. In his criticism of the *plaasroman*, Coetzee evidences the silences of which it is structurally composed and
thus dependent on:

True, the silences in the South African farm novel, particularly its silence about the place of the black man in the pastoral idyll, and the silence it creates when it puts into the mouth of the black countryman a white man's words ... speak more loudly now than they did fifty years ago. Our ears today are finely attuned to modes of silence.[64]

The central absence of the black man, a structural aspect of the *plaasroman*, is an indicator of the larger issue pertaining to the (im)possibilities of white writing on blackness. What such writing should include, or exclude would soon devolve into programmatic notions of personhood that would eclipse the surprise that constitutes the speech of the Other.[65]

As Richard Begam suggests, Coetzee's notion that white writing is unable to read blackness, anchors in a Levinasian-derived ethical form, through the acknowledgement "that there might be a form of writing, a form of speaking, a form of being, different from itself."[66] That is, the Other's dimensions remain opaque in their extension; one cannot apprehend, tame the Other.

Interestingly, in *Summertime*, as Margot questions Coetzee on his usage of the Khoi language, his reply is that such language can only be discerned through "grammars put together by missionaries in the old days. There are no speakers of Khoi languages left, not in South Africa. The languages are, for all practical purposes, dead" (S, 103). Writing then may enable a relation to the Other, but it remains a translation, different from the speech of the Other.

Coetzee's concern over white writing's relation to the usurpation of the racialised Other's voice, and an ethical impetus towards preserving its possible surprise by not assuming a more direct representation, presents also the acknowledgement of resistance by the racialised Other. The boy's internalised notion regarding those who have a right to the land is already a by-product of observation and an interest in going outside the finely defined parameters of *apartheid*'s inculcation of racial norms. The land belongs to Natives and Coloureds, with white people not considered as probable candidates. Yet, this is not based on an appreciation of African masculinity as intrinsically virile or violent. Rather, the racialised Other's masculinity is lauded not as a site of domination but that of a profound ethical relation with the land, a more contemplative, knowing outlook on the vicissitudes of life as a South African.

Notes

1. John Darwin, *After Tamerlane: The Rise & Fall of Global Empires, 1400–2000* (London: Penguin, 2008 [2007]), 51.
2. Eventually renamed *Cabo da Boa Esperança* [*Cape of Good Hope*] by King D. João II of Portugal, for the promising possibility of reaching India.
3. The rounding of the Cape was deemed a great achievement due to the roughness of the voyage. The Cape represented the point of access, or barrier, to further exploits in the Eastern world. As Anthony Parr considers, "just as America was initially perceived as a barrier to Europe's westward attempts on the Orient, so Africa represented an obstacle in the other direction" (105). The ambitions to surpass the Cape, presented as obstacle, a closed gate to the Eastern world, would come to be depicted in quite visual terms in the Martellus map in 1489, where the tip of Africa breaks the map's border. "To show Africa breaking the map frame," considers Parr, "is a symbolic statement that the continent is not confined to the *oikumene* [the known world], but it also suggests that Dias's voyage is a kind of transgression whose implications are not yet understood" (109). Anthony Parr, "Inventions of Africa," in *T'kama-Adamastor: Inventions of Africa in a South African Painting*, ed. Ivan Vladislavić (Johannesburg: University of the Witwatersrand, 2000), 99–109.
4. Robert Ross, *A Concise History of South Africa*, 2nd ed. (Cambridge: Cambridge University Press, 2008 [1999]), 22.
5. See Ross, *A Concise History of South Africa*, 22. Still regarding this event, South African President Thabo Mbeki, in a speech signalling the retirement of Nelson Mandela, would place the former president in a line of resistance whose ancient status would lead to the Khoikhoi victory over Dom Francisco Almeida. See David Johnson, "Remembering the Khoikhoi Victory over Dom Francisco Almeida at the Cape in 1510," *Postcolonial Studies* 12, no. 1 (2009): 107–30.
6. Michael Chapman, *Southern African Literatures* (Scottsville: University of Natal Press, 2003), 75.
7. A dichotomy celebrated and rigidified by the introduction, in the Renaissance, of the word "cannibal," "usually asserting the superiority of Christian Europe as well as legitimating violence against the indigenous inhabitants to which the European colonisers laid claim." See Shankar Raman, *Renaissance Literature and Postcolonial Studies* (Edinburgh: Edinburgh University Press, 2011), 26.
8. Homer, *The Odyssey*, trans. Walter Shewring (Oxford: Oxford University Press, 2008), 103.
9. Malvern Van Wyk Smith, "Shades of Adamastor: The Legacy of *The Lusiads*," in *The Cambridge History of South African Literature*, ed. David Attwell and Derek Attridge (Cambridge: Cambridge University Press, 2012), 118.
10. Homer, *The Odyssey*, 1.
11. Herodotus, *The Histories*, trans. Robin Waterfield (Oxford: Oxford University Press, 1998), 299.
12. Van Wyk Smith, *The Cambridge History of South African Literature*, 117.

13. "Seul, oisif, et toujours voisin du danger, l'homme Sauvage doit aimer à dormir, et avoir le sommeil léger comme les animaux, qui pensant peu, dorment, pour ainsi dire, tout le temps qu'ils ne pensent point." Jean-Jacques Rousseau, *Discours sur l'origine et les fondements de l'inegalité parmi les hommes* (Paris: Gallimard, 1969 [1754]), 70. Representations of the Hottentot in more aesthetically pleasant ways, being referred to as "children of nature" in the later eighteenth-century, would still reflect a paternalistic inflection at its core. See David Johnson, "French Representations of the Cape 'Hottentots': Jean Tavernier, Jean-Jacques Rousseau and François Levaillant," in *Imagining the Cape Colony: History, Literature, and the South African Nation* (Edinburgh: Edinburgh University Press, 2012), 35–63.

14. J. M. Coetzee, *White Writing: On the Culture of Letters in South Africa* (Braamfontein: Pentz Publishers, 2007 [1988]), 15.

15. "One of the many myths perpetuated in South African history held that colonists moved into an 'empy land'.... Clearly this served to legitimize the claims of whites to land occupation in a later period." See Nigel Worden, *The Making of Modern South Africa*, 5th ed. (Malden: Wiley-Blackwell, 2012 [1994]), 9.

16. Coetzee, *White Writing*, 2.

17. Africa as Europe's "*other* place" was constructed by "the rational, scientific observer mapping the territory, classifying the fauna and flora." See Chapman, *Southern African Literatures*, 75.

18. William J. Burchell, *Travels in the Interior of Southern Africa*, Volume I (London: Longman-Hurst-Rees-Orme and Brown, 1822), 178.

19. See William J. Burchell, *Hints on Emigration to the Cape of Good Hope* (London: J. Hatchard and Son, 1819), 17.

20. Ronald L. Jackson II and Murali Balaji, "Conceptualizing Current Discourses and Writing New Ones," in *Global Masculinities and Manhood*, ed. Ronald L. Jackson II and Murali Balaji (Urbana and Chicago: University of Illinois Press, 2011), 18–19.

21. Stephen Frosh, "Psychoanalysis, Colonialism, Racism," *Journal of Theoretical and Philosophical Psychology* 33, no. 3 (2013): 149.

22. As J. C. Kannemeyer points out, Jacobus Coetsé "is descended from a different line to that of J. M. Coetzee". See J. M. *Coetzee: A Life in Writing*, trans. Michiel Heyns (Johannesburg and Cape Town: Jonathan Ball Publishers, 2012), 20.

23. J. M. Coetzee, *Dusklands* (London: Vintage, 2004 [1974]), 80.

24. David Attwell, J. M. *Coetzee: South Africa and the Politics of Writing* (Berkeley: University of California Press, 1993), 36.

25. Coetzee, *Dusklands*, 79.

26. Coetzee, *Dusklands*, 79–80.

27. Coetzee, *Dusklands*, 106.

28. As stated by Albert Memmi: "On se plaît encore quelquefois à représenter le colonisateur comme un homme de grande taille, bronzé par le soleil, chaussé de demi-bottes, appuyé sur une pelle—car il ne dédaigne pas de mettre la main à l'ouvrage, fixant son regard au loin sur l'horizon de ses terres; entre deux actions contre la nature, il se prodigue aux hommes,

soigne les malades, et répand la culture, un noble aventurier enfin, un pionnier." See *Portrait du Colonisé/Portrait du Colonisateur* (Paris: Gallimard, 1985 [1957]), 29.

29. As Stephen Frosh argues, a purely psychological notion of racism is untenable. Instead, Frosh advances a psychosocial theory of racism, according to which "what is supposedly 'inside' does not stay there but leaks out and finds its place among networks of identification and relationality that are organized socially. These are also part of the "self": racist ideation is intense precisely because it is felt. The meaning of a 'social subject' is located here: each subject is constructed in and by the demands of (colonial) society, of course acting upon it in its own way, but nevertheless riven by it and inconceivable without it." "Psychoanalysis, Colonialism, Racism," 150.

30. Coetzee, *Dusklands*, 106.

31. Coetzee, *Dusklands*, 79.

32. Jessica Benjamin, *Shadow of the Other: Intersubjectivity and Gender in Psychoanalysis* (New York: Routledge, 1998), namely 86–87.

33. Coetzee, *Dusklands*, 81.

34. "For, in fashioning the thing, the bondsman's own negativity, his being-for-self, becomes an object for him only through his setting at nought the existing *shape* confronting him. But this objective *negative* moment is none other than the alien being before which it has trembled. Now, however, he destroys this alien negative moment, posits *himself* as a negative in the permanent order of things, and thereby becomes *for himself*, someone existing on his own account. In the lord, the being-for-self is an 'other' for the bondsman, or is only *for* him [i.e. is not his own]; in fear, the being-for-self is present in the bondsman himself; in fashioning the thing, he becomes aware that being-for-self belongs to *him*, that he himself exists essentially and actually in his own right. The shape does not become something other than himself through being made external to him; for it is precisely this shape that is his pure being-for-self, which in this externality is seen by him to be the truth." G. W. F. Hegel, *Phenomenology of Spirit*, trans. A. V. Miller (Oxford: Oxford University Press, 1977 [1807]), 118.

35. Hegel, *Phenomenology of Spirit*, 111.

36. As indicated in Ryszard Kapuściński, *The Other* (London: Verso, 2008 [2006]).

37. Frantz Fanon, *Peau Noire, Masques Blancs* (Paris: Seuil, 1952), 88.

38. "Certains se mettront en tête de nous rappeler que la situation est à double sens. Nous répondons que c'est faux. Le Noir n'a pas de résistance ontologique aux yeux du Blanc." See Fanon, *Peau Noire*, 88–89.

39. J. M. Coetzee, "The Mind of Apartheid: Geoffrey Cronjé (1907–)," *Social Dynamics* 17, no. 1 (1991): 2.

40. See Stephen Frosh, "The Other," *American Imago* 59 (2002): 389–407.

41. Jessica Benjamin, *The Bonds of Love: Psychoanalysis, Feminism, and the Problem of Domination* (New York: Pantheon Books, 1988), 53.

42. Coetzee, "The Mind of Apartheid," 2.

43. Stephen Frosh, "Psychoanalysis, Colonialism, Racism," 150.

44. Margrit Shildrick, "The Self's Clean and Proper Body," in *Embodying the Monster: Encounters with the Vulnerable Self*, ed. Margrit Shildrick (London: Sage, 2002), 54.

45. Luís Vaz de Camões, *Os Lusíadas*, ed. Emanuel Paulo Ramos (Porto: Porto Editora, 1996), 202.

46. Camões, *Os Lusíadas*, 204.

47. Camões, *Os Lusíadas*, 208.

48. Van Wyk Smith, *The Cambridge History of South African Literature*, 122.

49. Van Wyk Smith, *The Cambridge History of South African Literature*, 123.

50. Chapman, *Southern African Literatures*, 77. One of the more widely available uses of the Adamastor *Leitmotiv* is André Brink's *The First Life of Adamastor*. In this work the author questions the nature of the force behind Camões's concoction of the giant, advancing, for the sake of his novel, the following hypothesis: "Suppose there *were* an Adamastor, a model for the giant of Camoens' fanciful history; and suppose that original creature, spirit, or whatever he may have been, had survived through the centuries in a series of disparate successive avatars in order to continue watching over the Cape of Storms: how would *he* look back, from the perspective of the late twentieth century, on that original experience?" *The First Life of Adamastor* (London: Vintage, 2000 [1993]), 7.

51. In his 1917 *Introductory Lectures to Psycho-Analysis*, Freud would claim the legacy of radical disruption of the prevailing notion of human centeredness, in alluding to the works of both Copernicus and Darwin: "But human megalomania will have suffered its third and most wounding blow from the psychological research of the present time, which seeks to prove to the ego that it is not even master in its own house, but must content itself with scanty information of what is going on unconsciously in its mind. We psychoanalysts were not the first and not the only ones to utter this call to introspection; but it seems to be our fate to give it its most forcible expression and to support it with empirical material which affects every individual." "Introductory Lectures on Psycho-Analysis," in *The Standard Edition of the Complete Psychological Works of Sigmund Freud, Volume XVI (1916–1917): Introductory Lectures on Psycho-Analysis (Part III)* (London: Vintage, 1975 [1917]), 285.

52. A definition of the unconscious is found in Freud's *The Ego and the Id*, as a series of "very powerful psychic processes or notions … all of which can have a considerable effect on the subject's inner life, just like any other notions, but which themselves remain unconscious even though their *effects* may in turn become conscious as notions." *The Ego and the Id*, trans. John Reddick (London: Penguin, 2003 [1923]), 106.

53. As Tony Thwaites argues: "What psychoanalysis talks about is something that spills over its apparent boundaries: what seems to be internal is already out there in the world, and whatever is external stands to be already there deep within.… In that spilling-out and in the development of a logic that can describe it, psychoanalysis provides a framework rather different from those of the empirical human sciences of psychology and sociology. It offers ways of thinking not just of the individual, but of those dimensions which are always intimately part of the individual, though they incessantly spill over those boundaries into questions of the social, and the cultural, and the ideological. This is not even strictly speaking a matter of examining how the individual and the social are connected, for that would imply an initial separation which is then overcome. With psychoanalysis, it is a matter of thinking through how the human subject is always and already in the world, from the very outset." *Reading Freud: Psychoanalysis as Cultural Theory* (London: Sage, 2007), 3.

54. Julia Kristeva, *Étrangers à Nous-Mêmes* (Paris: Gallimard, 1988), 283–84.

55. Mtutuzeli Matshoba would be involved in the rising Black Consciousness movement in the early 1970s, his work being central in depicting black social conditions during *apartheid*. For further contextualisation, see Kelwyn Sole, "Political Fiction, Representation and the Canon: The Case of Mtutuzeli Matshoba," *English in Africa* 28, no. 2 (2001): 101–21.

56. Mtutuzeli Matshoba, "Call Me not a Man," in *A Land Apart: A South African Reader*, ed. André Brink and J. M. Coetzee (London: Faber and Faber, 1986 [1979]), 94.

57. Jacobus Adriaan du Pisani, "Hegemonic Masculinity in Afrikaner Nationalist Mobilisation, 1934–48," in *Masculinities in Politics and War: Gendering Modern History*, ed. Stefan Dudink, Karen Hagemann, and John Tosh (Manchester: Manchester University Press, 2004), 166.

58. Robert Morrell, "Of Boys and Men: Masculinity and Gender in Southern African Studies," *Journal of Southern African Studies* 24, no. 4 (1998): 616.

59. Keith Breckenridge argues for the existence of an "aesthetics of violence" present in the South African landscape, namely in farms where virulent violence "that white farmers displayed, even in its most elaborately sadistic forms, was rationalised and motivated by the idea of the paternalism." "The Allure of Violence: Men, Race and Masculinity on the South African Goldmines, 1900–1950," *Journal of Southern African Studies* 24, no. 4 (1998): 672. The progressive deterioration of the economic position of working class white men in the early decades of the twentieth century implied that relations between white and black workers would be increasingly defined by violence in the underground mining industry. This would result in confrontations with heavily gendered dynamics, as Breckenridge further argues: "In some instances, also, what was clearly intended as taxonomic violence, with white supervisors beating generic black subordinates, dissolved into dramatic dyadic encounters that could only be resolved by both parties agreeing to recognise each other as men" (673).

60. Amal Treacher Kabesh, *Postcolonial Masculinities: Emotions, Histories and Ethics* (Farnham, Surrey: Ashgate, 2013), 86.

61. Such affirmation espouses Levinasian ethics: "Autrui s'impose comme une exigence qui domine cette liberté et, dès lors, comme plus originelle que tout ce qui se passe en moi. Autrui dont la présence exceptionnelle s'inscrit dans l'impossibilité éthique où je suis de le tuer, indique la fin des pouvoirs. Si je ne peux plus pouvoir sur lui, c'est qu'il déborde absolument toute idée que je peux avoir de lui." Emmanuel Levinas, *Totalité et Infini: Essai sur L'Extériorité* (Paris: Kluwer Academic, 2014 [1961]), 86.

62. Neil Lazarus, *The Postcolonial Unconscious* (Cambridge: Cambridge University Press, 2011), 145.

63. The deep silence, akin to a hum, that the boy experiences in the graveyard, echoes the ending of Coetzee's *Foe*: "His mouth opens. From inside him comes a slow stream, without breath, without interruption. It flows up through his body and out upon me; it passes through the cabin, through the wreck; washing the cliffs and shores of the island, it runs northward and southward to the ends of the earth. Soft and cold, dark and unending, it beats against my eyelids, against the skin of my face." J. M. Coetzee, *Foe* (London: Penguin, 2010 [1986]), 157.

64. Coetzee, *White Writing*, 83–84.
65. That is Michael K.'s insinuation, that the black man, in being treated as less than human, may serve only towards feeding the fantasy of a personal story strictly delineated in terms of absolute suffering: "I have become an object of charity, he thought. Everywhere I go there are people waiting to exercise their forms of charity on me....They want me to open my heart and tell them the story of a life lived in cages. They want to hear about all the cages I have lived in, as if I were a budgie or a white mouse or a monkey." J. M. Coetzee, *Life & Times of Michael K* (London: Vintage, 2004 [1983]), 181.
66. Richard Begam, "Silence and Mut(e)ilation: White Writing in J. M. Coetzee's *Foe*," *The South Atlantic Quarterly* 93, no. 1 (1994): 126.

· 6 ·

"SHADES AND SHADOWS OF LIFE"

Women in Dark Times

To rediscover that love was like suddenly being transported to a super-state of life. It was the point at which all personal love had died in them. It was the point at which there were no private hungers to be kissed, loved, adored. And yet there was a feeling of being kissed by everything: by the air, the soft flow of life, people's smiles and friendships; and, propelled forward by the acquisition of this vast and universal love, they had moved among men again and again and told them they loved them. That was the essential nature of their love for each other. It had included all mankind, and so many things could be said about it, but the most important was that it equalized all things and all men.

Bessie Head, *A Question of Power*

Hopeful States

"Is that the fate of all women who become mixed up with artists," wonders young John, "to have their worst or their best extracted and worked into fiction?" (Y, 11). As already advanced, Coetzee understands white writing to be in tense relation with a responsability towards the representation of the racialised Other. Yet, in the redrawn schematics of power of the new South Africa, present already in the social struggle that preceded it and gave it form, there would be other Others whose claims would find voice.

In particular, women would find how some promises, notwithstanding its precarious nature, could indeed be achieved, as the consequence of continued fight for their voices to be heard. Considering, however, the silences and exclusion permeating the polity when it comes to women's livelihoods, one can re-enact John's question: what, indeed, may be the fate of women, not only in fiction but in the wider field of politics?

Adressing the overall specificities of imperialism, Gayatri Spivak suggests that the repression originated by colonialism, with its being linked to patriarchy, produced the impossibility for the subaltern's voice to be heard.[1] Spivak's consideration of the silencing of women provides a meeting point for postcolonial and gender scholarship. In considering women as the subaltern of the subaltern, Spivak more clearly delineates such a situation in a revision of her 1988 essay:

> Within the effaced itinerary of the subaltern subject, the track of sexual difference is doubly effaced. The question is not of female participation in insurgency, or the ground rules of the sexual division of labor, for which there is "evidence". It is, rather, that, both as object of colonialist historiography and as subject of insurgency, the ideological construction of gender keeps the male dominant. If, in the contest of colonial production, the subaltern has no history and cannot speak, the subaltern as female is even more deeply in shadow.[2]

Spivak is clear on how gender hierarchy produces less space for the voices of women, with the correlate of men overspending their opportunity to speak— even those within radical, progressive, *milieux*.

Long before Spivak, the question of men's sovereignity was also placed by Simone de Beauvoir. Questioning the lack of reciprocity between the sexes, Beauvoir's thesis would enunciate the societal pressures on women:

> Certains passages de la dialectique par laquelle Hegel définit le rapport du maître à l'esclave s'appliqueraient bien mieux au rapport de l'homme à la femme. Le privilège du Maître, dit-il, vient de ce qu'il affirme l'Esprit contre la Vie par le fait de risquer sa vie: mais en fait l'esclave vaincu a connu ce même risque; tandis que la femme est originellement un existant qui donne la Vie et ne risque pas sa vie; entre le mâle et elle il n'y a jamais eu de combat; la définition de Hegel s'applique singulièrement à elle....En vérité les femmes n'ont jamais opposé aux valeurs mâles des valeurs femelles: ce sont des hommes désireux de maintenir les prérogatives masculines qui ont inventé cette division; ils n'ont prétendu créer un domaine féminin—règle de la vie, de l'immanence—que pour y enfermer la femme; mais c'est par-delà toute spécification sexuelle que l'existant cherche dans le mouvement de sa transcendance sa justification: la soumission même des femmes en est la preuve. Ce qu'elles revendiquent

aujourd'hui c'est d'être reconnues comme existants au même titre que les hommes et non de soumettre l'existence à la vie, l'homme à son animalité.[3]

Beauvoir thus considers that Hegel's moment of recognition is also the demand of women—to meet as equals and not be subsumed in the societally male-defined Self.

Further feminist scholarship would explore the dimensions and possibilities of this moment of recognition. In the work of Jessica Benjamin, domination arises from a Self-interested, careless use of the Other, in the sense that this Other exists only to the extent that the Self may be validated. "The master's denial of the other's subjectivity," argues Benjamin, "leaves him faced with isolation as the only alternative to being engulfed by the dehumanized other. In either case, the master is actually alone, because the person he is with is no person at all."[4]

In these readings of the Hegelian dialectic arises the possible easy temptation to comply relatedness with assimilation, where the Other is the same as the Self, and thus phagocyted in the benefit of the Self-system. Contrary to such a framework, Levinas would argue that ethics is the place where one is questioned by the Other:

> On appelle cette mise en question de ma spontanéité par la présence d'Autrui, éthique. L'étrangeté d'Autrui—son irréductibilité à Moi—à mes pensées et à mes possessions, s'accomplit précisément comme une mise en question de ma spontanéité, comme éthique.[5]

The violence of colonial and gender orders attests to an understanding whereby Otherness is simply digested to favour one's understanding of oneself and, consequently, of the world. As Spivak further argues, the rigid cultural positioning of coloniser and colonised imply the "general epistemic violence of imperialism, the construction of a self-immolating colonial subject for the glorification of the social mission of the coloniser,"[6] drawn as it is in heavily gendered modes.

This attention to the gendered Other would materialise in the attempts at writing women's history, a sisyphean task for a social group who, in Beauvoir's understanding, had no collective past to speak of, or the capacity to organise into a community of struggle.[7] Notwithstanding its occlusion of certain historical aspects, Beauvoir's thesis would, in delineating the modes of alienation imposed on women, make available the notion of History as a field of contested representations, criss-crossed with power and violence.[8]

On this matter, Robert Young provides the "evidence" of women's engagement with liberatory struggles, by considering how women often exploited prescribed gender notions to their advantage, making use of colonial authorities' demeaning prejudice towards them.[9] Seen as non-threatening by authorities, women would, in the context of liberatory struggles, oftentimes perform the tasks that men couldn't.

In terms of the specificities of South African politics, the 1913 Bloemfontein campaign organised by women against residential passes would come to occupy a prevalent place in women's struggle for freedom.[10] Protesting against state-mandated passes, hundreds of women marched into the centre of town, clearly defying institutionalised norms by tearing their passes in front of the police. This event would illustrate not only to the state, but also to African men and white women, that black women could organise themselves in quite effective ways. Black women would also introduce their passive resistance practices into the African political community, derived from the teachings of Mahatma Gandhi.[11] In 1954, the Federation of South African Women, an organisation for all women, was created, and in 1956 "thousands of women marched on Pretoria to once more protest passes for women and the Women's Charter was formed."[12] The Charter would prove instrumental in influencing future documents in terms of women's equality.

White women, notwithstanding possible sympathies towards the specificities of black women's social predicaments, occupied a particularly ambiguous position in terms of power. "Barred from the corridors of formal power," and bound by a series of laws prescribed by men, white women however occupied places of power over colonised women and men. As such, "white women were not the hapless onlookers of empire but were ambiguously complicit both as colonizers and colonized, privileged and restricted, acted upon and acting."[13]

In a passage in *Boyhood*, a moment is described when, after the visit of a Coloured man, a discussion arises on what to do with the tea service that has been used. The contact with the Other, namely with the body of the racialised Other, is mediated by repulsion. "The custom, it appears, is that after a person of colour has drunk from a cup the cup must be smashed….However, in the end his mother simply washes the cup with bleach." (*B*, 157), the scene revealing the power of the white woman regarding the racialised Other, while at the same time indicating the possibility to disrupt further offense.[14]

In her 1974 novel *A Question of Power*, South African writer Bessie Head provides a compelling description of the difficult relation between women of different social backgrounds:

Elizabeth put the pie-dish on the sink and said, half-laughingly, half-vehemently: "Am I always in her company, or is she always in mine? The silly thing has so many false assumptions about life. I've never been able to get in a word about not liking her. She's stone-deaf and blind. She takes the inferiority of the black man so much for granted that she thinks nothing of telling us straight to our faces we are stupid and don't know anything. There's so many like her. They don't see the shades and shadows of life on black people's faces.[15]

In the above passage, Elizabeth, Head's protagonist, in a moment of frustration over her dealings with Danish aid worker Camilla, addresses how women may themselves reproduce inequality, through the perpetuation of stereotypes and a condescending attitude, based on the inability to understand the Other through more complex schematics.

Elizabeth's frustration with Camilla re-activates the South African colour barriers: "It was like living with permanent nervous tension, because you did not know why white people there had to go out of their way to hate you or loathe you. They were just born that way, hating people, and a black man or woman was just born to be hated."[16]

As Ronit Frenkel argues, colonial discourse's logic, with its binary system encompassing the division between coloniser and colonised, is actualised into *apartheid* discourse, with the formation of the different racial taxonomies, while partaking in patriarchal logic, through the dismissal of women as fragile, docile and sexually available.[17]

Facing this, post-*apartheid* South Africa, in its newfound vocabulary of amnesty and forgiveness, would come to inquire, with renewed force, the issues pertaining to responsibility and how—or if—historical culpability could be addressed: through the mode of confrontation or accommodation.[18] White writers, in dealing with the troubled past, would come to understand with pressing urgency the need to provide an answer to Breyten Breytenbach's question, found in his prison account of *apartheid* time: "But what does one do if you are White, if in fact you are part of the privileged minority in power?"[19]

Recuperating the theme of who may speak for whom, Linda Martín Alcoff suggests that, while such practices are irredeemably interconnected with suspicion, privilege and other aspects, it remains important to consider the consequences of such actions: "Will it enable the empowerment of oppressed peoples?"[20] In this vein, it is *apropos* to indicate how, in Coetzee's work, alongside the many silences and textual oversights, women occupy a central role in terms of, in Spivak's reasoning, the creation of an alternative to the Self that seeks to validate the codes of colonialism as universal.[21]

Poetesses of Interiority

Towards the end of *Boyhood*, young John's Oedipal rivalry presents a dark turn. His father, experienced as an outsider in his own house, an unwelcome presence in the domain of the young king, is contemplated in a decidedly negative fashion:

> His father is wearing pyjama pants and a cotton singlet. He has not shaved. There is a red V at his throat where sunburn gives way to the pallor of his chest. Beside the bed is a chamber-pot in which cigarette-stubs float in brownish urine. He has not seen anything uglier in his life. There are no pills. The man is not dying, merely sleeping. He does not have the courage to take sleeping-pills, just as he does not have the courage to go out and look for a job. (*B*, 159)

Contrary to this representation of the depressed father unable to provide for his family—a telling subversion of the mainstream account of gendered roles within *apartheid* time—, the mother is experienced as endlessly sacrificing herself towards the betterment of the family's situation: "She wants to sacrifice herself for her children.... But once she has sacrificed herself entirely, once she has sold the clothes off her back, sold her very shoes, and is walking around on bloody feet, where will that leave him?" (*B*, 158).

His mother's determined stance on her own sacrifice, in order to protect her children and, one may suggest, her husband, is the account of everyday sacrifice, extraordinary in its enactment, clear in its goals. In Jacques Derrida's terms, it may be considered as a kind of sacrifice on which society depends in order to reproduce itself.[22] An illustrated example of how society oftentimes demands work from groups who are otherwise marginalised is provided by Anne McClintock, while discussing popular imagery:

> Like white women, Africans (both women and men) are figured not as historic agents but as frames for the commodity, valued for *exhibition* alone. The working women, both black and white, who spent vast amounts of energy bleaching the white sheets, shirts, frills, aprons, cuffs and collars of imperial clothes are nowhere to be seen.[23]

John's mother's scene of sacrifice indicates also the woman's agency as labourer: "To tide them over until his father's new law practice begins to bring in money, his mother returns to teaching" (*B*, 151). Characteristic of a negative portrayal of the patriarch, the father is said to be "a child when it comes to money" (*B*, 154), and is eventually rescued in his debts by an Aunt Girlie, not without an ultimatum: he is to cease his law practice, an action confirmed in *Summertime*, as the father has opted for a bookkeeping job (*S*, 255).

Yet, tellingly, observing the downtrodden father is experienced as a shameful situation: "he wishes he were not here, witnessing the shame" (*B*, 160). Shame as the prevailing inscription in Coetzee's work goes to a great extent of providing a possible answer on its inability to portray explicit politics. As Señor C in *Diary of a Bad Year* argues, "the generation of white South Africans to which I belong, and the next generation, and perhaps the generation after that too, will go bowed under the shame of the crimes that were committed in their name."[24]

Regardless of the level of individual commitment to the crimes of humanity, such crimes will take hold in the children of those who draw some benefit, or continuous privilege from it. This is a thesis derived from *Dusklands*'s first novella, *The Vietnam War*, where protagonist Eugene Dawn, much like Jacobus Coetzee, actualises a mediation with the Other through the means of destruction, but with a more obvious sexual inflection, enacted in voyeuristic terms for a massified televised audience: "If spraying does not give the orgasm of the explosion (nothing has done more to sell the war to America than televised napalm strikes), it will always be more effective than high explosive in a campaign against the earth."[25]

The mediatised conflict generates not only support. Propaganda works as a stimulus for a nation to remain in war, but it also deteriorates human hearts in the process: "When I think of the heart that holds my secret I think of something closed and wet and black, like, say, the ball in the toilet cistern.... Guilt is a black poison.... Guilt was entering our homes through the TV cables."[26]

The warring nation then loses in the process of warfare its future, through the dehumanisation of children. The burden of violence, as enacted through guilt, generates a cross-generational traumatic experience. If "the father is authority, infallibility, ubiquity,"[27] such omnipotence is self-destructive, as it bears its fanged marks in its young. Eugene's destructive behaviour towards his one child is the culmination of a process in which alternative masculinity is not to be found: "How loud must I shout, how wide with passion must my eyes glare, how must my hands shake before he will believe that all is for the best, that I love him with a father's love, that I desire only that he should grow to be what I am not, a happy man?"[28]

Shame and guilt appear as *Leitmotiv* in Coetzee's work, as the assumed inevitable conditions of those who are embroiled in the business of war and colonisation. Eugene's guilt may be understood within the scope of the shame exhibited by the white writer in colonial settings. As indicated in the chapter "Art of One," Coetzee's work exhibits the shame of the privileged and, recalling Timothy Bewes's assertion, "the impossibility, even the obscenity, of a literary response to *apartheid*."[29]

According to Sara Ahmed, shame arises when "*the badness of an action is tranferred to me*, such that I feel myself to be bad and to have been 'found' or 'found out' as bad by others."[30] Shame possesses a narcissistic quality,[31] an emotion to be triggered in relation to others, when ideals are perceived to have been unmet. On the other hand, guilt is introjected, a perceived failure in attending to norms, rules, or prohibitions.[32] Guilt arises from a perceived possibility of having done harm to, or projecting harm towards, someone else. As Martha Nussbaum considers, "guilt focuses on an action (or a wish to act)," and already "recognises the rights of others," by aiming at a "restoration of the wholeness of the separate object or person."[33] Guilt remains an important aspect, for its reparatory motion, the possibility of acknowledging the aggression done to others, and the attempt at limiting the damage done.[34]

The white South African writer may not, however, be expiated of such a shameful state,[35] and, in this reading, Coetzee's work may very well be understood in a double mode: "both obligatory and reprehensible, impossible and inevitable,"[36] that is, shame is inescapable due to historical responsibility, with attempts to evade such shame proving even more shameful.

Such political stance necessarily informs the writing of the Other. In *Youth*, John wonders how the woman before him, in her nakedness, feels no shame. "Is it to taunt him," he wonders, "or do all nurses behave like this in private, dropping their clothes, scratching themselves, talking matter-of-factly about excretion, telling the same gross jokes that men tell in bars?" (Y, 14).

Tellingly, in Coetzee's novelistic work, Eugene Dawn and Jacobus Coetzee are superseded by Magda, the white Afrikaner woman in *In the Heart of the Country*. Located in an ambiguous geography and timeline, the narrative enacts the tense relations between subjugated identities, that of women and the black Other in a servant position. As Magda indicates, "I know nothing of Hendrik.... We have our places, Hendrik and I, in an old old code."[37]

Unlike Eugene or Jacobus, who seek to dominate the Other in order to create a sense of themselves, Magda develops a more sensitised philosophy of subjectivity, appropriately termed "the psychology of masters."[38] Such skills of observation enacted throughout a lifetime of isolation in the Afrikaner farm, conduct her to acknowledge her purported function in such a *milieu*: "Clenched beneath a pillow in a dim room, focussed on the kernel of pain, I am lost in the being of my being. This is what I was meant to be: a poetess of interiority, an explorer of the inwardness of stones, the emotions of ants, the consciousness of the thinking parts of the brain."[39]

Magda claims her powers over the poetry of inner life as a result of a cloistered existence. Such isolation from the tasks of labour, belonging as it does to the world of men, provide the use of observation as guide through such a life. Yet, this very quality is also found to be lacking, unsharpened as it is by the lack of worldly experience. Magda, it seems, can only acknowledge the conscious, rational parts of the brain, the suggestion being that there are other dimensions in existence, yet barred from comprehension.

Freud's linking of the psychoanalytic project with the decentring of human subjectivity based on the existence of the unconscious is again recaptured.[40] Coetzee may be read as indicating that Magda is in search of the unconscious, if by such a term we understand a quality that decentres the subject; and that the very process of the search for the unconscious, or unconscious elements, is all that one can really do: to suggest otherwise may be to continue on the direction of mastery over all elements.

In this vein, Magda is not so much barred from entering the unconscious. She is actually in the process of searching for its possible meanings, continually shaping them. Jean Laplanche considers such constant praxis as the only possible solution, itself always precarious and tense, of foregoing assimilation.[41] Magda wonders: "Is it possible that there is an explanation for all the things I do, and that that explanation lies inside me, like a key rattling in a can, waiting to be taken out and used to unlock the mystery?"[42] The question, itself mysterious, goes unanswered.

Thus, Eugene's grandiose ideal of "the self reading the self to the self in all infinity"[43] finds its disruption in gendered terms. Towards the end of the novella, Eugene ruminates on how "most of the trouble in my life has been caused by women,"[44] suggesting, however, more than simple blame. Women as outside the masculinised world of the military, the world of the authoritarian Father, are coded as the political alternative to such a masculine world bent on violence.

Magda as female narrator hosts a shift in narratorial voice within the work of Coetzee. One possible consequence of such shift is the introduction of greater ambivalence to the strict gendered system, previously organised in the language of omnipotence. Both Eugene and Jacobus partake in the authority of such system, whereas the white woman is located both inside and outside the privileged system of South African politics. Magda eventually recalls the masculine position of omnipotence—"What is there for me but dreary expansion to the limits of the universe?"[45]—, yet by being a woman such a place is never entirely hers to occupy.

Unlike Eugene and Jacobus, Magda possesses a greater understanding of the difficulties of constructing community and, by extension, the implications of a politics based on alternative. As Mike Marais argues, Magda's recognition of the coded interactions between master and slave as historically determined reveal her "dissatisfaction with the way in which her self has been defined by language."[46] Based as her relationship with Hendrik may be on old linguistic and behavouristic codes, there is an attempt at reforging such a framework, by acknowledging the suffering made upon others.

In seeking liberation, Coetzee's first female narrator allows the author to play more directly with the possibilities of madness as an alternative to current political systems, dominated by rationality; that is, madness in its literary form introduces an array of meanings and affects, namely in terms of the desire to shape the polity otherwise, that are not available to the vocabulary of the male coloniser.

By the novel's ending, Magda is visited by voices who demand her attention, and it is through these voices that the act of writing is made possible: "Her writing is her involuntary response to being visited by what is beyond her prisonhouse of language."[47] Through Magda, Coetzee expresses a more direct acknowledgement of the need for recognition as antidote for omnipotence, whereby the former may be understood in Coetzee's work as the capacity to not colonise the Other and subsume it into the Self. In this Other-led ethics, Magda recognises the centrality of the Other, the stranger whose presence disavows the centrality of the Self and disrupts the possibility of completion.[48] Yet, in true Coetzeean fashion, this movement towards recognition is never entirely resolved, hinting not only towards the metaphysical implications of the impossibility of bridging the gap between Self and Other to a point where the latter is assimilated into the former, but more poignantly insisting on the inviolable nature of South African politics during *apartheid*, directed as they were to the centrality of the hermetic Self.

Breytenbach's poignant question on the role of the privileged writer in South Africa may be actualised by employing Jacqueline Rose's reading of Coetzee's work. In Rose's account, and through her reading of *Disgrace*, an ethical question arises: "How do you get from dissociation, a consciously or unconsciously willed refusal to connect to the horrors going on around you, a drastic failure of historical imagination as we might call it, to empathy."[49] In a sense, the question may be posed as follows: how can a political project start being designed that purports to provide a language that may understand the urgency of Bessie Head's paradigmatic notion of "the shades and shadows of life"?

According to Laura Wright, it is the female narrators in Coetzee's work that allow the author to enter, in somewhat of a more direct way, the arena of the political.[50] By voicing women, and directing something of an imaginary and literary tranvestism—clearer as one advances in Coetzee's career, namely in the Elizabeth Costello character and the voluntary confusion between character and author—,[51] Coetzee is already engaging in a reshaping of authority, dismissing the masculine voice as purportedly unique. The powerful combination of guilt and shame, among other "ugly feelings,"[52] require "an art of engagement" with the surprise and mystery that form the Other.[53]

Some of these hard-learned lessons would seep into young John, as he feels embarassed in being referred to as "the little master" by Tryn, the house servant.[54] The megalomania of the *enfant terrible* bears also some degree of sophistication through being visited by the call for the Other's subjectivity. As a product of the sympathetic author, John is also Magda's heir.

Disputing the Story

With more than a hint of frustration, in *The Story of an African Farm*, Olive Schreiner's heroine Lyndall surmises the ways of the world in terms of the relations between men and women:

> We all enter the world little plastic beings, with so much natural force, perhaps, but for the rest— blank; and the world tells us what we are to be, and shapes us by the ends it sets before us. To you it says—*Work*; and to us it says—*Seem*! To you it says—As you approximate to man's highest ideal of God, as your arm is strong and your knowledge great, and the power to labour is with you, so shall you gain all that human heart desires. To us it says—Strength shall not help you, nor knowledge, nor labour. You shall gain what men gain, but by other means. And so the world makes men and women.[55]

Set in the 1860s, Schreiner's novel would exhibit the tensions in terms of the changing sexual mores of the late Victorian period. Equally, and as described by Coetzee himself, it would assume a central place in the tradition of the *plaasroman*.[56] While purporting to advance women's rights, by questioning their place in society, and the inherent injustice of pre-formulated societal designations given according to one's sex, *The Story of an African Farm* would exhibit the historical limitations of its time, as evidenced by the lack of sympathetic imagination in representing the dispossessed racialised Other.

In this cultural mould, some of the future white writers in South Africa would find the need to improve on their sympathetic imagination, *via* Schreiner, while acknowledging the existence of inherited silences. These heirs would come to understand the lack of easy political solutions, as it is reflected in Amal Treacher Kabesh's felicitous argument: "alongside more welcome understanding, there exists the knowledge of how aggressive, weak, vulnerable, frail, envious, full of the desire to obliterate self and others we can be."[57] In Coetzee's case, this would intimate the continuous, painful seeking of a framework that could eventually comply with the notion of the meeting of selves as presupposing an Encounter where both are mutually shaped, challenged and, hopefully, changed—that is, rewritten.

Women's speech, for the most part left unvoiced in more public spheres, need not say anything conclusive in terms of an essentialistic lack of agency on women's part, as a telling passage in *Boyhood* may suggest:

> It is the same in the kitchen. There are two women who work in the kitchen: Ros's wife Tryn, and Lientjie, his daughter from another marriage. They arrive at breakfast-time and leave after the midday meal, the main meal of the day, the meal that is here called dinner. So shy is Lientjie of strangers that she hides her face and giggles when spoken to. But if he stands at the kitchen door he can hear, passing between his aunt and the two women, a low stream of talk that he loves to eavesdrop on: the soft, comforting gossip of women, stories passed from ear to ear to ear, till not only the farm but the village at Fraserbug Road and the location outside the village are covered by the stories, and all the other farms of the district too: a soft white web of gossip spun over past and present, a web being spun at the same moment in other kitchens too, the Van Rensburg kitchen, the Alberts kitchen, the Nigrini kitchen, the various Botes kitchens: who is getting married to whom, whose mother-in-law is going to have an operation for what, whose son is doing well at school, whose daughter is in trouble, who visited whom, who wore what when. (85)

In the above, women constitute the core of the community, as they weave their stories and share those across a multitude of spaces. This community is also interracial, a meeting of masters and servants, who in the everyday go beyond the institutionalised boundaries of *apartheid* by sharing knowledge.

In representing this scene, Coetzee is alluding to the promises of the women's movement in South Africa, based on "self-affirmation and collective purpose," and the hope of bridging the gap between black and white women.[58]

At work is a strange element, apparently absent in the narratives of men: the latter seems singular, whereas the weaving of women's storytelling, composed of multiple aspects and covering a great deal of terrain, seems the stuff of intertextuality. Such a reading, to a certain point perhaps too general, may still see its merits if we understand, following Spivak, fiction and ethics as continuous tasks rather than clearly delineated events.[59] Intertextuality, in this particular sense, comprises the formations of texts and their reproduction in terms that, through their combination, may well elude and confuse the dominant political *milieu*.

This community, however, is already necessarily the product of epistemic violence. Underground, these stories are only heard in whispers. Such narratives, telling as they are in their capacity to organise webbed relations, reflect the systemic violence that is at the core of their silencing.

A marked representation of such violence is of a sexual nature, as exemplified at the beggining of *Youth*: "It is a job that the regular librarians, women for the most part, prefer not to do because the campus, up on the mountainside, is too bleak and lonely at night" (Y, 1). Coetzee here indicates the continuous aspect of violence against women in South Africa. "Gender based violence," notes Pumla Gqola, "is everywhere, commonplace, made to seem normal."[60] Adhering to a "cult of femininity,"[61] Gqola argues, maintains alive the dichotomy of public and private spaces: so-called empowered women may act in the former, yet the latter remain ruled by conservative notions of livelihood.

As such, notwithstanding the celebrated inclusion of gender rights in the Constitution, beneath its "heroic façade," as Shireen Hassim argues, "a vicious cocktail of violence, sexism and hatred brewed."[62] Further commenting on this matter, Helen Moffett argues that such rights "were crafted in a country contending not only with a legacy of racism, but one of manifest sexism, homophobia and xenophobia."[63] From the farm to the university, from rural to urban sites, sexual aggression has been a part of the South African landscape in both the pre and post-*apartheid* periods, with Hassim noting how such violence is imbricated in gender formations; how it has been a "persistent feature of masculinity in South Africa."[64]

The trial case of President Jacob Zuma may be understood, in its theatrical quality, as embodying the tensions of purported tradition and modernity;

how the new South Africa still presents challenges in terms of its considerations over the availability of women's bodies, and notions of sexual consent. Of course, Coetzee would engage elsewhere, and to a certain extent, with such arguments, holding it as one of the central themes in *Disgrace* where, tellingly, both black and white men are found guilty, to a degree or other, of sexual violence.[65]

Naming violence becomes a central strategy for redrawing political maps. In the first dated fragment of the notebooks that serve as the beginning to *Summertime*, the now-deceased John considers the corruption of the Afrikaner community, the trivialisation of violence, drawn from the encapsulated living on which such a community is based. "These," he laments, "are the men under whose dirty thumb he lives!" (6).

Much like John's story is irredeemeably interconnected with the dirty thumbs of such men, so is his own story possible of being narrated through the site of the Other. This is Julia's argument, when pressed by the persistent curiosity of Vincent about the dead John: "Mr. Vincent, I am perfectly aware it is John you want to hear about, not me" (S, 43). But Julie's decision is to go down another path: she will tell her story, interconnected as it is with John's, yet remaining hers altogether:

> But the only story involving John that I can tell, or the only one I am prepared to tell, is this one, namely the story of my life and his part in it, which is quite different, quite another matter, from the story of his life and my part in it. My story, the story of me, began years before John arrived on the scene and went on for years after he made his exit. (S, 43)

Julia's story surpasses the desired object of inquiry, John, as he is but a "minor character" (S, 44) in her own story. The truth of John's life is withheld, simply because it can never be told in absolute ways. There is always something lacking, some part that Julia or others can never, could never, access. Equally, and recalling Magda's search for the unconscious, John himself would never be able to provide a strictly truthful account of himself. In this paradigm, the narrative suspects the truthful agent, quasi-omnipotent in its claim to accede to the totality of verifiable truth, instead acknowledging as it does how one is inescapably "marked by a secret that may not be a secret but cannot be unlocked."[66]

Out of the five interviewees for Vincent's biography of John, four are women, with Martin's interview being the shortest. Much like Martin discusses the feeling of the Afrikaner's misplacement in South Africa, so he, as a man, seems to be out of place in this narrative. In this, we may propose that Coetzee re-activates a certain identification with the lives of women, through an Other-led ethics, whereby the Other commands and such a summons cannot be denied.

Towards providing an account of the framework employed by Coetzee, we may briefly return to his concern over the attributes of the writer: "Writing is not free expression. There is a sense in which writing is dialogic: a matter of awakening the countervoices in oneself and embarking upon speech with them."[67]

Seeking to understand the dialogue between mind and world, a dialogue that is always preoccupied with the wider social forces, for it finds its formation there, Coetzee provides an account of a dialogical novel as "one in which there is no dominating, central authorial consciousness, and therefore no claim to truth or authority, only competing voices and discourses."[68]

The poignant theme is, then, the overall poor characterisation of John in *Summertime*. If in both *Boyhood* and *Youth* there are undercurrents of megalomania and attempts at holding omnipotence, the descriptions of John in *Summertime* are in general those referring to a failed man, with a clear emphasis on his inability to be with others. "No, of course John did not love his father, he did not love anybody, he was not built for love" (S, 48). Margot adds the personal note: "does not even love himself" (S, 142). Thus the confident man is not to be found in John, wrecked as he is with shame, as per Adriana's description:

> This man was disembodied. He was divorced from his body. To him, the body was like one of those wooden puppets that you move with strings. You pull this string and the left arm moves, you pull that string and the right leg moves. And the real self sits up above, where you cannot see him, like the puppet-master pulling the string. (S, 198)

The cloistered Self, the overgrown mask that hides one's humanity recalls Magda's predicament, and her critique of the perversity of the Afrikaner world, as well as the eventual inability to escape for lack of alternative.

Could the narrative be offering humanity as the sole site of the woman? Could these poetesses of interiority, at first a sympathetic gesture of the author, be essentialised in such a restricted role? The narrative seems to argue otherwise. While it is clear that there is an effort to abase the determination of the masculine Self—the white, Afrikaner masculine Self—women are also seen as critical of a purported privilege to interiority. Magda's descendants they may be—Julia and the others are, after all, Coetzee's characters, oftentimes voicing an agency regarding the troubled accounts of biographical writing—yet they demonstrate being dismissive of a purported role as prophets of humanity. As argued by Julia: "I never had the feeling that he was with *me*, me in all my reality. Rather, it was as if he was engaged with some erotic image of me inside his head; perhaps even with some image of Woman with a capital W" (*S*, 52).

In this passage, societal fantasies are recognised in their importance in terms of shaping relations. Per Julia, John would be too immersed in a overly fantasised notion of woman—Woman—, aspiring to the idealised, forgetting the human. "How could this man of yours be a great man when he was not human?... Why do you think I, as a woman, could not respond to him?", questions Adriana (*S*, 199).

Thus these women actualise Magda's significance in Coetzee's work. Heirs of Magda, Julia and the others are biting in their critique of hegemonic masculinity's perceived enactments, revealing the dour truth of such fantasies. Daughters of a new land, their critique of the "Wooden Man" (*S*, 200) reaches the public sphere, arguing that the task of emotional work may be culturally extended to men.

As argued by Zília Osório de Castro, the continuous work in the field of women's histories provides not only the necessary re-assessment of past struggles and ideals, but finds its most important conclusion in the promise that it makes to the future: "By drawing attention to women who lived as real beings and made a mark on their own societies, notwithstanding criticism and polemic, women of today are reminded that there is a space yet to be built and to occupy in the very societies that they live in" (our translation).[69]

They had, after all, been doing work for quite some time. Mostly in the shadows of History, often silenced, often denied. To recover such powers of sharing and owning stories, moulding them to build community, is to redraw the hope for a different world.

There is, however, still hope for men in the redrawing of such maps. Much like Magda, so does John understand the talk of ants. His mother's "ant-like determination" is something that he is "all too familiar with" (*B*, 158). In this sense, mutuality arises, for in the relation to the Other one can start to understand the finesse of feelings.

Yet such mutuality is often curtailed, denied in its emancipatory principles, as both child and adult man exhibit the contradictions of living in politically strenuous times that demand a mode of masculinity societally constructed in terms of diminishing the importance and agency of the Other. Recalling the wider political panorama of violence and struggle that continuously questions if the aspirations of Schreiner's Lyndall, of seeing a future where "to be born a woman will not be to be born branded,"[70] may yet see fruition, one could say that the dream of such non-branding persists, in an often cruel climate, with ant-like determination.

Notes

1. The term "subaltern," following Antonio Gramsci, has been employed to depict the groups that find themselves in an oppressed position in terms of power structures. The question is one of "voice," whether those that find themselves oppressed may speak though, as Spivak puts it, such discourse is never isolated from hegemony. See Gayatri Chakravorty Spivak, "Can the Subaltern Speak?," in Marxism and the Interpretation of Culture, ed. Cary Nelson and Lawrence Grossberg (London: Macmillan, 1988), 271–313.
2. Gayatri Chakravorty Spivak, A Critique of Postcolonial Reason: Toward a History of the Vanishing Present (Cambridge, MA: Harvard University Press, 1999), 274.
3. Simone de Beauvoir, Le Deuxième Sexe I (Paris: Gallimard, 1976 [1949]), 116–17.
4. Jessica Benjamin, The Bonds of Love: Psychoanalysis, Feminism, and the Problem of Domination (New York: Pantheon Books, 1988), 65.
5. Emmanuel Levinas, Totalité et Infini: Essai sur L'Extériorité (Paris: Kluwer Academic, 2014 [1961]), 33.
6. Gayatri Chakravorty Spivak, "Three Women's Texts and a Critique of Imperialism," Critical Inquiry 12, no. 1 (1985): 251.
7. "C'est qu'elles n'ont pas les moyens concrets de se rassembler en une unité qui se poserait en s'opposant. Elles n'ont pas de passé, d'histoire, de religion qui leur soit propre; et elles n'ont pas comme les prolétaires une solidarité de travail et d'intérêts; il n'y a pas même entre elles cette promiscuité spatiale qui fait des Noirs d'Amérique, des Juifs des ghettos, des ouvriers de Saint-Dennis ou des usines Renault une communauté." Simone de Beauvoir, Le Deuxième Sexe I, 21.
8. As argued in Mthunzi Zungu and others, "HERstory: Writing Women into South African History," Agenda 28, no. 1 (2014): 7–17.
9. Robert Young, Postcolonialism: An Historical Introduction (Oxford: Blackwell, 2001), 363.
10. As Cherryl Walker summarises: "This anti-pass campaign represents the first large-scale entry of black women, operating in terms of the modern (non-tribal) political structure in South Africa, into the political arena." Women and Resistance in South Africa, 2nd ed. (Claremont, South Africa: David Philip Publishers, 1991 [1982]), 32.
11. For a more detailed account of the event, see Julia C. Wells, "Why Women Rebel: A Comparative Study of South African Women's Resistance in Bloemfontein (1913) and Johannesburg (1958)," Journal of Southern African Studies 10, no. 1 (1983): 55–70.

12. Anne McClintock, *Imperial Leather: Race, Gender and Sexuality in the Colonial Contest* (New York and London: Routledge, 1995), 381.

13. McClintock, *Imperial Leather*, 6.

14. Georgina Horrell, "A Whiter Shade of Pale: White Femininity as Guilty Masquerade in 'New' (White) South African Women's Writing," *Journal of Southern African Studies* 30, no. 4 (2004): 765–76.

15. Bessie Head, *A Question of Power* (Johannesburg: Penguin, 2011 [1974]), 83.

16. Head, *A Question of Power*, 12.

17. Ronit Frenkel, "Feminism and Contemporary Culture in South Africa," *African Studies* 67, no. 1 (2008): 1–9.

18. Michiel Heyns, "The Whole Country's Truth: Confession and Narrative in Recent White South African Writing," *Modern Fiction Studies* 46, no. 1 (2000): 42–66.

19. Breyten Breytenbach, *The True Confessions of an Albino Terrorist* (London: Faber and Faber, 1984), 73.

20. Linda Martín Alcoff, "The Problem of Speaking for Others," in *Who Can Speak? Authority and Critical Identity*, ed. Judith Roof and Robyn Wiegman (Urbana and Chicago: University of Illinois Press, 1995), 116.

21. Gayatri Chakravorty Spivak, "Theory in the Margin: Coetzee's *Foe* Reading Defoe's *Crusoe/Roxana*," *English in Africa* 17, no. 2 (1990): 5.

22. Derrida's example is of the millions of children that die of hunger and disease "without any moral or legal tribunal ever being considered competent to judge such a sacrifice, the sacrifice of others to avoid being sacrificed oneself. Not only is it true that such a society participates in this incalculabe sacrifice, it actually organizes it. The smooth functioning of its economic, political, and legal affairs, the smooth functioning of its moral discourse and good conscience presupposes the permanent operation of this sacrifice." *The Gift of Death*, trans. David Wills (Chicago: Chicago University Press, 1995), 86.

23. McClintock, *Imperial Leather*, 223.

24. J. M. Coetzee, *Diary of a Bad Year* (London: Vintage, 2008 [2007]), 44.

25. J. M. Coetzee, *Dusklands* (London: Vintage, 2004 [1974]), 29.

26. Coetzee, *Dusklands*, 48.

27. Coetzee, *Dusklands*, 21.

28. Coetzee, *Dusklands*, 38.

29. Timothy Bewes, "The Event of Shame in J. M. Coetzee," in *The Event of Postcolonial Shame* (Princeton: Princeton University Press, 2010), 138.

30. Sara Ahmed, "Shame Before Others," in *The Cultural Politics of Emotion*, 2nd ed., ed. Sara Ahmed (Edinburgh: Edinburgh University Press, 2014 [2004]), 105.

31. As Jeff McMahan argues, shame "requires the presence, or at least the imagined presence, of observers." "Torture and Collective Shame," in *J. M. Coetzee and Ethics*, ed. Anton Leist and Peter Singer (New York: Columbia University Press, 2010), 90.

32. See Adriaan van Heerden, "Disgrace, Desire, and the Dark Side of the New South Africa," in *J. M. Coetzee and Ethics*, 44–63.

33. Martha C. Nussbaum, "Inscribing the Face: Shame and Stigma," in *Hiding from Humanity: Disgust, Shame, and the Law*, ed. Martha C. Nussbaum (Princeton: Princeton University Press, 2004), 207.

34. Martha C. Nussbaum, *Upheavals of Thought: The Intelligence of Emotions* (Cambridge: Cambridge University Press, 2001), namely 206–24.

35. See Isidore Diala, "Nadine Gordimer, J. M. Coetzee, and Andre Brink: Guilt, Expiation, and the Reconciliation Process in Post-Apartheid South Africa," *Journal of Modern Literature* XXV, no. 2 (2002): 50–68.

36. Bewes, *The Event of Postcolonial Shame*, 150.

37. J. M. Coetzee, *In the Heart of the Country* (London: Vintage, 2004 [1977]), 27.

38. Coetzee, *In the Heart of the Country*, 36.

39. Coetzee, *In the Heart of the Country*, 38.

40. As Freud acknowledges in the initial section of *The Ego and the Id*, the notion of a human psychology that would not be defined in its entirety by conscious processes, but rather would also encompass unconscious ones, would be sure to meet with derision: "The division of the psychic realm into the conscious and the unconscious is the fundamental premiss of psychoanalysis; it alone enables psychoanalysis to understand the pathological processes that are such a common and important feature of psychic life, and to offer a systematic scientific account of them....To most people whose education is grounded in philosophy, the idea of a psychic realm that is not also a *conscious* one is so incomprehensible as to seem an absurdity easily refuted by plain, straightforward logic." *The Ego and the Id*, trans. John Reddick (London: Penguin, 2003 [1923]), 105.

41. "The permanence of the unconscious, the primacy of the address of the other—one of the functions of analysis is to uphold these truths, and it is the duty of the analyst to guarantee them the respect which is their due." Jean Laplanche, *New Foundations for Psychoanalysis*, trans. David Macey (Oxford: Basil Blackwell, 1989), 85.

42. Coetzee, *In the Heart of the Country*, 67.

43. Coetzee, *Dusklands*, 38.

44. Coetzee, *Dusklands*, 44.

45. Coetzee, *In the Heart of the Country*, 81.

46. Mike Marais, *Secretary of the Invisible: The Idea of Hospitality in the Fiction of J. M. Coetzee* (Amsterdam: Rodopi, 2009), 19.

47. Marais, *Secretary of the Invisible*, 24.

48. As Stephen Frosh argues: "We do not know the other; we know the other only as a subject we cannot fully know." "The Relational Ethics of Conflict and Identity," *Psychoanalysis, Culture & Society* 16, no. 3 (2011): 229.

49. Jacqueline Rose, "Apathy and Accountability: The Challenge of South Africa's Truth and Reconciliation Commission to the Intellectual in the Modern World," in *Not Being Able to Sleep: Psychoanalysis and the Modern World*, ed. Jacqueline Rose (London: Vintage, 2004), 233–34.

50. Laura Wright, "Displacing the Voice: South African Feminism and JM Coetzee's Female Narrators," *African Studies* 67, no. 1 (2008): 13.

51. As argued in Lucy Graham, "Textual Transvestism: The Female Voices of J. M. Coetzee," in *J. M. Coetzee and the Idea of the Public Intellectual*, ed. Jane Poyner (Ohio: Ohio University Press, 2006), 217–35.

52. Rita Barnard, "Ugly Feelings, Negative Dialectics: Reflections on Postapartheid Shame," *Safundi: The Journal of South African and American Studies* 13, no. 1–2 (2012): 151–70.

53. Amal Treacher Kabesh, *Postcolonial Masculinities: Emotions, Histories and Ethics* (Farnham, Surrey: Ashgate, 2013), 126.

54. As referenced by Rita Barnard, "Coetzee in/and Afrikaans," *Journal of Literary Studies* 25, no. 4 (2009): 95.

55. Olive Schreiner, *The Story of an African Farm* (Oxford: Oxford University Press, 1998 [1883]), 154–55.

56. See J. M. Coetzee, *White Writing: On the Culture of Letters in South Africa* (Braamfontein: Pentz Publishers, 2007 [1988]).

57. Amal Treacher Kabesh, "Something in the Air: Otherness, Recognition and Ethics," *Journal of Social Work Practice* 20, no. 1 (2006): 36.

58. Cherry Clayton, "Radical Transformations: Emergent Women's Voices in South Africa," *English in Africa* 17, no. 2 (1990): 27.

59. As argued in Gayatri Chakravorty Spivak, "Ethics and Politics in Tagore, Coetzee, and Certain Scenes of Teaching," in *An Aesthetic Education in the Era of Globalization*, ed. Gayatri Chakravorty Spivak (Cambridge, MA: Harvard University Press, 2012), 331.

60. Pumla Dineo Gqola, "How the 'Cult of Femininity' and Violent Masculinities Support Endemic Gender Based Violence in Contemporary South Africa," *African Identities* 5, no. 1 (2007): 118.

61. Gqola, "How the 'Cult of Femininity,'" 116.

62. Shireen Hassim, "Democracy's Shadows: Sexual Rights and Gender Politics in the Rape Trial of Jacob Zuma," *African Studies* 68, no. 1 (2009): 57. See also the argument advanced in "Fathers of the Nation" on the relation between the trial and a defense based on traditional values regarding black masculinity.

63. Helen Moffett, "'These Women, They Force Us to Rape Them': Rape as Narrative of Social Control in Post-Apartheid South Africa," *Journal of Southern African Studies* 32, no. 1 (2006): 142.

64. Hassim, "Democracy's Shadows," 66.

65. As argued in Lucy Valerie Graham, "Reading the Unspeakable: Rape in J. M. Coetzee's *Disgrace*," *Journal of Southern African Studies* 29, no. 2 (2003): 433–44.

66. Spivak, "Theory in the Margin," 16.

67. J. M. Coetzee, *Doubling the Point*, ed. David Attwell (Cambridge, MA: Harvard University Press, 1992 [1986]), 65. Writing as dialogic echoes Mikhail Bakhtin's philosophical work, namely his exploration of the dialogic in Dostoyevsky's work, the former considering that the latter was one of the writers who most precisely understood the need to introduce a non-authorial control over his creations. Mikhail Bakhtin, *Problems of Dostoyevsky's Poetics*, trans. Caryl Emerson (Minneapolis: University of Minnesota Press, 1984).

68. J. M. Coetzee, "Dostoyevsky: The Miraculous Years," in *Stranger Shores: Essays 1986–1999*, ed. J. M. Coetzee (London: Vintage, 2001), 144.

69. Zília Osório de Castro, "Nota de Abertura," *Faces de Eva. Estudos sobre a Mulher* 30 (2013): 6.

70. Schreiner, *The Story of an African Farm*, 154.

· 7 ·

QUEER OTHER

We have so much to learn from each other. There are better ways, they keep telling
me, capitalism is not the only way. We haven't nearly exhausted all the possibilities,
they say. We know that the future depends on everyone working together.
K. Sello Duiker, *The Quiet Violence of Dreams*

To a Happier Year

Summertime's first notebook fragment, with John's exclamation over the perilous men under whose thumb he finds himself after returning to South Africa,
bears an italicised note at its end, a writer's possible mental note to be picked
upon at a later date: "To be expanded on: his father's response to the times as
compared to his own; their differences, their (overriding) similarities" (S, 6).

The above may be read as a possible allusion to the experience of change
in the South African polity, tempered with a pessimism enacted through
inter-generational dialogue. Is change possible, or is it, as seems to be hinted
in the passage, a disguised version of the same? What could be the role of the
intellectually minded writer in such a context? Could the sympathetic writer,
in this sense, dare hope that the dreams of Lyndall and Magda finally find fruition in a democratic South Africa? Could, in the words of feminist-identified
Elizabeth Costello, a world be imagined in which "poverty, disease, illiteracy,

racism, sexism, homophobia, xenophobia, and the rest of the bad litany have been exorcised"?[1]

The post-1994 "rainbow nation" would present itself to the world as a beacon of hope for accommodating different narratives, underlined by a human rights rhetoric, particularly in its espousal of multiracialism and upholding non-discrimination based on gender or sexual orientation. This would be a clear attempt at making a distinction between the pre- and post-*apartheid* eras, seeking to take into account democratic structures that would allow for the "fullest range of human rights for all South African citizens".[2]

The "rainbow nation"—the rainbow already one of the most powerful international symbols for gay liberation—would, provocatively, adopt the term "coming out" as national metaphor: in 1998, Albie Sachs would famously consider that "it's not just the gay and lesbian community that is coming out," equating the new nation and its narratives of truth-telling and reconciliation as the grand project of "coming out".[3]

And yet, as Ryan Thoreson would argue, it would remain difficult to translate hopeful metaphors into concrete realities, as hostility towards dissident sexualities would often conflict with the general liberatory bent enunciated by Sachs.[4] What could, then, be the place of sexual dissidence in this new South Africa, in its "rehearsals and revisions of a new sense of imagined community and national identity"?[5]

As seen in the case of demands for gender equality, how the nation receives such new narratives, and the place it accords them, remains one of the main challenges of this new South Africa and, by extent, of the postcolonial world. In the particular case of homophobia,[6] the constitutionally consecrated rights of non-discrimination have provided renewed space for political demands in terms of acceding to better, safer living conditions.[7]

Yet, such attempts at creating both physical and psychical space for those still discriminated against, face the constant enemy of non-normative sexualities: its silencing. As Eve Kosofsky Sedgwick would explain on this particular topic:

> *Don't ask; You shouldn't know.* It didn't happen; it doesn't make any difference; it didn't mean anything; it doesn't have any interpretive consequences. Stop asking just here; stop asking just now; we know in advance the kind of difference that could be made by the invocation of *this* difference; it makes no difference; it doesn't mean.[8]

Homosexuality must not mean.[9] It is imposed that it be so. As anthropologist Miguel Vale de Almeida further considers, the figure of the homosexual is a synthesis of purported masculine failings, with homosexuality understood as

the "degenerescence of masculinity" (our translation).[10] In Connell's assertion, and in the vein of Almeida's assessment, "gayness, in patriarchal ideology, is the repository of whatever is symbolically expelled from hegemonic masculinity".[11] Following this note, the absence of meaning suggested by
Sedgwick is the compulsory maintenance of a certain gender order, whereby
homosexuality figures in monothematic presence, and complexity or political
agency are silenced or viewed askance.

A telling inscription in literary history appears in the form of E. M. Forster's *Maurice*.[12] Completed in 1914, it would only be published posthumously
in 1971. Its significance in the literary *plateau* is its happy ending. As Forster
himself argues: "A happy ending was imperative. I shouldn't have bothered
to write otherwise. I was determined that in fiction anyway two men should
fall in love and remain in it for the ever and ever that fiction allows, and in
this sense Maurice and Alec still roam the greenwood." Contrary to it ending "unhappily, with a lad dangling from a noose or with a suicide pact"—
what seemed to Forster a more aggreable ending in society's eyes –, the author
would opt for a more optimistic path: *Maurice*'s "happiness is its keynote".[13]

The depiction of homosexual love in a more humane way would, as Forster was able to predict, draw ire from the society of his time. Even within the
more relaxed halls of literature, house of imagination, love between men or
women would spark tension, revolt, ultimately resulting in protracted silence.
In this sense, Forster's dedication of *Maurice* "to a happier year" means the
hope of a time when same-sex desire would not be criminalised, or silenced.[14]

Such mechanics of silencing would be vital in colonialism, playing a central part in the way that homosexuality would be represented in non-Western
societies. Drawing upon various early anthropological accounts on sexuality
in African societies, Stephen Murray and Will Roscoe suggest that the presence of same-sex desire had been largely denied or silenced, with the prevailing notion that it would only be accounted for under the auspices of it being
an expression of situational, or opportunistic contexts:

> When homosexuality is acknowledged, its meaning and cultural significance are dis-
> counted and minimized. By claiming that homosexual relations are solely due to a
> lack of women, for example, or are part of a short-lived adolescent phase, the possi-
> bility of homoerotic desire—that an individual may actually want and find pleasure
> in another of the same sex—is effectively denied.[15]

Same-sex relations would, alongside an array of other sexual arrangements,
generally be employed at the service of the community, and would indeed be

present in pre-colonial African societies. Mark Epprecht provides the following examples:

> Abstinence or sex with males were thought to have had specific powers to prepare men for battle, as reported among the Azande in Central Africa/Sudan, the Tutsi kingdoms of the Great Lakes, and the Zulu, Ndebele and other Ngugi kingdoms in southern Africa. In the latter, the ruler's ability to control his subjects' sexuality was critical to the process of state formation in the late eighteenth and early nineteenth centuries.[16]

Entering the colonial period, knowledge based on Western-centric science would prove a central tool in organising power relations. Modernisation theory, stemming from Enlightenment views of rationality, would seek to provide "value-neutral scientific rationality and technical expertise" in order to "replace traditional religious beliefs, myths, and superstitions about nature and social relations."[17]

In such a project, the varied organisational systems of the multiple polities in Africa, with their own processes in terms of decision-making, would see their significance stripped away, in the case of such practices not falling in accord with European sensibilities. It would also be a heavily gendered project. As Mary Terrall argues, science in the seventeenth and eighteenth centuries would be enmeshed in stylised fantasies, with the male knowledge-seeking explorer, who braved the risks of the voyages in the pursuit of unraveling the natures of wilderness, providing the euphoric template for the acknowledgement of scientists as an integral part of the nation.[18]

Early anthropology would reveal the difficulties in understanding the complexity of sexual systems in their concrete contexts of research. Murray and Roscoe suggest these would stem from employing frameworks derivative of their own societies, thus adopting, willingly or otherwise, an ethnocentric attitude towards sexuality:

> For individuals from a society in which homosexuality is defined as a unitary, predominantly sexual phenomenom with fixed internal psychological motivations—and who have judged that phenomenon so harshly that even its leading social engineers and intellectuals are afraid to study or discuss the subject—the diversity of African homosexualities is, indeed, "all very confusing."[19]

A telling example of "scientific racism"—to employ Brenna Munro's description[20]—is inscribed in the narrative of *Proteus*, a 2003 South African movie directed by John Greyson.[21] The film's narrative, set in the eighteenth century, concerns the loving relationship between Claas Blank (a Khoikhoi man) and Rijkhaart Jacobsz (a Dutch sailor). The movie is inspired by real events: both men had been in a relationship for twenty years, eventually being accused of sodomy and executed.

A parallel narrative introduces the wider cultural context of sciencemaking, through a botanist's revelation of the processes of classifying plants and animals. This is a clear foreshadowing of the eventual rise of homosexuality as scientific category in the late nineteenth century, as the botanist engages with Claas in an attempt at extending botanic knowledge into racial categorisation, with the homosexual figuring as a lesser species.

As Michel Foucault argued, it would be in such a period that, through the combined efforts of scientific discourse, homosexuality as a category would emerge.[22] Historically located, categorical notions of human sexuality would emerge against a backdrop of heavy societal disquiet over purported national degeneracy, perceived in the decline of virility, impotence and overall tensions regarding masculinity.[23] And yet, as Jeffrey Weeks further argues, sexological categories as discursive practices did not extinguish the possibility of agency: sexology's proposed "restrictive definitions" would, however, also "put into language a host of definitions and meanings which could be played with, challenged, negated, and used."[24]

In the African context, religious and cultural fundamentalism would provide the gusto for a consideration of homosexuality as un-African. As Sokari Ekine argues, this would remain a problem even in the twenty-first century, with moral panic against homosexuality being clear in the cases of Nigeria, Uganda or Malawi, through recurrent state-mandated homophobic legislation.[25]

However, such fervent nationalist discourse, purporting to provide a remedy to the ills of the colonial past, is itself the product of selective amnesia. As already enunciated, same-sex desire would figure in the making of African societies in the pre-colonial period. The banning of such relations would be the byproduct of the colonial enterprise, through the mandates of Europeancentric conceptions of acceptability and morality within the field of human sexuality. An irony presents itself in the nationalist commanded discourse, for it is not homosexuality that is the purported alien within African systems of the polity, but indeed its disavowal, as Murray and Roscoe further argue:

> The first generation of postcolonial Africans was extremely reluctant to discuss the subject of homosexuality. For most, the negotiation of African identity remained tied to European standards of morality. In seeking to replace a "genuinely perverse"

with a "genuinely normal" Other, they drew on the same rhetoric employed in colonial discourse on native sexuality. As the medical model of homosexuality was being abandoned in the west, it was widely adopted in the developing world.[26]

The taboo over African homosexualities has its roots then on the systems of surveillance and regulation for its suppression. In this vein, Sylvia Tamale considers the use of homosexuality as un-African to be of a political nature, designed towards providing a reasoning for the maintenance of power:

> A whole generation of nationals was born and raised and came to maturity during their regime, and these rulers have become experts in the politics of distraction. Hence, instead of blaming political mismanagement and corruption for high unemployment, the high cost of living, and poor health facilities, the population is encouraged to focus, inter alia, on red herrings such as "the vice of homosexuality" and "the evil of prostitution" which are fished out of the sea of morality particularly when electoral accountability is looming.[27]

According to this argument, homophobia would be used as a political tool by some African leaders as effective means to achieve short term goals. Hence, in complying to homophobia as introduced by colonial discourse, the fathers of the nations are themselves reproducing such a discourse. In this, the South African Constitution constitutes a glowing alternative, while not meaning the absence of prejudice.

"We Have So Much to Learn From Each Other": Other Politics

In 1996, on the occasion of the passing of the Constitution, Thabo Mbeki would give a charismatic speech, titled "I Am an African". The speech bears an acknowledgement of the nation's cultural diversity, an attempt at indicating the ills of *apartheid* for having curtailed such possibilities, and the demonstration of the promises of the new nation. The Constitution, argued Mbeki, provides the template for a new community, free from the oppression that had thus far characterised it:

> It seeks to create the situation in which all our people shall be free from fear, including the fear of the oppression of one national group by another, the fear of the disempowerment of one social echelon by another, the fear of the use of state power to deny anybody their fundamental human rights and the fear of tyranny.[28]

Although homosexuality would be fully decriminalised in South Africa in 1998, a happier year for many, the dour reality of continued homophobia would prevent the date from being the idealistic site of Forster's conception. The democratic transition would hold its tensions, with an increasingly problematic view of constitutional rights as imposing modern values in traditional settings.

Thus, the constitutionally mandated rights would find themselves in tension with a national discourse that saw the heterosexualisation of the family as being under threat from so-called minority rights. South African masculinity contemporary to the rainbow era would, then, find itself at odds with purported attacks by what has been perceived as modern, Western-centric ideological mandates.

Such tensions would congeal under the form of denialism, particularly obvious in the field of women's and gay rights. As indicated in "Shades and Shadows of Life", systemic rape as a tool to police women's sexuality would figure in its brutal presence within the scope of the "rainbow nation".

Denialism as political strategy would be particularly present in the field of public health, both in terms of the dismissal of the statistics of sexual abuse and of cases of HIV/AIDS. Notwithstanding its existence in white, middle-class heterosexual communities, the latter continues to be associated with promiscuous homosexuality.[29] As would be common in other countries, social activists would heed the call for state recognition of the high numbers of infection.[30]

Mbeki himself would become known for his denialist stance. Deborah Posel considers that such denialism rests on more public racialised assumptions regarding violence: the black man as hyper-masculine, a legacy of colonialism.[31] On the contrary, Jacob Zuma would adopt a hyper-masculine posture, pleasing to both men and women who saw constitutional rights as defying the stability of heterosexual life.

Per Rosemary Jolly's argument, notwithstanding differing strategies, both men have sought to maintain intact a notion of the South African family that is seen as being under attack by an array of destabilising forces. In the case of Mbeki, the feared possible return of racialised stereotyping as provided by the colonial past possibly implied a consequent responsibility of acting as father of the nation and the censor of a purported crisis of masculinity as stemming from black men. In the case of Zuma, the growing demands of women in the public field, and its consequences on the continuation of men as dominating the sphere of familial relations, implied a return to the safe harbour of the heterosexual family romance.[32]

In this framework, the queer Other is seen as the bearer of chaos and social mischief. Observing black masculinity as hampered by homosexuality, even great writers such as Bessie Head would partake in a pathological discourse on the latter. As such, in A *Question of Power*, Head would see homosexuality as one of the perversions stemming from *apartheid*: "They and people in general accepted it as a disease one had to live with."[33]

Concerning white masculinity, with its conservative and silencing bent towards homosexuality, more recent cultural productions in South Africa allow a possible glimpse into the emerging contradictions and changes in the national landscape towards dissident sexualities. The 2011 South African movie *Skoonheid* (Afrikaans for "beauty")[34] portrays its main character, François van Heerden, as torn between his duties as a father and husband in the *locus* of the heterosexual white family, and his lust for a younger man, Christian Roodt, friend of the family.

The film has various, long wide shots of traditionally masculine locations, such as the construction site or the farm. In a revealing scene, a shot of the Afrikaner farm transitions to a sexual scene between François and another man, a meeting arranged through what is purported to be an underground network of white men who seek sexual pleasure while maintaining the outward, public appearance of family men.

Through the transition between masculine sites and the underground depiction of homosexual activity, the continued silencing of homosexuality within the construction of Afrikaner masculinity is brought to the fore.[35] The movie signals, however, how different generations connect with the reality of homosexuality in South Africa, with the indication that François is left inadequate in a place of growing acceptance.

As such, and subsisting through continued hostility, differing accounts of homosexuality would arise, with cultural production being a privileged site for dealing with the tensions of the new nation. From a depiction of homosexuality in monothematic, stereotypical tones,[36] the transition to democracy, notwithstanding its eventual flaws, would see celebrated writers such as Coetzee and Gordimer writing stories of white people adjusting to the times, with children not heterosexual. Coetzee's case would be the famous *Disgrace*, under the form of lesbian Lucy Lurie.

However, the most powerful inscription in literary form would be K. Sello Duiker's 2001 novel *The Quiet Violence of Dreams*.[37] Tshepo, Duiker's protagonist, would be the first black gay protagonist "to see his homosexuality as an inalienable part of his African identity."[38] Set in the period of 1998 to 2000, Duiker's novel explores how Tshepo comes to terms with his homosexuality, a tortuous road even within a society that has come to legislate against prejudice.

Tshepo's journey necessarily invites reflection on the public discourse on homosexuality, namely its pathologisation—the first part of the novel places Tshepo in a mental health institution, mirroring the historical treatment of homosexuality as a case of mental illness –, and also the notion of homosexuality as un-African. To the latter argument, Tshepo retorts as follows:

> I mean, people always say that black culture is rigid and doesn't accept things like homosexuals and lesbians. You know the argument—it's very unafrican. It's a lot of crap. In my experience that kind of thinking comes from urbanised blacks, people who've watered down the real origins of our culture and mixed it with notions from the Bible. It's stupid to even suggest that homosexuality and lesbianism are foreign to black culture. Long ago, long before whites, people were aware of all of this.[39]

Conjoining gender and postcolonial critique, Duiker understands homosexuality as part of the African landscape, and an escape from heteronormative masculinity, bent on domination and violence. At another point in the novel, another character places the question: "Who says violence has to be synonymous with men? Who says men can't be tender?"[40] Such inquiry on the constitutive aspects of masculinity composes Duiker's assertion of a renewed masculinity based on collaboration, equality, and self-determination—the central tenets of social movements.

Indeed, by the novel's ending it is the possibility of creating a community that is emphasised. Much like the underground network of women's stories in *Boyhood*, so does Tshepo come to be a part of an identical formation:

> I have met bankers, architects, poets, builders, miners, diplomats, engineers, labourers, waiters, sailors, firemen, soldiers, farmers, preachers, men worth their salt and men of integrity. They all go about the quiet business of telling me their secrets, sharing their wisdom. We have so much to learn from each other.[41]

The future depends on the collaborative potential of such a diverse cast: one must learn from each other. Contrary to dominant formulations of masculinity, it is clear that such men are "fragile",[42] not by means of sexual orientation but as a sign of social nature. Disconnected lives imply a regenerative pull towards being together: "We must think about each other, about how we feel, and what we will do to comfort each other."[43]

In *Boyhood*'s seventeenth chapter, the penultimate chapter, a telling description of the relation to the homosexual Other occurs. The chapter begins
with intimations of personal changes in John's life: he has stopped some of his
childhood pastimes, instead looking in the mirror for signs of physical changes.
He has not forgotten cricket, and yet he prefers the imagined game he concocts,
with his own rules, to the real thing: "When he plays real cricket he has to
concentrate all his energies on not flinching, not giving himself away" (B, 145).

As argued in "Family Outcast", both in cricket and in rugby, vital institutionalised sites of masculinity-making, he is often found to be inept—"he
hardly ever scores runs" (B, 145)—and equally dismissive of the physical contact that is core to such games: he is "frightened of being tackled" (B, 146).

In the aforementioned chapter in *Boyhood*, the narrative then turns to a
scene where John finds a sex manual in his mother's drawer and shares it with
his school friends. Whereas the other boys "pore avidly over it," John is left
disappointed with its technical potrayal of sex: "the drawings of the organs
look like diagrams in science books, and even in the section on postures there
is nothing exciting (inserting the male organ into the vagina sounds like an
enema)" (B, 147). Heterosexual sex is, thus, deprived of greater erotic qualities, and the possible site of abjection.

A third turn of the narrative concerns the budding relationship between
John and Theo Stavropoulos. Coming from a Greek family, Theo is also a
stranger in South Africa. Described as intellectually superior to John (B, 139),
both him and John study Greek, with Theo sitting squashed "against him in
his desk, underneath the picture of Jesus opening his chest to reveal a glowing ruby heart" (B, 148). Intimacy is alluded to, with both boys whispering
"Eudaimonia" back and forth, alluding to the Aristotelic designation for the
highest human good.

School rumours on Theo indicate him as "a *moffie*, a queer," yet John "is
not prepared to believe them" (B, 148).[44] A series of other textual signs appear
that indicate homosexuality is in consideration in this chapter. It is Brother
Gabriel who interrupts the two boys' idyllic, eroticised episode on friendship,
doing pride to his namesake, the biblical angel who would act as destroyer
of Sodom and Gomorrah. It is in this very act of interruption that the text
reveals its queer side, as it provides an anagram for a sexual scenario: "Brother
Gabriel pricks up his ears" (B, 149). Equally, in a possible intertextual reading,
the Greek origins of Theo may remind the Coetzeean reader of Greek poet
C. P. Cavafy, himself homosexual, and whose writings would name Coetzee's
third novel *Waiting for the Barbarians*.

As Theo escapes the proper aesthetics of dominant masculinity, defined in often physically rough criteria, signs of difference in terms of masculinity implicate the projection of tensions on masculinity-making onto those perceived as less so, therefore being taken as homosexual. In the passage, the queer one emerges as bad, to be avoided, the site of humiliation and scorn, yet John's resoluteness in not believing such rumours, and subsequently to become friends with Theo, signals resistance to the imposed norms of the group.

Contrary to the rough vocabulary of masculinity, Theo appears, in John's eyes, as an idealised figure: "his fine skin and his high colouring and his impeccable haircuts and the suave way he wears his clothes" (B, 148). Far from the derogatory discourse of the homosexual Other as a site of disease or revolting strangeness, both Theo and his family, as contrasted with the undesirability of John's own family, are represented through an aura of meticulous perfection and adoration. Theo's father is "a tall, elegantly dressed man with dark glasses." The mother "small and slim and dark". The older sister, "so beautiful, so expensively educated, so marriageable, that she is not allowed to be exposed to the gaze of Theo's friends" (B, 148). Theo is the unattainable figure, to be sought after and emulated.

The overall representation demarcates Theo and his family as the site of maturity. Contrary to John and his anxiety over his own family, it is implied that Theo does not share such childish anxieties regarding one's parents (B, 148–49). Furthermore, Theo reacts to ridicule "with equanimity" (B, 149). Confidently navigating the destructive bent of Others, Theo posits a mature, knowledgeable understanding of how to react to another's jeers, that is contrasted with the immature world of the boys who remain engulfed in anxious predicaments over one's sexuality and body: "sudden drops of tone, whisperings, outbursts of guffawing" (B, 148). In this, the purported homosexual Other is a site of agency, eluding humiliation:

> He expects Theo to be crushed by the experience: by the envy and malice of the other boarders, by the poor food, by the indignities of a life without privacy. He also expects Theo to have to submit to the same kind of haircut as everyone else. Yet somehow Theo manages to keep his hair elegantly styled; somehow, despite his name, despite being clumsy at sport, despite being thought to be a *moffie*, he maintains his suave smile, never complains, never allows himself to be humiliated. (B, 149)

The passage addresses some of John's own predicaments, namely his anxiety over collective sports and a certain sense of disconnection, as he understands that he does not fit the idealised image of white masculinity. Furthermore, John

worries that Theo shall be homogenised, giving place to the naturalised hap-
penings of masculine codes. Yet, Theo's singularity prevails. What distinguishes
him remains in place. In spite of the various shortcomings in terms of acceding
to masculinity, Theo remains a site of the eloquent alternative to such codes.

If Theo emerges as a figure of elegant dissidence over dominant masculinity, how can one understand John's desire to avenge Theo for all of the latter's
mistreatment at the hands of the Brothers and the other boys? It is important to
remember that in the first reference to Theo, the habitual positive description
of the character includes that he is always given the role of Marc Antony in the
Shakespearean play *Julius Caesar*. Coetzee finds in this situation the possibility
to actualise the demands of the "rainbow nation". Could the new South Africa
rely on the old codes of masculinity, enacted through a vocabulary of physicality,
aggressive and compulsory heterosexuality, and derision of the homosexual Other? Or, could the new nation learn something from Theo-cum-Marc Anthony?

The funeral speech, "the most famous speech in the play" (B, 129), is a
site of rebellion. As Daniel Juan Gil argues, such rebellion is not character-
related, but driven to criticise the modes of a politics "that orders social life
into rival factions demanding personal sacrifice in the name of public goods."[45]
Actualised in the figure of the *moffie*, the nation's elegant yet continuous outcast, such rebellion seems to act as an inquiry on the fabric of a nation that,
in purporting to provide a secure space for all, continuously derides those who
fall outside the norms, imbued as these are with *apartheid*-era prejudices.

Contrary to the paradigm of institutionalised masculinity, Theo as stranger
to such a system provides one of its most valuable antidotes. In questioning
the validity of a public discourse based on humiliation, Theo introduces the
intimate site of learning as the reasoning framework for personal development
and dissidence from the obscure workings of the unreasonable group. Theo
acts, then, much like his purported Shakespearean model: per Gil's reading,
what Antony as oppositional figure teaches Rome is "a grammar of interper-
sonal bonding that defines connections between bodies," such connections
being meant to "replace any politically mediated public life."[46] The narrative
understands the homosexual as a character in a torn relation with the state,
with state violence described as central in tearing the bond between people based on collective fabricated fear over the *moffie*. Yet, in the Coetzeean
narrative, the homosexual remains capable of upholding a sense of personal
dignity and singularity, despite this tumultuous context.

John's call to battle over Theo can, then, be read as professing compan-
ionship. John is Theo's ally for he recognises in him the beauty of human

relationship that augments a sense of being in the world, contrasted as it is with the stiffling, half-hearted and impatient enactment of dominant masculinity. As Derrida would argue, "the possibility of friendship lodges itself in the movement of my thought insofar as it requires, calls, desires the other, the necessity of the other, the cause of the other at the heart of the *cogito*."[47] John will do battle for Theo for in him he recognises a friend.

This obligation to the Other is also enacted in a different way throughout the trilogy. John's failed masculinity is, necessarily, accompanied by intimations of him possibly being homosexual.[48] We have seen, in "Art of One", how the episode in *Youth* where John shuns homosexuality is implicated in the construction of the failed man, projecting anxieties elsewhere. Equally, in Margot's purported narrative in *Summertime*, incessant questions over John's sexuality arise. Such intimations, however, conflate less with a purported negativity of homosexuality, but foremost with John carrying a lover's bleeding heart: "If he has no woman, is that because he has no feeling for women, and therefore women, herself included, respond by having no feeling for him? Is her cousin, if not a *moffie*, then a eunuch?" (S, 114).

The scandal to hegemonic masculinity is that such inability to connect emotionally oftentimes reveals its extent in terms of the inability to appear sexually seductive. "But there was a quality he did not have that a woman looks for in a man, a quality of strength, of manliness.... He was not a man, he was still a boy." (S, 171).

The logic presented may be drawn as follows: John is equated with being a *moffie*, an eunuch, due to his emotional distancing, this being characterised in the narrative as the necessary consequence of hegemonic masculinity's tenets in the white Afrikaner community: "She forgot: you do not ask a man to show you his poems, not in South Africa, not without reassuring him beforehand that it will be all right, he is not going to be mocked. What a country, where poetry is not a manly activity" (S, 130).

White masculinity is then understood as stifling, a masquerade that is recognised as producing serious negative consequences. John's poetry is what differentiates him from the Afrikaner *volk*: "Mr. Coetzee is not an Afrikaner, said Maria Regina. He has a beard. He writes poetry" (S, 157).

Poetry then is the way that John found to keep something of his emotions alive. In the tension between hegemonic masculinity and the possibility of Self-determination, poetry could be understood as an anchor in the midst of cultural turmoil.

The presence of poetry in an otherwise "wooden man" is what could eventually *queer* John, as it enunciates his derision of hegemonic masculinity's tenets—with the term "queer" used to indicate a difference that is perceived as exclusionary and aberrant.[49] "Queer" denotes the activity of critique, not only illuminating normative logic, at the same time critiquing it.[50] "Queer" marks homosexual visibility, at the same time as it makes demands for change at the institutional level.[51] Furthermore, the radicality of the term resides in the fact that it also delineates individual and collective political activity that subverts normative notions of identity, community and other political arrangements.[52] In this particular usage of the term, it is possible to argue that John is queer, rather than a "wooden man".

Notes

1. J. M. Coetzee, *Elizabeth Costello: Eight Lessons* (London: Secker & Warburg, 2003), 132.
2. William J. Spurlin, *Imperialism within the Margins: Queer Representation and the Politics of Culture in Southern Africa* (New York: Palgrave Macmillan, 2006), 78.
3. Quoted in Tim Trengove Jones, "Fiction and the Law: Recent Inscriptions of Gayness in South Africa," *Modern Fiction Studies* 46, no. 1 (2000): 114–15.
4. Ryan Richard Thoreson, "Somewhere Over the Rainbow Nation: Gay, Lesbian and Bisexual Activism in South Africa," *Journal of Southern African Studies* 34, no. 3 (2008): 679–97.
5. Spurlin, *Imperialism within the Margins*, 79.
6. "Homophobia" is employed as a term covering "a range of negative attitudes toward homosexuality and those who are or are perceived to be homosexual." See Patrick R. Ireland, "A Macro-Level Analysis of the Scope, Causes, and Consequences of Homophobia in Africa," *African Studies Review* 56, no. 2 (2003): 49. In such a definition, homophobia alludes also to its institutionalised nature, as it "can be sponsored by the state or by institutions like religious groups, the private sector, and the military" (49).
7. Mark Gevisser, "A Different Fight for Freedom: A History of South African Lesbian and Gay Organisation from the 1950s to 1990s," in *Defiant Desire: Gay and Lesbian Lives in South Africa*, ed. Mark Gevisser and Edwin Cameron (New York: Routledge, 1995), 14–86.
8. Eve Kosofsky Sedgwick, *Epistemology of the Closet* (Los Angeles: University of California Press, 2008), 53.
9. The term "homosexual" is here used as it more accurately reflects the conventions of sexuality employed throughout Coetzee's work. As Miguel Vale de Almeida warns, a methodological distinction must be drawn between homosexual behaviour—universal and trans-historic –, from homosexual identity, developed in specific historical circumstances. Miguel Vale de Almeida, "Teoria *Queer* e a Contestação da Categoria 'Género'", in *Indisciplinar a Teoria: Estudos Gays, Lésbicos e Queer*, ed. António Fernando Cascais (Lisboa: Fenda Edições, 2004), 91–98.

10. Miguel Vale de Almeida, A Chave do Armário: Homossexualidade, Casamento, Família (Lisboa: ICS, 2009), 31.

11. R. W. Connell, Masculinities, 2nd ed. (Cambridge: Polity Press, 2005 [1995]), 78.

12. E. M. Forster, Maurice (London: Penguin, 2005 [1971]).

13. E. M. Forster, "Terminal Note," in Maurice (London: Penguin, 2005 [1971]), 220.

14. Forster, "Terminal Note," 220.

15. Stephen O. Murray and Will Roscoe, "All Very Confusing," in Boy-Wives and Female Husbands: Studies of African Homosexualities, ed. Stephen O. Murray and Will Roscoe (London: Macmillan Press, 1998), xiii.

16. Marc Epprecht, Sexuality and Social Justice in Africa: Rethinking Homophobia and Forging Resistance (London: Zed Books, 2013), 113.

17. Sandra Harding, "Beyond Postcolonial Theory: Two Undertheorized Perspectives on Science and Technology," in The Postcolonial Science and Technology Studies Reader, ed. Sandra Harding (Durham and London: Duke University Press, 2011), 2.

18. Mary Terrall, "Heroic Narratives of Quest and Discovery," in The Postcolonial Science and Technology Studies Reader, ed. Sandra Harding (Durham and London: Duke University Press, 2011), 84–102.

19. Murray and Roscoe, Boy-Wives and Female Husbands, xv.

20. Brenna M. Munro, South Africa and the Dream of Love to Come: Queer Sexuality and the Struggle for Freedom (Minneapolis: Minneapolis University Press, 2012), 62. As Munro also points out, Proteus was shot at Robben Island, with the permission of the authorities, thus figuring as an example of the different cultural status of such productions in the "rainbow" era.

21. Proteus, directed by John Greyson (Pluck Productions, 2003).

22. "L'homosexualité s'est mise à parler d'elle-même, à revendiquer sa légitimité ou sa 'naturalité' et souvent dans le vocabulaire, avec les catégories par lesquelles elle était médicalement disqualifiée." Michel Foucault, Histoire de la Sexualité I: La Volonté de Savoir (Paris: Gallimard, 1976), 134.

23. Matt T. Reed, "Historicizing Inversion: Or, How to Make a Homosexual," History of the Human Sciences 14, no. 4 (2001): 1–29.

24. Jeffrey Weeks, Sexuality and Its Discontents (London: Routledge, 1985), 95.

25. See Sokari Ekine, "Contesting Narratives of Queer Africa," in Queer African Reader, ed. Sokari Ekine and Hakima Abbas (Dakar: Pambazuka Press, 2013), 78–91.

26. Murray and Roscoe, Boy-Wives and Female Husbands, xv–xvi.

27. Sylvia Tamale, "Confronting the Politics of Nonconforming Sexualities in Africa," African Studies Review 56, no. 2 (2013): 39.

28. Thabo Mbeki, "I Am an African," in The South Africa Reader: History, Culture, Politics, ed. Clifton Crais and Thomas V. McClendon (Durham and London: Duke University Press, 2014 [1994]): 478.

29. Steven Robins, "'Long Live Zackie, Long Live': AIDS Activism, Science and Citizenship after Apartheid", Journal of Southern African Studies 30, no. 3 (2004): 651–72.

30. As is the case of performer Pieter-Dirk Uys. See Darling! The Pieter-Dirk Uys Story, directed by Julian Shaw (Green Light Productions, 2007).

31. Deborah Posel, "The Scandal of Manhood: 'Baby Rape' and the Politicization of Sexual Violence in Post-Apartheid South Africa," *Culture, Health & Sexuality* 7, no. 3 (2005): 239–52.

32. See Rosemary Jolly, *Cultured Violence: Narrative, Social Suffering, and Engendering Human Rights in Contemporary South Africa* (Liverpool: Liverpool University Press, 2013), specifically 127–33.

33. Bessie Head, *A Question of Power* (Johannesburg: Penguin, 2011 [1974]), 41.

34. *Skoonheid*, directed by Oliver Hermanus (Swift Productions, 2011).

35. Theo Sonnekus, "'We're Not Faggots!': Masculinity, Homosexuality and the Representation of Afrikaner Men Who Have Sex With Men in the Film *Skoonheid* and Online," *South African Review of Sociology* 44, no. 1 (2013): 22–39.

36. Chris Dunton, "'Wheything Be Dat?' The Treatment of Homosexuality in African Literature," *Research in African Literatures* 20, no. 3 (1989): 422–48.

37. K. Sello Duiker, *The Quiet Violence of Dreams*, 2nd ed. (Cape Town: Kwela Books, 2014 [2001]).

38. Dobrota Pucherova, "Re-Imagining the Other: The Politics of Friendship in Three Twenty-First Century South African Novels," *Journal of Southern African Studies* 35, no. 4 (2009): 936.

39. Duiker, *The Quiet Violence of Dreams*, 329.

40. Duiker, *The Quiet Violence of Dreams*, 400.

41. Duiker, *The Quiet Violence of Dreams*, 607.

42. Duiker, *The Quiet Violence of Dreams*, 607.

43. Duiker, *The Quiet Violence of Dreams*, 608.

44. "*Moffie*" is a derogatory term in South African slang. One of its possible senses alludes to effeminacy or homosexuality in men. See Shaun de Waal, "On 'Moffie'", in *Defiant Desire: Gay and Lesbian Lives in South Africa*, ed. Mark Gevisser and Edwin Cameron (New York: Routledge, 1995), xiii.

45. Daniel Juan Gil, "'Bare Life': Political Order and the Specter of Antisocial Being in Shakespeare's *Julius Caesar*," *Common Knowledge* 13, no. 1 (2007): 70.

46. Gil, "'Bare Life'", 70.

47. Jacques Derrida, "Politics of Friendship," *American Imago* 50, no. 3 (1993): 362.

48. "Post-1994 Coetzee appears to allow himself considerable leeway in dwelling upon, gentling, fondling in script, if not male bodies, then androgynous parts of male bodies." Elleke Boehmer, "Queer Bodies," in *J. M. Coetzee in Context and Theory*, ed. Elleke Boehmer, Katy Iddiols, and Robert Eaglestone (London: Continuum, 2009), 126.

49. "'Queer' can refer to: the open mesh of possibilities, gaps, overlaps, dissonances and resonances, lapses and excesses of meaning when the constituent elements of anyone's gender, of anyone's sexuality aren't made (or *can't be* made) to signify monolithically." Eve Kosofsky Sedgwick, "Queer and Now," in *Tendencies* (London: Routledge, 1994), 7.

50. Ken Corbett, "More Life: Centrality and Marginality in Human Development," *Psychoanalytic Dialogues* 11, no. 3 (2001): 315.

51. As further argued by David Glover and Cora Kaplan, *Genders*, 2nd ed. (New York: Routledge, 2009 [2000]); see 114–46.

52. The same argument is employed by Vale de Almeida, "Teoria Queer," 97.

CONCLUSIONS

I no longer know which story I am trying to write. Who could keep going in a straight line with so many stories, like feral siblings, separated and each running wild, chasing each other's tales?

Zoë Wicomb, *David's Story*

We began the present work by suggesting how gender and postcolonial studies, both in their academic presence and otherwise, are committed to inquire over the possibilities of community-making. John Maxwell Coetzee, one of the most prominent of writers in contemporaneity, given his influence, could have something to say regarding the matter. And yet, Coetzee seems to be adamant in foregoing any kind of involvement in such a political project: "I am not a herald of community or anything else.... I am someone who has intimations of freedom (as every chained prisoner has) and constructs representations—which are shadows themselves—of people slipping their chains and turning their faces to the light."[1]

The above passage, taken at face value, makes one wonder what, if anything at all, Coetzee may contribute to such interested scholarship and everyday political practice. To take such a position would be, however, to acknowledge that one has learned nothing of relevance regarding this writer's provocative way of being in the world. For the truth of the matter—and one can employ such an expression cognisant of its contested significance regarding this writer's work—is that Coetzee has always been mired in the grasp of politics, either by attempting to imagine otherwise in the context of *apartheid*, when the pull was to a fervent realist account of the times; or, post-*apartheid*, through the insistence of resisting historical and cultural amnesia, in the understanding that the past is ever present, rearing its head in oftentimes unpredictable ways, yet surely taking a stand in shaping the present. For the most part, his has been his own way, firmly standing for the notion that we cannot live in a community that is outside contradictions. This has been his stake— the writer turned therapist turned writer.

The time of unbridled hope that characterised the democratic turn of South Africa would eventually meet the disenchantment of the persistence of historical repetition of violent enactments. In May 2008, the nation would witness widespread xenophobic attacks, resulting in the killing of over sixty people across the country. In 16 August 2012, Marikana police shootings of miners on strike would underline continuing social inequality.[2] Most recently, in 2015, xenophobic outbreaks would again make the headlines, reminding the world, who had just recently celebrated twenty years of South African democracy, how promises of equality and freedom are so difficult to maintain. Coetzee's doubts over the prevalence of the magical moment that underscored South Africa's transition to democracy would, frustratingly enough, prove to hold their point.

In this work, we have argued that the violence that has long haunted the South African landscape is, in part, the enactment of rigid notions of masculinity, drawn through various time periods, yet whose origins may be located in imperial and *apartheid* codes of conduct. Coetzee's pessimistic view of Afrikanerdom results in his creation of a John who espouses various moments of dissidence towards established history, thus providing a nod to alternative sites of history making. The Afrikaner fathers of the nation provide the optimal *locus* of authority; yet their story is mired in the blood, suffering and exclusion of Others, violence validated through sanctimonious myth-making. The boy's questioning regarding the undesirability of the Others of Afrikanerdom indicates a break with the coded messages of white masculinity in *apartheid* time. Eventually, the nation would, indeed, receive a long sought father after all, Nelson Mandela, whose intelligent and meticulous masculine performances would, in the later period of his life, be employed towards augmenting the possibilities for community. Laughter and cries of welcoming freedom replaced the tortured sounds of killing and despair—even if only for a certain period of time.

Derision of coded sites of masculinity-making, such as the Boy Scouts or literary institutions, is a double edged sword, resulting not only in the augmenting powers of imagination, but also in the loss of privilege. In this, John is never the angelic child, waiting for the full breath of redemption and blissful existence at the end of his travels, as could be argued would be the reasoning behind the autobiographical moment in the democratic transition. For Coetzee's Afrikaner child, there is no complete path of atonement for the father's sins, only to remain aware of historical complicity, and the evident responsibility to live within an ethical outlook for the Other's well-being. The project thus installed is one of continuous demand, never an easy task. Such subversion of *apartheid*'s manichean mode persists through a framework that allows for an engagement with an Other, that is necessarily in excess of the Self, and to whom that Self depends in a strained, yet necessary, relation, thus dismantling the Cartesian hope for an irrevocable unitary subject, as reality is agitated in its univocal comprehension by the irruption of an-Other's presence. Continuous in its presence, surprising in its moments of eruption.

The espousal of a failed Self in the trilogy can, then, be understood as the rejection of the male dominant authority, providing a tentative solution towards abandoning *apartheid*'s manichean discourse and allowing for a possible answer to "the post-Enlightenment subject encountering heterogeneity and difference in previously unimagined and urgent senses."[3]

As Breytenbach evinces, the place of death reveals the possibility of resolving political issues: "There was an antithesis between myself and my fellow-Afrikaners that I had to resolve. The alternative would be to keep silent, to fade out. I had to die, as it were, in order to stop dying."[4] So it is in Coetzee's architected death that the omnipotent Self of colonial discourse, of the Afrikaner *volk*, of a certain period of Western history, meets its own dissolution. In seeking to write John's biography, Vincent—and, by extension, the reader—learned that the narrativisation of the masculine Self, historically dated from colonial time, may be derided and observed in less than gallant ways by the Other of such a system. The testimony of the Other, then, enunciates what is lacking in the appraisal of a traditional notion of a life: its merits are surely there, but human contact is more than the discourse of public life can ever account for. Writing the Other as dismissing what has been historically considered as the universal Self provides the reverse political account in terms of the colonialist discourse.

We may further assign this as the logical conclusion in Coetzeean frame-work: the totality of dominant modes of masculinity, criticised and presented in their destructive goals, would never simply be exchanged for the totality of peace. Rather, the articulation of the painful, long process of change, with its noted confusion, despair, and necessary ambiguity, ironically claims a greater status to the realities of the workings of human society. In this, one may agree with Mike Marais when positing Coetzee as a writer intent in disrupting any and all totality, wherein totality is the attempted erasure of the Other: "The community implied by the concern for and with the Other in Coetzee's fiction is grounded in recognition of difference and is, therefore, always incomplete. Given the futural nature of an ethical community, it is Coetzee's ethical re-sponsibility to continue his interruptive engagement with political totalities in the present."[5]

In this particular sense, one may very well conclude that writing is the queerest of activities. Certainly strange, in the more obvious use of the term, to *apartheid*'s exclusionary bent. Yet, bridging societal taboos in the name of the responsibility towards the Other is the *locus* of the trilogy, accompanied as it is by the notion of how unstable, precarious, such location is. And, clearly, how hegemonic masculinity is antithetical to such a process, with the need to redraw gendered formations based on collaboration, mutuality, acceptance of weaknesses and of vulnerabilities.

What can most certainly be suggested is that in the continuous search for an ethics that may provide some source of possibility of living together in what is increasingly becoming a more violent, more dangerous world, mascu-linity in its singularity and plurality, local and global meanings, will be one of the focus of discussion, inevitably dissent, within such ethics. To this project, one may rely on Coetzee as the perennial gadfly. *Contra* Coetzee, *via* Coetzee: either way, a community of discussion is being elaborated, limits and testing of the imagination are being discussed. Perhaps, in the world that such practices may create, the madwoman with a bycicle may see her promises of independ-ence achieved; Adamastor may shed his monstrous carapace; and the queer Other may teach the nation a lesson or two about the politics of friendship and how to erect community around such codes.

It should again be noted how nascent the field of assessing the representa-tions of masculinities in Coetzee's work is. As such, much work is to be done still within the particular universe of Coetzee's *oeuvre*. For our main suggestion towards future work in this nascent field, however, we should like to honour the intertextual basis of Coetzee's writing. Times have indeed changed, and as they progress, we have unfortunately lost esteemed figures of South African culture, namely Nadine Gordimer and André Brink. Of the often named "Holy Trinity" of South African literature, only Coetzee remains. Surely, this disposition of South African literature may be criticised, as it betrays the ways in which cultural specificities are marketed in the global arena.

Contrary to such ignorance, Coetzee has proved to be a steady hand in raising awareness of local cultural productions. His international recognition and evident efforts have proved instrumental in giving voice to a new generation of South African writers, such as Damon Galgut, Ivan Vladislavić, Lauren Beukes or Zoë Wicomb. With their own idiosyncrasies, styles and commitments, this new generation is necessarily engaging in different ways with the actuality of gendered, sexual and other types of politics in the post-*apartheid*, postcolonial world, in a sense a possible reflexive place that Coetzee opened for others to be able to experience in perhaps freer a manner. An important work would be to assess how their own consideration over gendered, and in particular masculine, formations, is necessarily indebted to Coetzee's presence in the cultural field. It will prove instrumental for scholarship to understand how the new generation engages with the gaps and the silences of the social, such work being in large part initiated by Coetzee in his inimitable way.

To Coetzee, then, and through his favoured site of the woman narrator, the last words:

> It is the roaming gangs I fear, the sullen-mouthed boys, rapacious as sharks, on whom the first shade of the prison house is already beginning to close. Children scorning childhood, the time of wonder, the growing time of the soul. Their souls, their organs of wonder, stunted, petrified. And on the other side of the great divide their white cousins, soul-stunted too, spinning themselves tighter and tighter into their sleepy cocoons. Swimming lessons, riding lessons, ballet lessons; cricket on the lawn; lives passed within walled gardens guarded by bulldogs; children of paradise, blond, innocent, shining with angelic light, soft as *putti*. Their residence the limbo of the unborn, their innocence the innocence of bee grubs, plump and white, drenched in honey, absorbing sweetness through their soft skins. Slumbrous their souls, bliss-filled, abstracted.[6]

Notes

1. J. M. Coetzee, Doubling the Point, ed. David Attwell (Cambridge, MA: Harvard University Press, 1992 [1986]), 341.
2. A contextualisation of these examples of violence in South Africa is found in Derek Hook, (Post)Apartheid Conditions (Cape Town: HSRC Press, 2014), 1–3.

3. David Attwell, "Coetzee's Estrangements," *NOVEL: A Forum on Fiction* 41, no. 2–3 (2008): 233.
4. Breyten Breytenbach, "'I am not an Afrikaner any more,'" *Index on Censorship* 12, no. 3 (1983): 4.
5. Mike Marais, "'Little Enough, Less Than Little: Nothing': Ethics, Engagement and Change in the Fiction of J. M. Coetzee," *MFS Modern Fiction Studies* 46, no. 1 (2000): 180.
6. J. M. Coetzee, *Age of Iron* (London: Penguin, 2010 [1990]), 17.

BIBLIOGRAPHY

Primary Bibliography

A) Texts Studied

Coetzee, J. M. *Boyhood: Scenes from Provincial Life*. London: Vintage, 1998 [1997].
—. *Youth*. London: Vintage, 2003 [2002].
—. *Summertime: Scenes from Provincial Life*. London: Vintage, 2010 [2009].
—. *Scenes from Provincial Life*. London: Harvill Secker, 2011.

B) Other Texts by Coetzee

Dusklands. London: Vintage, 2004 [1974].
In the Heart of the Country. London: Vintage, 2004 [1977].
Waiting for the Barbarians. London: Vintage, 2004 [1980].
Life & Times of Michael K. London: Vintage, 2004 [1983].
"Truth in Autobiography". Unpublished Inaugural Lecture, University of Cape Town, 1984.
Foe. London: Penguin, 2010 [1986].
White Writing: On the Culture of Letters in South Africa. Braamfontein: Pentz Publishers, 2007 [1988].
Age of Iron. London: Penguin, 2010 [1990].

"The Mind of *Apartheid*: Geoffrey Cronjé (1907–)." *Social Dynamics* 17, no. 1 (1991): 1–35.
Doubling the Point, edited by David Attwell. Cambridge, MA: Harvard University Press, 1992.
"The Manuscript Revisions of Beckett's *Watt*." In *Doubling the Point*, edited by David Attwell, 39–42. 1992 [1972].
"Samuel Beckett and the Temptations of Style." In *Doubling the Point*, edited by David Attwell, 43–53. 1992 [1973].
"Captain America in American Mythology." In *Doubling the Point*, edited by David Attwell, 107–14. 1992 [1976].
"Achterberg's 'Ballade van de gasfitter.'" In *Doubling the Point*, edited by David Attwell, 69–90. 1992 [1978].
"Notes on Rugby." In *Doubling the Point*, edited by David Attwell, 121–26. 1992 [1978].
"Jerusalem Prize Acceptance Speech." In *Doubling the Point*, edited by David Attwell, 96–99. 1992 [1986].
"Confession and Double Thoughts: Tolstoy, Rousseau, Dostoevsky." In *Doubling the Point*, edited by David Attwell, 251–93. 1992 [1986].
"The Taint of the Pornographic: Defending (Against) *Lady Chatterley*." In *Doubling the Point*, edited by David Attwell, 302–14. 1992 [1988].
"Homage." *The Threepenny Review* 53 (1993): 5–7.
Master of Petersburg. London: Vintage, 2004 [1994].
Giving Offense: Essays on Censorship. Chicago: Chicago University Press, 1996.
"A Fiction of the Truth." *Sydney Morning Herald*, November 27, 1999.
Disgrace. London: Vintage, 2000 [1999].
The Lives of Animals. Princeton: Princeton University Press, 1999.
"Daniel Defoe, *Robinson Crusoe*." In *Stranger Shores: Essays 1986–1999*, 20–26. London: Vintage, 2001.
"Dostoyevsky: The Miraculous Years." In *Stranger Shores: Essays 1986–1999*, 134–48. London: Vintage, 2001.
"What is a Classic?" In *Stranger Shores: Essays 1986–1999*, 1–19. London: Vintage, 2001.
Elizabeth Costello: Eight Lessons. London: Secker and Warburg, 2003.
The Nobel Lecture in Literature. New York: Penguin, 2004.
Slow Man. London: Vintage, 2006 [2005].
"Samuel Beckett in Cape Town—An Imaginary History." In *Beckett Remembering, Remembering Beckett: A Centenary Celebration*, edited by James Knowlson and Elizabeth Knowlson, 74–77. London: Bloomsbury, 2006.
Diary of a Bad Year. London: Vintage, 2008 [2007].
"Storm Over Young Goethe," *New York of Books* 59, no. 7 (2012). Accessed September 15, 2013. http://www.nybooks.com/articles/archives/2012/apr/26/storm-over-young-goethe/.
The Childhood of Jesus. London: Harvill Secker, 2013.
"On Nelson Mandela (1918–2013)." *New York Review of Books*, January 9, 2014. Accessed March 23, 2014. http://www.nybooks.com/articles/archives/2014/jan/09/nelson-mandela-1918-2013/.

C) Other Texts by Various Authors

Auster, Paul, and J. M. Coetzee. *Here and Now: Letters 2008–2011*. New York: Viking, 2013.

Baden-Powell, Robert. *Scouting for Boys*, edited by Elleke Boehmer. Oxford: Oxford University Press, 2004 [1908].

Beckett, Samuel. *Watt*, edited by C. J. Ackerley. London: Faber and Faber, 2009 [1953].

Breytenbach, Breyten. *The True Confessions of an Albino Terrorist*. London: Faber and Faber, 1984.

Brink, André. *On the Contrary: Being the Life of a Famous Rebel, Soldier, Traveller, Explorer, Reader, Builder, Scribe, Latinist, Lover and Liar*. London: Martin Secker & Warburg Limited, 1993.

——. *The First Life of Adamastor*. London: Vintage, 2000 [1993].

Camões, Luís Vaz de. *Os Lusíadas*, edited by Emanuel Paulo Ramos. Porto: Porto Editora, 1996.

Conrad, Joseph. "Heart of Darkness." In *Heart of Darkness and Other Tales*, edited by Cedric Watts, rev. ed., 101–87. New York: Oxford University Press, 2002 [1899].

——. *Lord Jim*. Oxford: Oxford University Press, 2008 [1900].

——. "Youth: A Narrative." In *Heart of Darkness and Other Tales*, edited by Cedric Watts, rev. ed., 69–99. New York: Oxford University Press, 2002 [1902].

——. *The Shadow-Line*. Oxford: Oxford University Press, 2009 [1917].

Coetzee, J. M., and Arabella Kurtz. *The Good Story: Exchanges on Truth, Fiction and Psychotherapy*. Harvill Secker: London, 2015.

Defoe, Daniel. *Robinson Crusoe*. Oxford: Oxford University Press, 2007 [1719].

Duiker, K. Sello. *The Quiet Violence of Dreams*, 2nd ed. Cape Town: Kwela Books, 2014 [2001].

Forster, E. M. *Maurice*. London: Penguin, 2005 [1971].

——. "Terminal Note." In *Maurice*, 219–224. London: Penguin, 2005 [1971].

Fugard, Athol. *Tsotsi*. Edinburgh: Canongate Books, 2009 [1979].

Galgut, Damon. "My Version of Home." In *A City Imagined*, edited by Stephen Watson, 12–20. Johannesburg: Penguin, 2006.

Goethe, Johann Wolfgang von. *The Sufferings of Young Werther*, translated and edited by Stanley Corngold. New York: W. W. Norton & Company, 2012 [1774].

——. *Le Divan Occidental-Oriental*, translated by Henri Lichtenberger. Paris: Éditions Aubier Montaigne, 1950 [1819].

Head, Bessie. *A Question of Power*. Johannesburg: Penguin, 2011 [1974].

Herodotus. *The Histories*, translated by Robin Waterfield. Oxford: Oxford University Press, 1998.

Homer. *The Odyssey*, translated by Walter Shewring. Oxford: Oxford University Press, 2008.

Hughes, Thomas. *Tom Brown's Schooldays*. Oxford: Oxford University Press, 1989.

Joyce, James. *A Portrait of the Artist as a Young Man*. Oxford: Oxford University Press, 2000 [1916].

Kipling, Rudyard. *Kim*. Oxford: Oxford University Press, 2008 [1901].

——. "If." In *Selected Poems*, 134. London: Penguin, 1993 [1910].

Mandela, Nelson. *Long Walk to Freedom*. London: Abacus, 1995 [1994].

Matshoba, Mtutuzeli. "Call Me not a Man." In *A Land Apart: A South African Reader*, edited by André Brink and J. M. Coetzee, 94–104. London: Faber and Faber, 1986 [1979].

Naipaul, V. S. *The Mimic Men*. London: Picador, 2011 [1967].

Osborne, John. *Look Back in Anger*. London: Faber, 1960 [1956].

Rhys, Jean. *Voyage in the Dark*. London: Penguin, 2000 [1934].

Said, Edward. *Out of Place: A Memoir*. New York: Alfred A. Knopf, 1999.

Schreiner, Olive. *The Story of an African Farm*. Oxford: Oxford University Press, 1998 [1883].

Tolstoy, Leo. *Childhood, Boyhood, Youth*, translated by Rosemary Edmonds. London: Penguin Books, 1964 [1852, 1854, 1857].

Secondary Bibliography

A) Criticism on Coetzee

Ackerley, Chris. "Style: Coetzee and Beckett." In *A Companion to the Works of J. M. Coetzee*, edited by Tim Mehigan, 23–38. New York: Camden House, 2011.

Attridge, Derek. *J. M. Coetzee and the Ethics of Reading*. Chicago: The University of Chicago Press, 2004.

Attwell, David. *J. M. Coetzee: South Africa and the Politics of Writing*. Berkeley: University of California Press, 1993.

—. "Coetzee's Estrangements." *NOVEL: A Forum on Fiction* 41, nos. 2–3 (2008): 229–43.

—. *J. M. Coetzee and the Life of Writing*. New York: Viking, 2015.

Barnard, Rita. "Coetzee in/and Afrikaans." *Journal of Literary Studies* 25, no. 4 (2009): 84–105.

Begam, Richard. "Silence and Mut(e)ilation: White Writing in J. M. Coetzee's *Foe*." *The South Atlantic Quarterly* 93, no. 1 (1994): 111–29.

Boehmer, Elleke. "Not Saying Sorry, Not Speaking Pain: Gender Implications in *Disgrace*." *Interventions: International Journal of Postcolonial Studies* 4, no. 3 (2002): 342–51.

—. "Sorry, Sorrier, Sorriest. The Gendering of Contrition in J. M. Coetzee's *Disgrace*." In *J. M. Coetzee and the Idea of the Public Intellectual*, edited by Jane Poyner, 135–47. Athens: Ohio University Press, 2006.

—. "Queer Bodies." In *J. M. Coetzee in Context and Theory*, edited by Elleke Boehmer, Katy Iddiols, and Robert Eaglestone, 123–34. London: Continuum, 2009.

Buikema, Rosemarie. "O Conteúdo da Forma e Outras Políticas Textuais. Configurações de Nação e Cidadania em *Disgrace* e *Agaat*." *Revista Crítica de Ciências Sociais* 89, trans. Isabel Pedro dos Santos (2010): 55–69.

Cantor, Paul A. "Happy Days in the Veld: Beckett and Coetzee's *In the Heart of the Country*." *South Atlantic Quarterly* 93, no. 1 (1994): 83–110.

Cardoen, Sam. "The Grounds of Cynical Self-Doubt: J. M. Coetzee's *Boyhood*, *Youth* and *Summertime*." *Journal of Literary Studies* 30, no. 1 (2014): 94–112.

Collingwood-Whittick, Sheila. "Autobiography as *Autre*biography: The Fictionalisation of the Self in JM Coetzee's *Boyhood: Scenes from Provincial Life.*" *Commonwealth* 24, no. 1 (2001): 13–23.

Coovadia, Imraan. "Coetzee In and Out of Cape Town." *Kritika Kultura* 18 (2012): 103–15.

Diala, Isidore. "Nadine Gordimer, J. M. Coetzee, and Andre Brink: Guilt, Expiation, and the Reconciliation Process in Post-*Apartheid* South Africa." *Journal of Modern Literature* XXV, no. 2 (2002): 50–68.

Engle, Lars. "Being Literary in the Wrong Way, Time, and Place: J. M. Coetzee's *Youth.*" *English Studies in Africa* 49, no. 2 (2006): 29–49.

Gordimer, Nadine. "The Idea of Gardening." *New York Review of Books*, February 2, 1984. Accessed April 3, 2012. http://www.nybooks.com/articles/archives/1984/feb/02/the-idea-of-gardening/.

Graham, Lucy Valerie. "Reading the Unspeakable: Rape in J. M. Coetzee's Disgrace." *Journal of Southern African Studies* 29, no. 2 (2003): 433–44.

—. "Textual Transvestism: The Female Voices of J. M. Coetzee." In *J. M. Coetzee and the Idea of the Public Intellectual*, edited by Jane Poyner, 217–35. Ohio: Ohio University Press, 2006.

Grzeda, Paulina. "The Ethico-Politics of Autobiographical Writings: J. M. Coetzee's *Boyhood, Youth* and *Summertime.*" *Werkwinkel* 7, no. 2 (2012): 77–101.

Head, Dominic. *J. M. Coetzee.* Cambridge: Cambridge University Press, 1997.

—. *The Cambridge Introduction to J. M. Coetzee.* Cambridge: Cambridge University Press, 2009.

Jacobs, J. U. "(N)either Afrikaner (n)or English: Cultural Cross-over in J. M. Coetzee's *Summertime.*" *English Academy Review: Southern African Journal of English Studies* 28, no. 1 (2011): 39–52.

Kannemeyer, J. C. *J. M. Coetzee: A Life in Writing*, translated by Michiel Heyns. Johannesburg and Cape Town: Jonathan Ball Publishers, 2012.

Kellman, Steven G. "J. M. Coetzee and Samuel Beckett: The Translingual Link." *Comparative Literature Studies* 33, no. 2 (1996): 161–72.

Kermode, Frank. "Fictioneering." *London Review of Books*, October 9, 2009. Accessed July 23, 2012. http://www.lrb.co.uk/v31/n19/frank-kermode/fictioneering.

Klopper, Dirk. "Critical Fictions in JM Coetzee's *Boyhood* and *Youth.*" *Scrutiny2: Issues in English Studies in Southern Africa* 11, no. 1 (2006): 22–31.

Kossew, Sue. "Scenes from Provincial Life (1997–2009)." In *A Companion to the Works of J. M. Coetzee*, edited by Tim Mehigan, 9–22. Rochester & New York: Camden House, 2011.

Kusek, Robert. "Writing Oneself, Writing the Other: J. M. Coetzee's Fictional Autobiography in *Boyhood, Youth* and *Summertime.*" *Werkwinkel* 7, no. 1 (2012): 97–116.

Lear, Jonathan. "The Ethical Thought of J. M. Coetzee." *Raritan* 28, no. 1 (2008): 68–97.

Lee, Hermione. "Heart of Stone: J. M. Coetzee." In *Body Parts: Essays on Life-Writing*, edited by Hermione Lee, 167–76. London: Pimlico, 2008.

Lenta, Margaret. "*Autre*biography: J. M. Coetzee's *Boyhood* and *Youth.*" *English in Africa* 30, no. 1 (2003): 157–69.

Marais, Mike. "'Little Enough, Less Than Little: Nothing': Ethics, Engagement and Change in the Fiction of J. M. Coetzee." *MFS Modern Fiction Studies* 46, no. 1 (2000): 159–82.

—. *Secretary of the Invisible: The Idea of Hospitality in the Fiction of J. M. Coetzee*. Amsterdam: Rodopi, 2009.

Mcmahan, Jeff. "Torture and Collective Shame." In *J. M. Coetzee and Ethics*, edited by Anton Leist and Peter Singer, 89–105. New York: Columbia University Press, 2010.

Meihuizen, N. C. T. "Beckett and Coetzee: Alternative Identities." *Literator* 32, no. 1 (2011): 1–19.

Meskell, Lynn, and Lindsay Weiss. "Coetzee on South Africa's Past: Remembering in the Time of Forgetting." *American Anthropologist* 108, no. 1 (2006): 88–99.

Onselen, Charles van. "A Childhood on the Edge of History." *London Review of Books*, February 5, 1998. Accessed July 17, 2012. http://www.lrb.co.uk/v20/n03/charles-van-onselen/a-childhood-on-the-edge-of-history.

Parks, Tim. "The Education of 'John Coetzee'." *New York Review of Books*, February 11, 2010. Accessed July 11, 2012. http://www.nybooks.com/articles/archives/2010/feb/11/the-education-of-john-coetzee/.

Parry, Benita. "Speech and Silence in The Fictions of J. M. Coetzee." In *Writing South Africa: Literature, Apartheid, and Democracy, 1970–1995*, edited by Derek Attridge and Rosemary Jolly, 149–65. Cambridge: Cambridge University Press, 1998.

Prentice, Chris. "Foe." In *A Companion to the Works of J. M. Coetzee*, edited by Tim Mehigan, 91–112. Rochester &, New York: Camden House, 2011.

Rose, Jacqueline. "Apathy and Accountability: The Challenge of South Africa's Truth and Reconciliation Commission to the Intellectual in the Modern World." In *Not Being Able to Sleep: Psychoanalysis and the Modern World*, edited by Jacqueline Rose, 216–37. London: Vintage, 2004.

Sheehan, Paul. "The Disasters of *Youth*: Coetzee and Geomodernism." *Twentieth-Century Literature* 57, no. 1 (2011): 20–33.

Smuts, Eckard. "J. M. Coetzee and the Politics of Selfhood." *English in Africa* 39, no. 1 (2012): 21–36.

Spivak, Gayatri Chakravorty. "Theory in the Margin: Coetzee's *Foe* Reading Defoe's *Crusoe/Roxana*." *English in Africa* 17, no. 2 (1990): 1–23.

—. "Ethics and Politics in Tagore, Coetzee, and Certain Scenes of Teaching." In *An Aesthetic Education in the Era of Globalization*, edited by Gayatri Chakravorty Spivak, 316–334. Cambridge, MA: Harvard University Press, 2012.

Twidle, Hedley. "Getting Past Coetzee." *Financial Times*, December 28, 2012. Accessed September 28, 2013. http://www.ft.com/cms/s/2/d2a3d68a-4923-11e2-9225-00144feab49a.html#axzz2Gk4csP8i>.

Van Heerden, Adriaan. "Disgrace, Desire, and the Dark Side of the New South Africa." In *J. M. Coetzee and Ethics*, edited by Anton Leist and Peter Singer, 44–63. New York: Columbia University Press, 2010.

Vermeulen, Pieter. "Wordsworth's Disgrace: The Insistence of South Africa in J.M. Coetzee's *Boyhood* and *Youth*." *Journal of Literary Studies* 23, no. 3 (2007): 179–99.

Yeoh, Gilbert. "J. M. Coetzee and Samuel Beckett: Nothingness, Minimalism and Indeterminacy." *ARIEL: A Review of International English Literature* 31, no. 4, (2000): 117–37.

Woessner, Martin. "Coetzee's Critique of Reason." In J. M. *Coetzee and Ethics*, edited by Anton Leist and Peter Singer, 223–47. New York: Columbia University Press, 2010.

Wright, Laura. "Displacing the Voice: South African Feminism and JM Coetzee's Female Narrators." *African Studies* 67, no. 1 (2008): 11–31.

Yekani, Elahe Haschemi. *The Privilege of Crisis: Narratives of Masculinities in Colonial and Postcolonial Literature, Photography and Film*. Frankfurt: Campus Verlag, 2011.

B) Masculinities and Gender Theory

Amâncio, Lígia. "A(s) Masculinidade(s) em Que-Estão." In *Aprender a ser Homem: Construindo Masculinidades*, edited by Lígia Amâncio, 13–27. Lisboa: Livros Horizonte, 2004.

Bahri, Deepika. "Feminism in/and Postcolonialism." In *The Cambridge Companion to Postcolonial Literary Studies*, edited by Neil Lazarus, 199–220. Cambridge: Cambridge University Press, 2004.

Barbosa, Madalena. *Que Força é Essa*. Lisboa: Sextante Editora, 2008.

Beauvoir, Simone de. *Le Deuxième Sexe I*. Paris: Gallimard, 1976 [1949].

—. *Le Deuxième Sexe II*. Paris: Gallimard, 1976 [1949].

Becker-Cantarino, Barbara. "Goethe and Gender." In *The Cambridge Companion to Goethe*, edited by Lesley Sharpe, 179–92. Cambridge: Cambridge University Press, 2002.

Beynon, John. *Masculinities and Culture*. Buckingham: Open University Press, 2002.

Benjamin, Jessica. *The Bonds of Love: Psychoanalysis, Feminism, and the Problem of Domination*. New York: Pantheon Books, 1988.

—. *Like Subjects, Love Objects: Essays on Recognition and Sexual Difference*. New Haven and London: Yale University Press, 1995.

—. *Shadow of the Other: Intersubjectivity and Gender in Psychoanalysis*. New York: Routledge, 1998.

Bhabha, Homi K. "Are you a Man or a Mouse?" In *Constructing Masculinity*, edited by Maurice Berger, Brian Wallis, and Simon Watson, 57–65. New York: Routledge, 1995.

Boehmer, Elleke. "Edward Said and (the Postcolonial Occlusion of) Gender." In *Edward Said and the Literary, Social, and Political World*, edited by Ranjan Ghosh, 124–36. New York: Routledge, 2009.

Breckenridge, Keith. "The Allure of Violence: Men, Race and Masculinity on the South African Goldmines, 1900–1950." *Journal of Southern African Studies* 24, no. 4 (1998): 669–93.

Brittan, Arthur. "Masculinities and Masculinism." In *The Masculinities Reader*, edited by Stephen M. Whitehead and Frank J. Barrett, 51–55. Cambridge: Polity Press, 2001.

Butler, Judith. *Gender Trouble*, 2nd ed. New York: Routledge, 1999 [1990].

—. "Gender." In *Feminism and Psychoanalysis: A Critical Dictionary*, edited by Elizabeth Wright, 140–45. Cambridge, MA: Blackwell, 1992.

—. *Giving an Account of Oneself*. New York: Fordham University Press, 2005.

Clayton, Cherry. "Radical Transformations: Emergent Women's Voices in South Africa." *English in Africa* 17, no. 2 (1990): 25–36.

Coltrane, Scott. "Theorizing Masculinities in Contemporary Social Science." In *Theorizing Masculinities*, edited by Harry Brod and Michael Kaufman, 39–60. London: Sage, 1994.

Connell, R. W. "Masculinities and Globalization." *Men and Masculinities* 1, no. 1 (1998): 3–23.

—. "The Social Organization of Masculinity." In *The Masculinities Reader*, edited by Stephen M. Whitehead and Frank J. Barrett, 30–50. Cambridge: Polity Press, 2001.

—. *Masculinities*, 2nd ed. Cambridge: Polity Press, 2005 [1995].

—. *Gender*. Cambridge: Polity Press, 2002.

—. "Change Among the Gatekeepers: Men, Masculinities, and Gender Equality in the Global Arena." *Signs* 30, no. 3 (2005): 1801–25.

—. *Gender: In World Perspective*, 2nd ed. Cambridge: Polity Press, 2009 [2002].

—, and James Messerschmidt. "Hegemonic Masculinity: Rethinking the Concept." *Gender & Society* 19 (2005): 829–59.

Corbett, Ken. "More Life: Centrality and Marginality in Human Development." *Psychoanalytic Dialogues* 11, no. 3 (2001): 313–35.

—. "Gender Now." *Psychoanalytic Dialogues* 18 (2008): 838–56.

—. *Boyhoods: Rethinking Masculinities*. New Haven and London: Yale University Press, 2009.

Cornwall, Andrea. "Introduction: Perspectives on Gender in Africa." In *Readings in Gender in Africa*, edited by Andrea Cornwall, 1–19. Oxford: James Currey, 2005.

Crenshaw, Kimberlé. "Demarginalizing the Intersection of Race and Sex: A Black Feminist Critique of Antidiscrimination Doctrine, Feminist Theory and Antiracist Politics." *The University of Chicago Legal Forum* 140 (1989): 139–67.

Cruise, Edwina. "Women, Sexuality, and the Family in Tolstoy." In *The Cambridge Companion to Tolstoy*, edited by Donna Tussing Orwin, 191–205. Cambridge: Cambridge University Press, 2002.

Davis, Kathy. "Intersectionality as Buzzword: A Sociology of Science Perspective on what Makes a Feminist Theory Successful." *Feminist Theory* 9, no. 1 (2008): 67–85.

Dawson, Graham. *British Adventure, Empire and the Imagining of Masculinities*. New York: Routledge, 1994.

Dunton, Chris. "'Wheything Be Dat?' The Treatment of Homosexuality in African Literature." *Research in African Literatures* 20, no. 3 (1989): 422–48.

Ekine, Sokari. "Contesting Narratives of Queer Africa." In *Queer African Reader*, edited by Sokari Ekine and Hakima Abbas, 78–91. Dakar: Pambazuka Press, 2013.

Epprecht, Marc. *Sexuality and Social Justice in Africa: Rethinking Homophobia and Forging Resistance*. London: Zed Books, 2013.

Forth, Christopher E. *Masculinity in the Modern West: Gender, Civilization and the Body*. New York: Palgrave Macmillan, 2008.

Foucault, Michel. *Histoire de la Sexualité I: La Volonté de Savoir*. Paris: Gallimard, 1976.

Frenkel, Ronit. "Feminism and Contemporary Culture in South Africa." *African Studies* 67, no. 1 (2008): 1–9.

Freud, Sigmund. "Three Essays on Sexual Theory." In *The Psychology of Love*, translated by Shaun Whiteside, 111–220. London: Penguin, 2006 [1905].

Gevisser, Mark. "A Different Fight for Freedom: A History of South African Lesbian and Gay Organisation from the 1950s to 1990s." In *Defiant Desire: Gay and Lesbian Lives in South Africa*, edited by Mark Gevisser and Edwin Cameron, 14–86. New York: Routledge, 1995.

Gilbert, James. *Men in the Middle: Searching for Masculinity in the 1950s*. Chicago: University of Chicago Press, 2005.

Gilmore, David. *Manhood in the Making: Cultural Concepts of Masculinity*. London: Yale University Press, 1990.

Glover, David and Cora Kaplan. *Genders*, 2nd ed. New York: Routledge, 2009 [2000].

Gqola, Pumla Dineo. "How the 'Cult of Femininity' and Violent Masculinities Support Endemic Gender Based Violence in Contemporary South Africa." *African Identities* 5, no. 1 (2007): 111–24.

Graydon, Jan. "'But it's More than a Game. It's an Institution.' Feminist Perspectives on Sport." *Feminist Review* 13 (1983): 5–16.

Harding, Sandra. *Sciences from Below: Feminisms, Postcolonialities, and Modernities*. Durham and London: Duke University Press, 2008.

Hassim, Shireen. "Democracy's Shadows: Sexual Rights and Gender Politics in the Rape Trial of Jacob Zuma." *African Studies* 68, no. 1 (2009): 57–77.

Hearn, Jeff and David L. Collinson. "Theorizing Unities and Differences between Men and between Masculinities." In *Theorizing Masculinities*, edited by Harry Brod and Michael Kaufman, 97–118. London: Sage, 1994.

hooks, bell. *Ain't I a Woman: Black Women and Feminism*. Cambridge: South End Press, 1981.

—. *Feminist Theory: From Margin to Center*, 2nd ed. London: Pluto Press, 2000 [1984].

—. *Feminism is for Everybody: Passionate Politics*. London: Pluto Press, 2000.

Horlacher, Stefan. "Charting the Field of Masculinity Studies; Or, Toward a Literary History of Masculinities." In *Constructions of Masculinity in British Literature from the Middle Ages to the Present*, edited by Stefan Horlacher, 3–18. New York: Palgrave Macmillan, 2011.

Horrell, Georgina. "A Whiter Shade of Pale: White Femininity as Guilty Masquerade in 'New' (White) South African Women's Writing." *Journal of Southern African Studies* 30, no. 4 (2004): 765–76.

Hunt, Nancy Rose. "Introduction." *Gender & History* 8, no. 3 (1996): 323–37.

Ireland, Patrick R. "A Macro-Level Analysis of the Scope, Causes, and Consequences of Homophobia in Africa." *African Studies Review* 56, no. 2 (2003): 47–66.

Jackson II, Ronald L., and Murali Balaji. "Conceptualizing Current Discourses and Writing New Ones." In *Global Masculinities and Manhood*, edited by Ronald L. Jackson II and Murali Balaji, 17–30. Urbana, Chicago: University of Illinois Press, 2011.

Jeffers, Jennifer M. *Beckett's Masculinity*. New York: Palgrave, 2009.

Jones, Tim Trengove. "Fiction and the Law: Recent Inscriptions of Gayness in South Africa." *Modern Fiction Studies* 46, no. 1 (2000): 114–36.

Kabesh, Amal Treacher. "Something in the Air: Otherness, Recognition and Ethics." *Journal of Social Work Practice* 20, no. 1 (2006): 27–37.

—. "Injurious Imperialism: Reflecting on My Father." *Journal of Postcolonial Writing* 45, no. 3 (2009): 341–50.

—. *Postcolonial Masculinities: Emotions, Histories and Ethics.* Farnham, Surrey: Ashgate, 2013.

Kimmel, Michael S. *The History of Men: Essays on the History of American and British Masculinities.* New York: State University of New York Press, 2005.

—. *Manhood in America: A Cultural History,* 2nd ed. Oxford: Oxford University Press, 2006 [1996].

—, and Abby L. Ferber. "Toward a Pedagogy of the Oppressor." In *Privilege: A Reader,* edited by Michael S. Kimmel and Abby L. Ferber, 1–10. Cambridge: Westview Press, 2003.

—, Jeff Hearn, and R. W. Connell (eds.), *Handbook of Studies on Men & Masculinities.* Thousand Oaks, CA: Sage, 2005.

Kobus Du Pisani. "Puritanism Transformed: Afrikaner Masculinities in the *Apartheid* and Post-*Apartheid* Period." In *Changing Men in Southern Africa,* edited by Robert Morrell, 157–175. London: Zed Books, 2001.

Lea, Daniel, and Berthhold Schoene. "Introduction to the Special Section on Literary Masculinities," *Men and Masculinities* 4, no. 4 (2002): 319–21.

Mangan, J. A. *"Manufactured Masculinity": Making Imperial Manliness, Morality and Militarism.* New York: Routledge, 2012.

Mcclintock, Anne. *Imperial Leather: Race, Gender and Sexuality in the Colonial Contest.* New York and London: Routledge, 1995.

Mcintosh, Peggy. "White Privilege and Male Privilege: A Personal Account of Coming to see Correspondences Through Work in Women's Studies." In *Privilege: A Reader,* edited by Michael S. Kimmel and Abby L. Ferber, 147–60. Cambridge: Westview Press, 2003.

Miller, Toby. "Masculinity." In *A Companion to Gender Studies,* edited by Philomena Essed, David Theo Goldberg, and Audrey Kobayashi, 114–31. Oxford: Blackwell, 2005.

Moffett, Helen. "'These Women, They Force Us to Rape Them': Rape as Narrative of Social Control in Post-*Apartheid* South Africa." *Journal of Southern African Studies* 32, no. 1 (2006): 129–44.

Mohanty, Chandra Talpade. *Feminism without Borders: Decolonizing Theory, Practicing Solidarity.* Durham and London: Duke University Press, 2003.

—. "Under Western Eyes: Feminist Scholarship and Colonial Discourses." *Feminist Review* 30 (1988): 61–88.

Mooney, Katie. "'Ducktails, Flick-Knives and Pugnacity': Subcultural and Hegemonic Masculinities in South Africa, 1948–1960." *Journal of Southern African Studies* 24, no. 4 (1998): 753–74.

Morrell, Robert. "Of Boys and Men: Masculinity and Gender in Southern African Studies." *Journal of Southern African Studies* 24, no. 4 (1998): 605–30.

—. *From Boys to Gentlemen: Settler Masculinity in Colonial Natal 1880–1920.* Pretoria: University of South Africa, 2001.

—. "The Times of Change: Men and Masculinity in South Africa." In *Changing Men in Southern Africa,* edited by Robert Morrellm, 3–37. London: Zed Books, 2001.

—. "Men, Movements, and Gender Transformation in South Africa." In *African Masculinities: Men in Africa from the Late Nineteenth Century to the Present,* edited by Ouzgane Lahoucine and Robert Morrell, 271–88. New York: Palgrave Macmillan, 2005.

—, Rachel Jewkes, and Graham Lindegger. "Hegemonic Masculinity/Masculinities in South Africa: Culture, Power, and Gender Politics." *Men and Masculinities* 15, no. 1 (2012): 11–30.

—, and others. "Hegemonic Masculinity: Reviewing the Gendered Analysis of Men's Power in South Africa." *South African Review of Sociology* 44, no. 1 (2013): 3–21.

Munro, Brenna M. *South Africa and the Dream of Love to Come: Queer Sexuality and the Struggle for Freedom.* Minneapolis: Minneapolis University Press, 2012.

—. "Nelson, Winnie, and the Politics of Gender." In *The Cambridge Companion to Nelson Mandela*, edited by Rita Barnard, 92–112. Cambridge: Cambridge University Press, 2014.

Murray, Stephen O., and Will Roscoe. "All Very Confusing." In *Boy-Wives and Female Husbands: Studies of African Homosexualities*, edited by Stephen O. Murray and Will Roscoe, xi–xxii. London: Macmillan Press, 1998.

Newton, Judith. "Masculinity Studies: The Longed for Profeminist Movement for Academic Men?" In *Masculinity Studies & Feminist Theory: New Directions*, edited by Judith Kegan Gardiner, 176–92. New York: Columbia University Press, 2002.

Nortwick, Thomas Van. *Imagining Men: Ideals of Masculinity in Ancient Greek Culture.* London: Praeger, 2008.

Osório de Castro, Zília. "Nota de Abertura." *Faces de Eva. Estudos sobre a Mulher* 30 (2013): 5–6.

Penedo, Susana López. *El Laberinto Queer.* Barcelona: EGALES, 2008.

Posel, Deborah. "The Scandal of Manhood: 'Baby Rape' and the Politicization of Sexual Violence in Post-Apartheid South Africa." *Culture, Health & Sexuality* 7, no. 3 (2005): 239–52.

Pucherova, Dobrota. "'Land of my Sons': The Politics of Gender in Black Consciousness Poetry." *Journal of Postcolonial Writing* 45, no. 3 (2009): 331–40.

—. "Re-Imagining the Other: The Politics of Friendship in Three Twenty-First Century South African Novels." *Journal of Southern African Studies* 35, no. 4 (2009): 929–43.

Quindeau, Ilka. *Seduction and Desire: The Psychoanalytic Theory of Sexuality since Freud*, translated by John Bendix. London: Karnac, 2013.

Ratele, Kopano. "Currents Against Gender Transformation of South African Men: Relocating Marginality to the Centre of Research and Theory of Masculinities." *NORMA: International Journal for Masculinity Studies* 9, no. 1 (2014): 30–44.

Reed, Matt T. "Historicizing Inversion: Or, How to Make a Homosexual." *History of the Human Sciences* 14, no. 4 (2001): 1–29.

Roberts, Benjamin B. *Sex and Drugs before Rock "N" Roll: Youth Culture and Masculinity during Holland's Golden Age.* Amsterdam: Amsterdam University Press, 2012.

Robins, Steven. "'Long Live Zackie, Long Live': AIDS Activism, Science and Citizenship after Apartheid." *Journal of Southern African Studies* 30, no. 3 (2004): 651–72.

Rose, Sonya O. "Temperate Heroes: Concepts of Masculinity in Second World War Britain." In *Masculinities in Politics and War: Gendering Modern History*, edited by Stefan Dudink, Karen Hagemann, and John Tosh, 177–95. Manchester: Manchester University Press, 2004.

Sampath, Niels. "'Crabs in a Bucket': Reforming Male Identities in Trinidad." In *The Masculinities Reader*, edited by Stephen M. Whitehead and Frank J. Barrett, 330–40. Cambridge: Polity Press, 2001.

Schoene-Harwood, Berthold. *Writing Men: Literary Masculinities from Frankenstein to the New Man*. Edinburgh: Edinburgh University Press, 2000.

Sedgwick, Eve Kosofsky. *Between Men: English Literature and Male Homosocial Desire*. New York: Columbia University Press, 1985.

—. "Queer and Now." In *Tendencies*, 1–19. London: Routledge, 1994.

—. *Epistemology of the Closet*. Los Angeles: University of California Press, 2008.

Segal, Lynne. *Is the Future Female?: Troubled Thoughts on Contemporary Feminism*. New York: Peter Bedrick Books, 1988.

—. *Slow Motion: Changing Masculinities, Changing Men*, 3rd ed. London: Palgrave Macmillan, 2007 [1990].

—. "Freud and Feminism: A Century of Contradiction." *Feminism & Psychology* 6, no. 2 (1996): 290–97.

—. *Why Feminism?: Gender, Psychology, Politics*. New York: Columbia University Press, 1999.

—. *Making Trouble: Life and Politics*. London: Serpent's Tail, 2007.

Sinha, Mrinalini. *Colonial Masculinity: The "Manly Englishman" and the "Effeminate Bengali" in the Late Nineteenth Century*. Manchester and New York: Manchester University Press, 1995.

—. "Giving Masculinity a History: Some Contributions from the Historiography of Colonial India." *Gender & History* 11, no. 3 (1999): 445–60.

Sole, Kelwyn. "Political Fiction, Representation and the Canon: The Case of Mtutuzeli Matshoba." *English in Africa* 28, no. 2 (2001): 101–21.

Sonnekus, Theo. "'We're Not Faggots!': Masculinity, Homosexuality and the Representation of Afrikaner Men Who Have Sex With Men in the Film *Skoonheid* and Online." *South African Review of Sociology* 44, no. 1 (2013): 22–39.

Spurlin, William J. *Imperialism within the Margins: Queer Representation and the Politics of Culture in Southern Africa*. New York: Palgrave Macmillan, 2006.

Swart, Sandra. "A Boer and His Gun and His Wife are Three Things Always Together: Republican Masculinity and the 1914 Rebellion." *Journal of Southern African Studies* 24, no. 4 (1998): 737–51.

Tamale, Sylvia. "Confronting the Politics of Nonconforming Sexualities in Africa." *African Studies Review* 56, no. 2 (2013): 31–45.

Tavares, Manuela. *Movimentos de Mulheres em Portugal—Décadas de 70 e 80*. Lisboa: Livros Horizonte, 2000.

Thoreson, Ryan Richard. "Somewhere Over the Rainbow Nation: Gay, Lesbian and Bisexual Activism in South Africa." *Journal of Southern African Studies* 34, no. 3 (2008): 679–97.

Tong, Rosemarie Putnam. *Feminist Thought*, 3rd ed. Boulder, CO: Westview Press, 2008 [1998].

Tosh, John. *A Man's Place: Masculinity and the Middle-Class Home in Victorian England*. New Haven and London: Yale University Press, 2007.

Treacher, Amal. "Postcolonial Subjectivity: Masculinity, Shame, and Memory." *Ethnic and Racial Studies* 30, no. 2 (2007): 281–99.

Unterhalter, Elaine. "The Work of the Nation: Heroic Masculinity in South African Autobiographical Writing of the Anti-*Apartheid* Struggle." *The European Journal of Development Research* 12, no. 2 (2000): 157–78.

Vale de Almeida, Miguel. "Teoria *Queer* e a Contestação da Categoria 'Género.'" In *Indisciplinar a Teoria: Estudos Gays, Lésbicos e Queer*, edited by António Fernando Cascais, 91–98. Lisboa: Fenda Edições, 2004.

—. *A Chave do Armário: Homossexualidade, Casamento, Família.* Lisboa: ICS, 2009.

Visagie, Andries. "White Masculinity and the African Other: *Die werfbobbejaan* by Alexander Strachan." *Alternation* 9, no. 1 (2002): 131–41.

Volkmann, Laurenz. "Fortified Masculinity: Daniel Defoe's *Robinson Crusoe* as a Literary Emblem of Western Male Identity." In *Constructions of Masculinity in British Literature from the Middle Ages to the Present*, edited by Stefan Horlacher, 129–46. New York: Palgrave Macmillan, 2011.

Waal, Shaun de. "On 'Moffie.'" In *Defiant Desire: Gay and Lesbian Lives in South Africa*, edited by Mark Gevisser and Edwin Cameron, xiii. New York: Routledge, 1995.

Waetjen, Thembisa. *Workers and Warriors: Masculinity and the Struggle for Nation in South Africa.* Urbana and Chicago: University of Illinois Press, 2004.

Walker, Cherryl. *Women and Resistance in South Africa*, 2nd ed. Claremont, South Africa: David Philip Publishers, 1991 [1982].

Walker, Liz. "Men Behaving Differently: South African Men since 1994." *Culture, Health & Sexuality: An International Journal for Research, Intervention and Care* 7, no. 3 (2005): 225–38.

Walters, Margaret. *Feminism: A Very Short Introduction.* Oxford: Oxford University Press, 2005.

Weeks, Jeffrey. *Sexuality and its Discontents.* London: Routledge, 1985.

Wells, Julia C. "Why Women Rebel: A Comparative Study of South African Women's Resistance in Bloemfontein (1913) and Johannesburg (1958)." *Journal of Southern African Studies* 10, no. 1 (1983): 55–70.

Wiegman, Robyn. "Unmaking: Men and Masculinity in Feminist Theory." In *Masculinity Studies & Feminist Theory: New Directions*, edited by Judith Kegan Gardiner, 31–59. New York: Columbia University Press, 2002.

Winn, William E. "Tom Brown's Schooldays and the Development of 'Muscular Christianity.'" *Church History* 29, no. 1 (1960): 64–73.

Woollacott, Angela. *Gender and Empire.* New York: Palgrave Macmillan, 2006.

Worden, Nigel. "Demanding Satisfaction: Violence, Masculinity and Honour in Late Eighteenth-Century Cape Town." *Kronos* 35 (2009): 32–47.

Zungu, Mthunzi, and others. "HERstory: Writing Women into South African History." *Agenda* 28, no. 1 (2014): 7–17.

C) Postcolonial and Cultural Theory

Ahmed, Sara. "Shame Before Others." In *The Cultural Politics of Emotion*, 2nd ed., 101–21. Edinburgh: Edinburgh University Press, 2014 [2004].

Alcoff, Linda Martín. "The Problem of Speaking for Others." In *Who Can Speak? Authority and Critical Identity*, edited by Judith Roof and Robyn Wiegman, 97–119. Urbana and Chicago: University of Illinois Press, 1995.

Allison, Scott T., and George R. Goethals. *Heroes: What They Do and Why We Need Them.* Oxford: Oxford University Press, 2011.

Anderson, Linda. *Autobiography*, 2nd ed. New York: Routledge, 2011 [2001].

Bakhtin, Mikhail. *Problems of Dostoyevsky's Poetics*, translated by Caryl Emerson. Minneapolis: University of Minnesota Press, 1984.

Barnard, Rita. "Ugly Feelings, Negative Dialectics: Reflections on Postapartheid Shame." *Safundi: The Journal of South African and American Studies* 13, nos. 1–2 (2012): 151–70.

Barthes, Roland. "The Death of the Author." In *Image-Music-Text*, translated by Stephen Heath, 142–48. London: Fontana, 1977 [1968].

Bethlehem, Louise. "The Pleasures of the Political: *Apartheid* and Postapartheid South African Fiction." In *Teaching the African Novel*, edited by Gaurav Desai, 222–45. New York: The Modern Language Association of America, 2009.

Bewes, Timothy. *The Event of Postcolonial Shame.* Princeton: Princeton University Press, 2010.

Bhabha, Homi K. *The Location of Culture.* New York: Routledge, 1994.

Boehmer, Elleke. *Colonial and Postcolonial Literature: Migrant Metaphors*, 2nd ed. Oxford: Oxford University Press, 2005 [1995].

—, and Frances Gouda. "Postcolonial Studies in the Context of the 'Diasporic' Netherlands." In *The Postcolonial Low Countries: Literature, Colonialism and Multiculturalism*, edited by Elleke Boehmer and Sarah de Mul, 25–44. Lanham: Lexington Books, 2012.

Coelho, Maria Teresa Pinto. *Ilhas, Batalhas e Aventura: Imagens de África no Romance de Império Britânico do Último Quartel do Século XIX e Início do Século XX.* Lisboa: Edições Colibri, 2004.

Darwin, John. *After Tamerlane: The Rise & Fall of Global Empires, 1400–2000.* London: Penguin, 2008 [2007].

Derrida, Jacques. "Politics of Friendship." *American Imago* 50, no. 3 (1993): 353–91.

—. *The Gift of Death*, translated by David Wills. Chicago: Chicago University Press, 1995.

Descartes, René. *A Discourse on the Method*, translated by Ian Maclean. Oxford: Oxford University Press, 2008.

Ehrenreich, Barbara. *The Hearts of Men: American Dreams and the Flight from Commitment.* New York: Random House, 1983.

Fanon, Frantz. *Peau Noire, Masques Blancs.* Paris: Seuil, 1952.

—. *Les Damnés de la Terre.* Paris: La Découverte and Syros, 2002 [1961].

Foucault, Michel. "What is an Author?" In *Language, Counter-Memory, Practice: Selected Essays and Interviews*, edited by Donald F. Bouchard, 113–38. New York: Cornell University Press, 1977 [1969].

Freud, Sigmund. "Introductory Lectures on Psycho-Analysis." In *The Standard Edition of the Complete Psychological Works of Sigmund Freud, Volume XVI (1916–1917): Introductory Lectures on Psycho-Analysis (Part III)*, 241–463. London: Vintage, 1975 [1917].

—. *The Ego and the Id*, translated by John Reddick. London: Penguin, 2003 [1923].

—. "Introductory Lectures on Psychoanalysis: New Series." In *An Outline of Psychoanalysis*, translated by Helena Ragg-Kirkby, 1–172. London: Penguin, 2003 [1933].

Frosh, Stephen. "The Other." *American Imago* 59 (2002): 389–407.

—. *For and Against Psychoanalysis*, 2nd ed. New York: Routledge, 2006 [1997].

—. "The Relational Ethics of Conflict and Identity." *Psychoanalysis, Culture & Society* 16, no. 3 (2011): 225–43.

—. "Psychoanalysis, Colonialism, Racism." *Journal of Theoretical and Philosophical Psychology* 33, no. 3 (2013): 141–54.

Gandhi, Leela. *Postcolonial Theory: A Critical Introduction*. Crows Nest: Allen and Unwin, 1998.

Gil, Daniel Juan. "'Bare Life': Political Order and the Specter of Antisocial Being in Shakespeare's *Julius Caesar*." *Common Knowledge* 13, no. 1 (2007): 67–79.

Gramsci, Antonio. *Selections from the Prison Notebooks*, edited and translated by Quintin Hoare and Geoffrey Nowell Smith. New York: International Publishers, 1971.

Green, Martin. *Dreams of Adventure, Deeds of Empire*. New York: Basic Books, 1979.

Hall, Stuart. "The Neo-Liberal Revolution." *Cultural Studies* 25, no. 6 (2011): 705–28.

Harding, Sandra. "Beyond Postcolonial Theory: Two Undertheorized Perspectives on Science and Technology." In *The Postcolonial Science and Technology Studies Reader*, edited by Sandra Harding, 1–31. Durham and London: Duke University Press, 2011.

Harvey, David. *A Brief History of Neoliberalism*. Oxford: Oxford University Press, 2007.

Hegel, G. W. F. *Phenomenology of Spirit*, translated by A. V. Miller. Oxford: Oxford University Press, 1977 [1807].

Kant, Immanuel. *An Answer to the Question: "What is Enlightenment?"*, translated by H. B. Nisbet. London: Penguin, 2009 [1784].

Kapuściński, Ryszard. *The Other*. London: Verso, 2008 [2006].

Kristeva, Julia. *Étrangers à Nous-Mêmes*. Paris: Gallimard, 1988.

Laplanche, Jean. *New Foundations for Psychoanalysis*, translated by David Macey. Oxford: Basil Blackwell, 1989.

Lawrence, Karen R. "Orlando's Voyage Out." *Modern Fiction Studies* 38, no. 1 (1992): 253–77.

Lazarus, Neil. *The Postcolonial Unconscious*. Cambridge: Cambridge University Press, 2011.

Lejeune, Philippe. "The Autobiographical Contract." In *French Literary Theory Today*, edited by Tzvetan Todorov, 192–222. Cambridge: Cambridge University Press, 1982.

Levinas, Emmanuel. *Totalité et Infini: Essai sur L'Extériorité*. Paris: Kluwer Academic, 2014 [1961].

Levine, Philippa. *The British Empire: Sunrise to Sunset*. Harlow: Pearson Education Limited, 2007.

Loomba, Ania. *Colonialism/Postcolonialism*, 2nd ed. New York: Routledge, 2005 [1998].

Loxley, Diana. *Problematic Shores: The Literature of Islands*. London: Macmillan Press, 1990.

Madden, Patrick. "The 'New Memoir.'" In *The Cambridge Companion to Autobiography*, edited by Maria DiBattista and Emily Wittman, 222–36. Cambridge: Cambridge University Press, 2014.

Man, Paul de. "Autobiography as De-Facement." *MLN* 94, no. 5 (1979): 919–930.

Mccall, Leslie. "The Complexity of Intersectionality." *Signs* 30, no. 3 (2005): 1771–800.

Memmi, Albert. *Portrait du Colonisé/Portrait du Colonisateur*. Paris: Gallimard, 1985 [1957].

Mullaney, Julie. *Postcolonial Literatures in Context*. London: Continuum, 2010.

Nussbaum, Martha C. *Upheavals of Thought: The Intelligence of Emotions*. Cambridge: Cambridge University Press, 2001.

—. "Inscribing the Face: Shame and Stigma." In *Hiding from Humanity: Disgust, Shame, and the Law*, 172–221. Princeton: Princeton University Press, 2004.

Patterson, Steven. "Postcards from the Raj." *Patterns of Prejudice* 40, no. 2 (2006): 142–58.

Prilleltensky, Isaac. "The Role of Power in Wellness, Oppression, and Liberation: The Promise of Psychopolitical Validity." *Journal of Community Psychology* 36, no. 2 (2008): 116–36.

—, and Geoffrey Nelson. *Doing Psychology Critically: Making a Difference in Diverse Settings*. New York: Palgrave Macmillan, 2002.

Raman, Shankar. *Renaissance Literature and Postcolonial Studies*. Edinburgh: Edinburgh University Press, 2011.

Rousseau, Jean-Jacques. *Discours sur l'origine et les fondements de l'inegalité parmi les hommes*. Paris: Gallimard, 1969 [1754].

—. *Les Confessions*. Paris: Gallimard, 2009 [1782–789].

Rowbotham, Sheila. *Promise of a Dream: Remembering the Sixties*. London: Allen Lane, 2000.

Ruddick, Nicholas. "The Fantastic Fiction of the *Fin de Siècle*." In *The Cambridge Companion to the Fin de Siècle*, edited by Gail Marshall, 189–206. Cambridge: Cambridge University Press, 2007.

Said, Edward. *Orientalism*. London: Penguin, 2003 [1978].

—. *Culture and Imperialism*. London: Vintage, 1994 [1993].

Sagan, Carl, *Cosmos*. New York: Ballantine Books, 2013 [1980].

Sanches, Manuela Ribeiro. "Afinidades Selectivas. Edward W. Said e a Perspectiva Pós-Colonial." In *Pensamento Crítico Contemporâneo*, edited by UNIPOP, 344–62. Lisboa: Edições 70, 2014.

Sandhu, Sukhdev. *London Calling: How Black and Asian Writers Imagined a City*. London: Harper, 2004.

Scott, John. *Power*. Cambridge: Polity Press, 2001.

Shildrick, Margrit. "The Self's Clean and Proper Body." In *Embodying the Monster: Encounters with the Vulnerable Self*, 48–67. London: Sage, 2002.

Spivak, Gayatri Chakravorty. "Three Women's Texts and a Critique of Imperialism." *Critical Inquiry* 12, no. 1 (1985): 243–61.

—. "Can the Subaltern Speak?" In *Marxism and the Interpretation of Culture*, edited by Cary Nelson and Lawrence Grossbergm, 271–313. London: Macmillan, 1988.

—. *A Critique of Postcolonial Reason: Toward a History of the Vanishing Present*. Cambridge, MA: Harvard University Press, 1999.

Stevenson, Randall. *The Oxford English Literary History Volume 12. 1960–2000: The Last of England?* Oxford: Oxford University Press, 2004.

Sullivan, Zohreh T. *Narratives of Empire: The Fictions of Rudyard Kipling*. Cambridge: Cambridge University Press, 1993.

Terrall, Mary. "Heroic Narratives of Quest and Discovery." In *The Postcolonial Science and Technology Studies Reader*, edited by Sandra Harding, 84–102. Durham and London: Duke University Press, 2011.

Thwaites, Tony. *Reading Freud: Psychoanalysis as Cultural Theory*. London: Sage, 2007.

Trivedi, Harish. "'Arguing with the Himalayas'? Edward Said on Rudyard Kipling." In *Kipling and Beyond: Patriotism, Globalisation and Postcolonialism*, edited by Caroline Rooney and Kaori Nagai, 120–43. New York: Palgrave Macmillan, 2010.

Trovão, Susana. "Comparing Postcolonial Identity Formations: Legacies of Portuguese and British Colonialisms in East Africa." *Social Identities* 18, no. 3 (2012): 261–80.

Turchi, Peter. *Maps of the Imagination: The Writer as Cartographer*. Texas: Trinity University Press, 2004.

Williams, Raymond. *Politics of Modernism: Against the New Conformists*. London: Verso, 2007.

Yegenoglu, Meyda. *Colonial Fantasies*. Cambridge: Cambridge University Press, 1998.

Young, Iris Marion. *Justice and the Politics of Difference*. Princeton: Princeton University Press, 1990.

Young, Robert J. C. *Torn Halves: Political Conflict in Literary and Cultural Theory*. Manchester: Manchester University Press, 1996.

—. *Postcolonialism: An Historical Introduction*. Oxford: Blackwell, 2001.

—. *Postcolonialism: A Very Short Introduction*. Oxford: Oxford University Press, 2003.

D) British and South African Culture and History

Adriaan du Pisani, Jacobus. "Hegemonic Masculinity in Afrikaner Nationalist Mobilisation, 1934–48." In *Masculinities in Politics and War: Gendering Modern History*, edited by Stefan Dudink, Karen Hagemann and John Tosh, 157–76. Manchester: Manchester University Press, 2004.

Beckford-Smith, Vivian. "South African Urban History, Racial Segregation and the Unique Case of Cape Town?" *Journal of Southern African Studies* 21, no. 1 (1995): 63–78.

Boehmer, Elleke. "Introduction." In Robert Baden-Powell, *Scouting for Boys*, edited by Elleke Boehmer, xi–xxxix. Oxford: Oxford University Press, 2004 [1908].

—. "Postcolonial Terrorist: The Example of Nelson Mandela." *Parallax* 11, no. 4 (2005): 46–55.

—. *Nelson Mandela: A Very Short Introduction*. Oxford: Oxford University Press, 2008.

Breytenbach, Breyten. "'I am Not an Afrikaner Any More.'" *Index on Censorship* 12, no. 3 (1983): 3–6.

Brink, André. "Stories of History: Reimagining the Past in Post-*Apartheid* Narrative." In *Negotiating the Past: The Making of Memory in South Africa*, edited by Sarah Nuttall and Carli Coetzee, 29–42. Cape Town: Oxford University Press, 1998.

—. "Post-*Apartheid* Literature: A Personal View." In *J. M. Coetzee in Context and Theory*, edited by Elleke Boehmer, Katy Iddiols, and Robert Eaglestone, 11–19. London: Continuum, 2009.

Bristow, Joseph. *Empire Boys: Adventures in a Man's World.* London: Harper Collins Academic, 1991.

Brook, Dominic. *Never Had It So Good: A History of Britain from Suez to the Beatles, 1956–1963.* London: Little, Brown, 2005.

Burchell, William J. *Hints on Emigration to the Cape of Good Hope.* London: J. Hatchard and Son, 1819.

—. *Travels in the Interior of Southern Africa, Volume I.* London: Longman-Hurst-Rees-Orme and Brown, 1822.

Comaroff, Jean, and John L. Comaroff. "Naturing the Nation: Aliens, Apocalypse and the Postcolonial State." *Journal of Southern African Studies* 27, no. 3 (2001): 627–51.

Chapman, Michael. *Southern African Literatures.* Scottsville: University of Natal Press, 2003.

Davis, Emily S. "1980s South African Fiction and the Romance of Resistance." In *Rethinking the Romance Genre: Global Intimacies in Contemporary Literary and Visual Culture,* 27–62. New York: Palgrave Macmillan, 2013.

Filatova, Irina. "The Lasting Legacy: The Soviet Theory of the National-Democratic Revolution and South Africa." *South African Historical Journal* 64, no. 3 (2012): 507–37.

Flower-Smith, Malcolm, and Edmund Yorke. *Mafeking! The Story of a Siege* Weltevredenpark, South Africa: Covos-Day Books, 2000.

Giliomee, Hermann. *The Afrikaners: Biography of a People.* London: Hurst & Company, 2011.

Gordimer, Nadine. *Living in Hope and History.* London: Bloomsbury Publishing, 1999.

Grobler, Jackie. "The Retief Massacre of 6 February 1838 Revisited." *Historia* 56, no. 2 (2011): 113–32.

Hamilton, Carolyn, Bernard K. Mbenga, and Robert Ross. "The Production of Preindustrial South African History." In *The Cambridge History of South Africa, Volume 1: From Early Times to 1885,* edited by Robert Ross, Anne Kelk Mager, and Bill Nasson, 1–62. Cambridge: Cambridge University Press, 2010.

Heyns, Michiel. "The Whole Country's Truth: Confession and Narrative in Recent White South African Writing." *Modern Fiction Studies* 46, no. 1 (2000): 42–66.

Holt, Richard. *Sport and the British: A Modern History.* Oxford: Clarendon Press, 1989.

Hook, Derek. *(Post)Apartheid Conditions.* Cape Town: HSRC Press, 2014.

Huggins, Mike. *The Victorians and Sport.* London and New York: Hambledon and London, 2004.

Hyam, Ronald, and Peter Henshaw. *The Lion and the Springbok: Britain and South Africa Since the Boer War.* Cambridge: Cambridge University Press, 2003.

Jeal, Tim. *Baden-Powell,* rev. ed. New Haven and London: Yale University Press, 2001 [1989].

Johnson, David. "Remembering the Khoikhoi Victory over Dom Francisco Almeida at the Cape in 1510." *Postcolonial Studies* 12, no. 1 (2009): 107–30.

—. "French Representations of the Cape 'Hottentots': Jean Tavernier, Jean-Jacques Rousseau and François Levaillant." In *Imagining the Cape Colony: History, Literature, and the South African Nation,* 35–63. Edinburgh: Edinburgh University Press, 2012.

Jolly, Rosemary. *Cultured Violence: Narrative, Social Suffering, and Engendering Human Rights in Contemporary South Africa.* Liverpool: Liverpool University Press, 2013.

Jules-Rosette, Bennetta, and David B. Coplan. "'Nkosi Sikelel' iAfrika': From Independent Spirit to Political Mobilization." *Cahier d'Études Africaines* XLIV, nos. 1–2 (2004): 343–67.

Krog, Antjie. *Country of my Skull*. London: Jonathan Cape, 1998.

Kuper, Adam. "The Death of Piet Retief." *Social Anthropology* 4, no. 2 (1996): 133–43.

Lodge, Tom. *Sharpeville: An Apartheid Massacre and its Consequences*. Oxford: Oxford University Press, 2011.

Mamdani, Mahmood. "Amnesty or Impunity? A Preliminary Critique of the Report of the Truth and Reconciliation Commission of South Africa (TRC)." *Diacritics* 32, nos. 3–4 (2002): 33–59.

Maylam, Paul. "Explaining the *Apartheid* City: 20 Years of South African Urban Historiography." *Journal of Southern African Studies* 21, no. 1 (1995): 19–38.

Mbeki, Thabo. "I Am an African." In *The South Africa Reader: History, Culture, Politics*, edited by Clifton Crais and Thomas V. McClendon, 475–80. Durham and London: Duke University Press, 2014 [1994].

Mcclelland, Keith, and Sonya Rose. "Citizenship and Empire, 1867–1928." In *At Home with the Empire: Metropolitan Culture and the Imperial World*, edited by Catherine Hall and Sonya O. Rose, 275–97. Cambridge: Cambridge University Press, 2006.

Nuttall, Sarah. "Telling 'Free' Stories? Memory and Democracy in South African Autobiography since 1994." In *Negotiating the Past: The Making of Memory in South Africa*, edited by Sarah Nuttall and Carli Coetzee, 75–88. Cape Town: Oxford University Press, 1998.

Oliveira, Pedro Aires de. *Os Despojos da Aliança. A Grã-Bretanha e a Questão Colonial Portuguesa, 1945–975*. Lisboa: Tinta da China, 2007.

Parr, Anthony. "Inventions of Africa." In *T'kama-Adamastor: Inventions of Africa in a South African Painting*, edited by Ivan Vladislavić, 99–109. Johannesburg: University of the Witwatersrand, 2000.

Penn, Nigel. "The Fatal Passion of Brewer Menssink." In *Rogues, Rebels and Runaways: Eighteenth-Century Cape Characters*, 9–72. Cape Town: David Philip Publishers, 1999.

—. "Estienne Barbier: An Eighteenth-Century Cape Social Bandit." In *Rogues, Rebels and Runaways: Eighteenth-Century Cape Characters*, 101–29. Cape Town: David Philip Publishers, 1999.

Ross, Robert. *A Concise History of South Africa*, 2nd ed. Cambridge: Cambridge University Press, 2008 [1999].

Sachs, Albie. *The Strange Alchemy of Life and Law*. Oxford: Oxford University Press, 2009.

Spilhaus, M. Whiting. "The Story of Simon van der Stel." In *Company's Men*, 93–171. Cape Town: John Malherbe Pty Ltd, 1973.

Summerfield, Penny. "Dunkirk and the Popular Memory of Britain at War, 1940–58." *Journal of Contemporary History* 45, no. 4 (2010): 788–811.

Tutu, Desmond. *No Future without Forgiveness*. London: Random House, 1999.

Van wyk Smith, Malvern. "Shades of Adamastor: The Legacy of *The Lusiads*." In *The Cambridge History of South African Literature*, edited by David Attwell and Derek Attridge, 117–37. Cambridge: Cambridge University Press, 2012.

Worden, Nigel. *The Making of Modern South Africa*, 5th ed. Malden: Wiley-Blackwell, 2012 [1994].

E) Nation and Nationalism

Anderson, Benedict. *Imagined Communities*. London: Verso, 2006 [1983].

Balibar, Etienne, and Immanuel Wallerstein. *Race, Nation, Class: Ambiguous Identities*, translated by Etienne Balibar and Chris Turner. London: Verso, 1991 [1988].

Barnard, Rita. "Rewriting the Nation." In *The Cambridge History of South African Literature*, edited by David Attwell and Derek Attridge, 652–75. Cambridge: Cambridge University Press, 2012.

Bhabha, Homi K. "Introduction: Narrating the Nation." In *Nation and Narration*, edited by Homi K. Bhabha, 1–7. New York: Routledge, 1990.

Boehmer, Elleke. *Stories of Women: Gender and Narrative in the Postcolonial Nation*. Manchester: Manchester University Press, 2005.

Butler, Judith and Gayatri Chakravorty Spivak. *Who Sings the Nation-State?* Calcutta: Seagull Books, 2007.

Chatterjee, Partha. "Whose Imagined Community?" In *Empire and Nation: Selected* Essays, 23–36. New York: Columbia University Press, 2010 [1991].

Enloe, Cynthia. *Bananas, Beaches and Bases: Making Feminist Sense of International Politics*, rev. ed. Berkeley and Los Angeles: University of California Press, 2000 [1989].

Gellner, Ernest. *Nations and Nationalism*. Oxford: Basil Blackwell Publishers Limited, 1983.

Hobsbawm, Eric. *Nations and Nationalism since 1780: Programme, Myth, Reality*, 2nd ed. Cambridge: Cambridge University Press, 2012 [1990].

Livy. *The Rise of Rome*, Books 1–5, translated by T. J. Luce. Oxford: Oxford University Press, 1998.

Mcclintock, Anne. "Family Feuds: Gender, Nationalism and the Family." *Feminist Review* 44 (1993): 61–80.

Nagel, Joane. "Masculinity and Nationalism: Gender and Sexuality in the Making of Nations." *Ethnic and Racial Studies* 21, no. 2 (1998): 242–69.

Renan, Ernest. "What is a Nation?" In *Nation and Narration*, translated by Martin Thom and edited by Homi K. Bhabha, 8–22. Oxon: Routledge, 1990 [1882].

Renouvin, Pierre, and Jean Baptiste Renouvelle. "El Sentimiento Nacional." In *Introducción a la Historia de Las Relaciones Internacionales*, translated by Abdiel Macías Arvizu, 171–209. Mexico: Fondo de Cultura Económica, 2000 [1991].

Smith, Anthony D. *Myths and Memories of the Nation*. Oxford: Oxford University Press, 1999.

West, Lois A. "Nation." In *A Companion to Gender Studies*, edited by Philomena Essed, David Theo Goldberg, and Audrey Kobayashi, 145–59. Oxford: Blackwell, 2005.

F) Films

Alfie. Directed by Lewis Gilbert. Paramount Pictures, 1966.

Darling! The Pieter-Dirk Uys Story. Directed by Julian Shaw. Green Light Productions, 2007.

District 9. Directed by Neill Blomkamp. TriStar Pictures, 2009.

Proteus. Directed by John Greyson. Pluck Productions, 2003.

Saturday Night and Sunday Morning. Directed by Tony Richardson. Woodfall Film Productions, 1960.

Skoonheid. Directed by Oliver Hermanus. Swift Productions, 2011.

The Loneliness of the Long Distance Runner. Directed by Tony Richardson. Woodfall Film Productions, 1962.

Zulu. Directed by Cy Endfield. Diamond Films, 1964.

INDEX

MASCULINITY STUDIES

Literary and Cultural Representations

Josep M. Armengol
General Editor

In line with the latest trends within masculinity scholarship, the books appearing in the Masculinity Studies series deal with representations of masculinities in culture, in general, and literature, in particular. The aim of this series is twofold. On the one hand, it focuses on studies that question traditionally normative representations of masculinities. On the other, it seeks to highlight new alternative representations of manhood, looking for more egalitarian models of manhood in and through literature and culture. Besides literary representations, the series is open to studies of masculinity in cinema, theatre, music, as well as all kinds of artistic and visual representations.

For further information about the series and submitting manuscripts, please contact:

Peter Lang Publishing, Inc.
Acquisitions Department
29 Broadway, 18th floor
New York, New York 10006

To order, please contact our Customer Service Department at:

800-770-LANG (within the U.S.)
212-647-7706 (outside the U.S.)
212-647-7707 FAX
CustomerService@plang.com

Or browse online by series at:
www.peterlang.com